TREVOR GRIFFITHS was born in Manchester in 1935. He became a teacher and then a Further Education Officer for the BBC before turning to full-time writing in 1972. He is now widely regarded as one of the most important and influential contemporary British dramatists. His stage plays include *Occupations, Comedians* and *The Party*. Griffiths has consistently concentrated on work in film and television for which he has written episodes in popular series, single plays such as *Through The Night, All Good Men* and *Country*, the series *Bill Brand* about the career of a left Labour MP and adaptations of D. H. Lawrence and Chekhov. He co-wrote the film *Reds. Judgement Over The Dead* was first screened in the United Kingdom and the United States in 1985 under the title *The Last Place on Earth*.

Trevor Griffiths

JUDGEMENT OVER THE DEAD

The screenplay of
THE LAST PLACE ON EARTH

Verso is the imprint of **New Left Books**

British Library
Cataloguing in Publication Data

Griffiths, Trevor, *1935–*
    Judgement over the dead : Scott & Amundsen's race
    to the South Pole.
    I. Title
    822'.914   PR6057.R52

First published 1986
© Trevor Griffiths

Verso
15 Greek Street, London W1V 5LF

Typeset in Palatino by
Cover to Cover, Cambridge

Printed by The Thetford Press
Thetford, Norfolk

ISBN 0–86091–120–9
ISBN 0–86091–826–8 Pbk

CONTENTS

For Gill Cliff,
without whose work, belief, commitment and creativity,
these texts could not have been written.
With love and thanks.

TRUTH IS OTHERWISE

Trevor Griffiths in conversation with Misha Glenny

Q. *The Last Place on Earth* was an enormous project and your decision to work on it cannot have been taken lightly. How did the idea come up in the first place and why did you take it on?

A. The idea came to me in the form of the book, *Scott & Amundsen*, sent to me by a producer and director, who were keen to make a television film series of it. I read the book pretty well at one sitting and recognized it would be a major engagement. I was not convinced on first reading that I really wanted to do it though I was attracted by many of the elements of the piece, particularly by the width of research that had gone into Huntford's work and the striking dislocation of our sense of the past that came out of it. But I was very suspicious of those parts of my own response which I call Boy's Own, as it were. There was something about a man's world and Edwardian days that sounded vaguely . . . that felt slightly comic strip or boy's comic. And I wasn't sure that I could find a politics within this piece that could be inserted into a contemporary discourse and the present struggle. So at first I refused the offer of the series.

Q. And when was that, roughly?

A. It was 1980, at Christmas. But I did say that it was

a project that really ought to be taken on and if they didn't find a suitable person to write the piece at the end of their searches they should come back and talk to me again. And about ten months later the producer came back and asked again and I said I'd read it again. And I don't know too clearly what happened in that year, but we were a year closer to Falklands, that's for sure, and maybe one could feel the build up to the Falklands in advance or something, some recrudescence of imperialist ideology . . . feeling . . . silliness. But anyway I read it again and said yes I want to do this, but I have very specific ways in which I want to do it. That took a long time to discuss. At that time the film was going to be shot by Roland Joffé, and I've got to say that that was probably part of the reason why I wanted to do it. He is a fine director, politically very interesting, and certainly a person I can work with and have worked well with in the past. It came at a time when I was seeking to do more writing and less production, as it were. There had been a couple of productions where I committed myself full-time to the work, six months in each case, and where I began to feel that (a) I was learning very little about production itself and (b) my contribution had not been as significant in the final quality of the pieces as previously I had always hoped for. So I felt with this piece that while it was an enormous project I could probably save myself the task of committing myself to the whole production which was going to take a year, in the arctic or wherever, and get on with more texts. With Roland in charge it seemed to me that I could handle that. So I agreed to do it. Work comes up in different ways. There are things which you create from yourself. Then there is another large terrain of work where projects come at you from producers or directors or actors or whoever. They draw your attention to something for one purpose but you inevitably see for another one, and write it quite differently from the way in which a production was originally imagined. I mean this is like *Reds*, in that it came from the industry. My response to it was not an industry response, but a personal writer's response to say what is there out of this massive lump of pages which can be carved into a Play for Today, which is always I suppose the first question I ask about any work.

Q.   Although it's an important exception, I think that while the industry threw it at you, it is worth bearing in mind that Roland Joffé was involved.

The problem of authorial control over film or television productions is not new to you and we'll be discussing this with detailed reference to *The Last Place on Earth* later on. Firstly can you outline basic structural difficulties faced by any author working in TV as opposed to theatre?

A.   TV is run by controllers and controllers are so called for fairly obvious reasons, because they seek control over the form and content of the material they transmit. Theatres are on the whole cottage industries at a quite different level of capital development. They are fairly openly dealing in ideas with less risk capital at stake. I'm talking about the sort of theatre I do, not West End theatre. Theatre has a very long history and a whole set of traditions has emerged through that history which are to do with art, to do with artists, and codes of practice; ways of seeing art and artists, which are bedded into how people do things in theatre, developed over the years. All of those I think can be used to increase authorial control and author status within the process of concretizing a text. The other thing to remember about a theatre text is that it will be produced in many different ways by many different people in many different countries, so that the text is the one constant element in a moving feast, a changing product or production. TV and film, you get one go at it. The text simply serves the higher text which is the thing itself: the TV film, the cinema film, that is the real text and the text you write, that the writer writes, will be deemed good or bad depending on how well it serves the interests of those who wish to make the film. And those interests, because of the higher capital involved, will not simply be another artist, a director, a star actor or whatever. They will be producers on behalf of capital. Although the playwright starts in the theatre, by the time he finds a process, a working process within TV he has already been relegated to maybe the level of lighting engineer or something of this sort. (I'm talking about pre-existing hierarchies, I don't approve of those hierarchies, but I'm simply trying to give an indication of where the author comes, where the writer comes.) Author is not a word that is used by the way in TV, except by those seeking very high status as producers and directors. We are talking about writers not authors, we are talking about script not about text.

It's worth talking about the contract too; the basic negotiation between art and capital. The contract in film is very clear. Any writing, notes for a character, notes for a sequence, images, jottings, draft treatments, sub-structures, all characters created, all language used on a page, including dialogue, stage directions and so on, all that you use in making the text, all of those belong to the producer. They don't belong at any point, not even at the point of creation, as it were, which may be in some ideational sphere, to the person creating them. Now I'm not arguing that they *should* belong to the individual person, that isn't my thrust. My thrust is that they belong to somebody else, and that they belong basically to the agents of capital. This is not the case in the theatre. The text belongs to the playwright, and his play, the production of his play will depend on his consent. If theatres want to do a play, they have to get a license to do it and that license is controlled by the author or his agent.

Q. Whereas the only leverage you have if a TV play of yours is performed abroad, say if you are unhappy with the edit that has been sold to the US, is to withdraw your name from the project. You cannot prevent the play being performed there, the only thing you can do is symbolic. Withdraw your name from the product. It is down to a level of symbols.

A. Absolutely. So what are we saying? That a principle structural difficulty of working in TV is that you start from a relatively low status *vis-à-vis* other sorts of worker in the process. Writers, playwrights in TV are still struggling for proper representation at the point of production, in the processes of production. And struggle is the word. You really do have to fight and each new production is a new site of struggle, because nothing is inherited, nothing is transmitted to the next production. You are dealing with different people, different companies, and those companies are dealing with hundreds of writers a year, and the quotidian experience of dealing with such writers is, for the company anyway, that they are buyable; that they are movable around; that they are interchangeable; and that what they do, while it might be felt important, is only initially important in serving as the seed for a product, which can then be parcelled, promoted, marketed and so on. So it's a very difficult terrain in which to work and one where I think it would be folly, deeply unrealistic, to imagine that you will ever come out of that process with a 100% production which celebrates, affirms the meanings and values of the piece that you have written.

Q. Sure, but in the very nature of TV production you cannot possibly hope to come out with that 100% production and in a certain sense you do not have the technical facilities to do so. You are not a lighting engineer, and there are lighting engineers who know what they are doing. It strikes me that in much of your work in TV and film, the director has often been a key problem, and of course the producer. We have frqeuently discussed a number of directors who you have come into conflict with. However as directors they have a right to a creative interpretation of the screenplay. You decided to go ahead with Joffé because you had a confidence in him to produce something along the lines that you were intending. But usually you will come into what seems to me will be irreconcilable conflicts with directors. They will have their ideas, they will be in the cutting room editing the piece, and although they may consult with you, they will inevitably feel that the final responsibility for the piece will be theirs and not yours. Can you see any way around this conflict between director and author, or is the only solution for you, the writer, to direct your own script?

A. I'm not yet at the point where I believe that that is the only solution. If I did I would be in some despair, I think. I mean, directing is not writing, and the only first-level skill I would seek to lay claim to is the ability to write dramatic texts. There is no doubt of the sphere of the director and the sphere of the writer. I see them not as in any way separate. I don't know what the geometric term is, but they do in fact intercept, and there is a decent space within the intersections of the two circles, spheres. I'm worried about the idea of a creative interpretation of a screenplay, but I think I know what the question means. Almost anything could fall within that notion of a creative interpretation. Harold Pinter's play *Old Times*. The only production I saw was by Luchino Visconti in a theatre in Rome where he set the play in a boxing ring. And as I watched the play, I had read the text, I watched the play in Italian and it was clear that Visconti was telling us about Visconti. Well Visconti is 'a great artist' and it may be he knew a thing or two about Roman audiences, they actually wanted to know more about Visconti than Pinter's latest statement on the world. But it is a very wide terrain we allow here. I would say: OK sure, a creative interpretation or whatever, yes; but there has to be something in which this interpretation is based, and that's the text, and in some way you have to rationally justify the interpretation you are making at every point as it unfolds. The problem is that directors on the whole don't work that way. They don't because of the industrial process in which they are engaged. They are dealing with a million tiny things most of the time. They are not dealing with that 'creative interpretation of the text', because they are dealing with whether they can actually get all that furniture from Rotterdam to Frobisher Bay in time to shoot *anything*. They are dealing with the problem of there being no snow when they get there and they are supposed to do the polar ice-cap in the next three days. They are dealing with problem of dogs and dog handlers, I'm just referring to *The Last Place On Earth*, but it's true of everything you seek to do. They are dealing with logistics.

Q. Logistical problems are essentially beyond their control. They also have their own individual needs and desires, their own career prospects.

A.   Yes indeed, and their own understanding of a text which
seeks to say something about the way history is recorded and
transmitted. What they bring to the piece is what they feel they
know about the world and its workings. And quite often that
will be massively inappropriate to the task in hand. I've had
different feelings at different points over the last fifteen or
twenty years. I began by thinking I need Marxist directors for
Marxist texts or socialist directors for socialists texts, and then I
thought I'd made a big discovery that we didn't need that, that
in fact in some ways the more politically illiterate the director
was, the freer he was to embrace and affirm those elements of
the text which, as it were, *weren't* foregrounded, in a thinner
notation than ideological exchanges, the political problematic of
the piece and all the rest of it. I have worked very effectively
with say Michael Lindsay-Hogg, who is an absolutely classic
liberal, American, *decontracté*, shrewd, very creative, very free-
flowing in some ways, and with that sort of sensibility coming
to a hard text like *Occupations*, he makes certain discoveries that
hard-left sensibilities possibly would not have, so there were
great gains to be had there. I have worked very successfully
with directors of that kind. Then there are times when that does
not work at all, when what has to be celebrated in the directorial
process is the nub of the piece, the axis of the piece, whatever
you want to call it. There the limitation of the political sensibility of the director becomes crucial as I see it. You can see the
piece leaking away in production, because it simply is not
understood that those things at the heart of the piece are *there*,
they are *actually* there, that is the point. There is a way of doing
realist texts which denies what they are about and simply celebrates their effects.

Q.   I presume that is particularly true for something like *The
Last Place On Earth* which is much more complex in its approach to
cultural and social superstructures than say *Occupations*. The
terrain is clearly political there.

A.   I just want to add one thing which I think is important. To see this thing as a contest between writer and director is proper. It is where power lies, but what one looks for is a working process which involves everybody, everybody who works on a piece and involves them totally, so we are not just talking about a director's response to the text on which he bases his creative interpretation. We are also talking about actors and craftsmen of all kinds, researchers, costume people and wigging and make up. This is a huge conglomerate of different sorts of craft skills and talents, of histories. As they are presently constituted within the TV industry, they are all isolates, they are all isolated skills, talents to be drawn on by the directors and producers. When you have tasted the other, when you have embraced the always messy but always rewarding collective process, as for example we began to achieve on *Bill Brand* – I'm talking about TV, I'm not talking about fringe theatre – then you begin to sense what is possible for working in TV.

What I am at pains to stress, I think, is also that I still haven't thrown out the notion that another person to direct is a good idea, other than the author, other than the writer. There is something about getting coolness around the heat and objectivity around subjectivity and just *secondness* – second guessing, second thinking, second imagining – which is enormously valuable. Working in isolation, which is what writing has become largely, this sort of writing anyway, has its own traps. I've always argued that what we're interested in are the best ideas in the best form that we can achieve. Who has those ideas? The ownership of the idea is the least important thing. What is important is to unlock people's capacities, everybody involved in the production, to this common aim, which is to say something worthwhile and to say it well. What constitutes worthwhileness and wellness will be to some extent determined by the people one works with. If you can create a circumstance, a process in which everybody is working on all engines, and not what we have at the moment where most crews though they are heroic, tend to operate on just a couple, because they know that they've got to work again, somewhere else, another way, another mode of production, another shit at the top. Their alienation from the thing they produce is as rapid as anybody's.

Q. Did you talk to anyone on the crew at any length, other than the director – cameraman, lighting, props etc?

A. Generally in a production where I am committed to the production and post-production process, which starts really with casting the director, yes I do talk to as many people as I can and at length. This was a production that I wasn't going to commit myself to in quite that way, so it was problematic for me to create time away from writing the text to do this. A key person in this production for me was the designer. His name is Maurice Kane and he is hugely gifted. In some ways when we were without somebody steering the boat, it was Maurice's spirit and his time which kept this thing going. I still have work that he did on this text, when he drew almost every shot. Quite extraordinary. We shared ideas about the text for a long time. I learnt a lot from him. I have never been so close to a designer in the whole of my working practice. That I did. I spent less time with cameras, make-up. I did spend some time with costume. I spent time with actors which is key, very important. Everybody writes in a certain tone of voice, and actors coming to it for the first time need pointing, they need help. Doing a Brecht play is different from doing a Chekhov, doing a Chekhov is different from a Strindberg. If you're going to treat things seriously as text and not just as script, then I think any help that you can get from the source of the text is very valuable.

Q. There were some fairly remarkable performances. Martin Shaw as Scott performed brilliantly, although one associates him normally with his roles in *The Professionals* and *Who Dares Wins.*

A. Absolutely, but Martin's very interesting because he's got a fairly extensive history of serious work, I mean of not doing *The Professionals.* I saw him in a Filipo play at the National Theatre in the early 70s. I saw him in *A Street Car Named Desire*, in which he played Stanley very persuasively. It's a considerable part and he played it very intelligently. I had absolutely no worries about Martin's capacity to do this job. Pretty powerful, committed, whole-hearted, whole-brained performance. Of course I think the achievement of the director in directing was to draw from this vast conglomeration of different sorts of acting styles and talents an ultimately single voice and performance. As the plays themselves go into the race for the pole and so on, I think the director did get the class tone right of the British and for the Norwegians. The Norwegians did a lot of that themselves. It reminded me somewhat of Richard Eyre's brilliant work in *Country*, in finding that single voice of performance for the class he is dealing with. And that voice is not just how people say their lines, I mean by the voice the whole tonal, gestural inflection, the whole way in which they create a people in the world, that world, those people.

Q. I think the single most telling relationship in *The Last Place On Earth* was between Scott and 'Birdy' Bowers, which expressed precisely all that you are saying about tonal, gestural relationships.

A. Yes, that was extraordinary, and it is worth mentioning the very different journeys of style and tone and aspiration which those two actors have taken through British theatre and drama. Until this day the guy playing 'Birdy', Sylvester McCoy, is an alternative actor, essentially of the Fringe, or a certain place within the Fringe, really Ken Campbell's Roadshow. Improvised performance, a lot of stage cartoon work, a lot of risking all in different venues every night with no fixed pattern of response established in the audience by the institution of the theatre. The Roadshow went in pubs, youth clubs, factories, on the street and whatever. Sylvester is very much of that, and looking at the much more conventional career and experience of Martin, you get an idea of what the director does in bringing, in harnessing all that stuff, in orchestrating it, bringing it into a modality. This you need – this a writer needs.

Q. Maybe this is the area where you can expect positive co-operation from a director. Had he not been succesful with the actors on *The Last Place On Earth*, then things could have collapsed catastrophically.

A. Absolutely, and what we could have got is a set of idiosyncratic characters who in no way cohere as representatives of a class in action – an imperial class in action. These things have to be said, and these are the things that directors at their best do.

Q. By British TV standards *The Last Place On Earth* was not cheap and it went overbudget as well. Given the strain on resources, what were the problems you came up against in terms of which scenes were shot, which were cut etc? And how were you able to influence what was happening in the production process given that the original director was not going ahead with the project?

A. My original director, Roland Joffé, was not going ahead with the project. The director that we finally decided was the best person for the job, Phillip Saville, left after two weeks into production. The third director, Marek Kanievska, was enlisted on the wing, as it were, for four weeks, while we found a fourth director to take over the whole piece. That raised certain problems, no question. One of the reasons we spent a great deal of money during the first eight weeks of the production was that the first permanent director cast the play with me and the producer, and then left. When Ferdinand Fairfax came to become the permanent director of the piece some weeks later, he wanted to do a fair bit of recasting, all contracts had to be honoured, so actors were paid up as if they had done the whole thing. New actors came in and took salary as well. So that was extraordinarily expensive. The new director, because he was a good one wanted to have a say in everything. A lot of decisions had already been made – we had had four months of pre-production with a director now departed. Now this is major. In

Hollywood they would close down on that. So there was re-casting, redesigning, rethinking about the text and so on. It's worth saying that the texts that I had created were much too long for slots of fifty-two minutes. This is something that I haven't solved as a writer, because I'm not sure that solving that problem does not bring worse problems in its wake.

Q. That is a very serious problem. Everything you have written is very carefully constructed, and if something has to go, the text as a whole will be seriously altered. Did you anticipate this, was it so much of a surprise to you when parts had to go?

A. The problem is this. So you have too much text for the slots afforded. We can say that in operational terms that the texts are too long. But they are only too long for TV, they are only too long for that production. If there were another production available at greater length, they might not be too long. My problem is, I cannot prioritize the length of slottage, the length of time on air, over all the other considerations that you have to work with when you start on a project. If I write a Play for Today, it's as long as it is. If it's 96 minutes, then it's 96 minutes. In a sense you don't know what you need in the final cut until you see what you've made of what you've made – what has been made of the text. It may be that on the page every moment is required to tell the story, establish the problematic or whatever. But it may be that because of the brilliance of a particular piece of lighting or a combination of lighting, performance, angle and cutting, Scene 3 is already saying something you felt it neces-sary to say in Scene 39 again, or to amplify. If it's already there in its amplified form now, that element of Scene 39 is no longer necessary. Now TV, which is industrial line process, would like you to make all those determinations in advance, because it doesn't want to shoot what it doesn't use. And says look 'you've got seven hours, please write seven hours'. Okay so we write twenty minutes more and play around with that. The only image I can think of off hand is sculpture. You start with a bloody-great block of stuff, and out of it you produce this thing.

Now the one thing you know is: the thing you create is not going to be bigger than the block of stuff, but it might be nearly as big, or it might be very small indeed. The question is should you have started with a smaller block of stuff. My view is that a writer's got enough to consider without having to consider how long it should be. Now of course we don't work in complete vacuums, so I internalize, I have absorbed a great deal of understanding and experience of working in TV, so that I know within limits what is long and what is short. But one thing is certain the restructuring of an overlong piece of text can only be done by the person who did the text in the first place. Because only that person in my view knows the relationships between the pieces as it were. If we take text to mean web, which is indeed its origin, in the web you cut a piece here at this point of the web and all the tensioning disappears along whole strands of the play, and you need somebody who makes threads to be there – you can't have somebody who cuts cloth! That was the problem. Because I had produced overlong texts, and because I wasn't in the front seat with the director driving, the car, the truck of the production, it then fell to others to determine what should stay and what should go. And those weren't the only considerations about whether it was too long or not. Major considerations were how much of the scenes have we got left to shoot, how much are they going to cost us? Given that we're overspending and all the rest of it. And so the pressure always came down on those elements of the text which were non-narrative, which didn't help advance the narrative, and since tendentially TV drama series are implacably about narrative, about action, about carrying the story on and on, a lot of the stuff, e.g. the dream sequences that I wrote; the social and historical context of imperial Britain at the beginning of this century; certain relationships within the text, Kathleen and Nansen for example, these things tended to represent areas of provocation and danger, or areas of massive resource use, expenditure. These disappeared without trace.

Q. Presumably a first edit was made and shown for your approval.

A. I came in much earlier than that. I came in on the rushes. I saw many, many dozens of hours of rushes on videotape that were sent back to England. I was looking at them while working on other things, but I was in daily telephone contact with Frobisher Bay, with the director, Ferdie Fairfax. We had long discussions about what he'd shot, what he'd yet to shoot, what it was necessary to do in order to recover moments lost in scenes, so there was a great deal of work going on there. This material was being sent back to England and assembled, rough assembly according to notes indicated, obviously in the text itself, but also by the director. So there was a full-time editor working on the stuff in London. When all the shooting had been done, then you get the long rough-cuts, which in this case was done by the director and the editor. Then I came in to see it, and then I had to discover what had been shot, what had not been shot and what had been shot badly, making nonsense of itself and the rest of the piece. And those are separate things. Then you've got to pitch in, the rough-cut is of course way overlength, so you've got pressure on you as to how much you can actually use. Then you've got to try and make a new text, as it were, from the rubble of the old text. You've got to get a new text which is a stronger building than the one you pulled down. You can argue that you ought to be able to do that in a different way, not after the event when it's too late to shoot anything, your actors have gone and all the rest of it.

We haven't discussed certain key things that happened during the shooting in the arctic. One was that the original producer was converted into an executive producer. He was separated from the means of power. The new producer was inserted by Central to keep the overspend down. Everybody knew there was an overspend, but the overspend had to be very, very rigidly supervised. This man issued a list of scenes which would not be shot. That list was 112 scenes. Now it's true that a proportion of those, maybe as many as 30% were single shot scenes, establishing scenes, ice against the bow of a ship, or somebody feeding dogs, or somebody carving a seal. Relatively simple scenes, but nevertheless, time-consuming, you had to get the right time of day, the right props, dogs and seals etc. Some of them were actually the key scenes as far as narrative, character, sense of period go. There they were in a great glob to be cut. I saw this telex with the 112 scenes listed. I went through the text and saw which each of them was. Then I rang Central and told them that I was pulling out, that my name would no longer be borne by this series. I wrote to the director and the principal actors – I sent a telegram, wishing them well and indicating that I was no longer part of the production. The upshot of that was new deliberations set in motion by Central. I worked for about six weeks out but connected directly with the director who would not accept that I was out of the process and argued that he would stand as guardian of the text, as it were, against all comers. On the whole he did a fairly good job and we reinstated a fairly high proportion of the key scenes.

The savaging was retrieved to an extent. Then I was confronted by what we had and what we didn't have. Then I had to work to find the best way through the material we had and the material we didn't have. A great deal of rewriting took place, incidentally, by telephone, as scenes were not to be shot, so that the content of those scenes somehow had to be repositioned within scenes that were going to be shot. So that was also a huge problem. Ideally I would have been out there and on the job. This problem of not being able to be on the spot, having it always mediated through this personal rapport, took its toll. Took its toll on other work as well. I was writing *Fatherland** at the time and this was delayed by eight months as a direct result of the newly perceived need to immerse myself in, I won't call it a rescue job because that is too self-referring. But certainly I had to put a great deal of thought and time into this production even though I wasn't there.

Q. Let's move on to the other problems affecting the production. Needless to say the screenplay was not produced in an ideological vacuum. In Powerplays Mike Poole and John Wyver suggest that Beatty's alterations to your script of *Reds* were motivated by the growing anti-communism in the US during the late 70s and early 80s. The implication is that Beatty would

---

* A film dealing with the German question to be released later this year.

have realised your script more faithfully if the historical conjuncture had allowed it. I think this exaggerates Beatty's commitment to politics but there is an element of truth in it. Hostility to *The Last Place On Earth* was potentially even greater, because added to the broader ideological pressures which may have influenced Beatty, the screenplay had to contend with objections raised by the powerful lobby comprising Scott's relatives and those of other British Antarctic Expedition members. In what ways were the politics of the television production affected by these external factors?

A.   There was a general anti-communism in the United States and it got worse during the seventies and early eighties. It became more pronounced, it became more focussed on cultural productions. But Beatty was dealing with historical characters who were, broadly speaking, unknown. Few had really heard of Louise Bryant, save historians and a few socialists. John Reed was a figure about whom people would say 'wasn't he . . . ?' and then something roughly adjacent.

Q.   They may have heard of *Ten Days That Shook The World*.

A.   Yes, but they'd certainly never read it. There's not too much evidence that Beatty had read *Ten Days That Shook The World*. When we come to Scott anyway, and imperial Britain in the first two decades of this century, we are talking about people with very high profile still, still taught in schools. I mean I did my research on that, there is no question about that. And we are talking about a piece of a country's history that has become mythologized into a timeless presence as it were. The spirit of Scott is with us today. Palpable, breathing in the way we perceive the world, the way we seek to change it or retain it. That was fierce and that was fierce in the writing. One sensed the atrocious audacity of this strange man Huntford in wanting to deconstruct the myth of Scott and construct the history, the real history of that expedition and that period. And also to construct for the first time in English the juxtaposed expedition, the expedition which took place at the same time as Scott's but was carefully filleted out of the myth that was transmitted. So in writing one was aware of all that and it seemed to me important that it would have been fatuous to seek to cartoonize the character or the events. One had to be very sane and very sober about what was going on, about what actually took place. I do use a word, but it is a word that I try and avoid – one had to be fairly factual, fairly low-key about the extent of chaos inside that man's and that expedition's preparations, and that country's expeditions. In a way that's no different from getting Gramsci, say, 'right' in *Occupations*, but in another way it's very different indeed, because you're not dealing with somebody about whom very little is known by this society. At the same time the problem of history remains, whether you're dealing with Gramsci or Kronstadt or 1968 or Scott. I don't believe that I made any significant changes in method or approach, but I was conscious from the outset that the piece had to be meticulous, it had to be built from a base. That made for a very difficult writing period. It took me 17 or 18 months to write the screenplay, and I had to read so much more extensively. I had to read the principal sources in English on which Huntford had based his thesis. And I had to go beyond that because I am a writer, a dramatist, who needs to know different things from the historiography, from the history. So the hostility was potentially even greater than that which had greeted *Reds*. Now you come to production and you've got people inside TV who for whatever reason want to do this. You've got the process itself, which isn't the best in the world for getting all these meticulous things built up. It's very higgedly-piggedly, it's very slapdash. And then you've got from a very early stage interest groups, pressure groups, people who represent those values in their own lives and seeking to defend them. Those people are exerting pressure in different ways on different people. I had a number of letters from Lord Kennet. Some of them unconsciously insulting, some of them couched in interrogatives but with some textual orders, as it were, lodged within them.

Q. When was this? After the first draft?

A. Yes, this was when the text was circulating. Once you get beyond a certain point in a production, the play gets into the hands of agents and actors, all sorts of people get hold of the text, it becomes a thing in itself for a while, and sure enough the text was in the hands of the Peter Scott and Kennet. They began to mobilize their resources, and you've got to remember that there was a history of such mobilization against Huntford anyway. There is a whole history to be told there.

Q. That's an interesting point. Huntford's work was a book. Until there was a TV production, the book was containable.

A. Yes. Absolutely.

Q. As soon as you move into TV, then opponents of the thesis have got to start mobilizing properly.

A. Yes, because TV has educative and reeducative functions because of its reach, you know, a book of history simply won't reach such an audience.

Q. I had no idea of the debunking of the Scott myth until *The Last Place On Earth*, and generally read literary pages quite carefully.

A. Yes, and the book had been in circulation about three years before I got hold of it. I had actually seen Huntford on TV on *Pebble Mill at One* defending the book against Kennet, so it had inscribed itself a little on my unconscious, but I had not gone out and bought the book, it hadn't fallen into my hands in any other way until I was sent it by the producer. He'd certainly made a mark with this piece, but it had been contained, because it was ultimately containable. Its cultural form made that containment possible. Once you get into TV then you are really in the stream, and you've got to employ very different strategies. Some of these strategies – the less said the better. For example, I believe that there was a more or less serious attempt to co-opt certain key personnel involved in the production to a different way of making it from the one that the text suggested or insisted on. I don't think it is politic to be more specific than that, but there was an attempt to subvert the production, and that attempt, though I won't believe finally that it was successful, nevertheless became inscribed on the process and became part of the problem. Now I don't believe that this was ever the case with *Reds*. I don't believe there was a John Reed faction, or a Louise Bryant faction that was actively seeking to co-opt key personnel within the production to subvert the intentions of the text, whatever those were by the time that Beatty and others had finished with it. I know that wasn't the case, I suspect, put it no more strongly than that, I suspect it was the case in *The Last Place On Earth*.

There was also, and this is on record, a concerted attempt by those interest groupings to prevent production taking place. There were approaches to the board, to the IBA, and people were enlisted in these approaches, The Royal Geographical Society and others, to seek to have this piece shelved, not made. When those failed then the *quid pro quo* for that was that they were on a private basis given an undertaking that they would see the finished series in advance of its transmission, and in advance even of its press showing. I fought along with the director and other creative workers in the process, I fought tooth and nail to prevent that showing from taking place. It seemed to me to represent a very serious breach with tradition, with the way of doing things. You don't show work to interested parties who might, having seen it, be in a stronger position to frame the public response. And they did, they quite clearly did to some extent, because of their friends in the other media, crucially the press. They did achieve something of their goal. By seeing the series and then priming an eager press, a press that wants controversy, they did prime them, they did frame the way in which this thing would be treated. There was a very powerful attempt to discount this series in so far as it was historical. The historicity of the piece was challenged from the outset. Not with evidences but with authoritative statements that simply went uninspected. It then became a very difficult terrain in which to fight for the piece, because it is clear that this was never an attempt to do a documentary reconstruction of the two expeditions. On the other hand documentary actuality was at the heart of the piece – historical research had been done by everyone involved. And some of the things that were picked on, for example that a seal should have been a block when it was being carved up, when it had palpably been killed a bare two hours before, somehow became pivotal – and that became the whole way of looking at it: if this is not true, what else is true. It's very interesting the way in which the piece was framed as a deliberate attempt to assasinate the historical character of Scott. You know, when you examine the piece, it follows Huntford's trajectory, which is to say, there were two expeditions. The British account of that time actually leaves out, for the most part, one of those expeditions – the one that got to the pole and came back without losing a life, that one is left out of the story. Now let's look at the story again with that included. That's the first thing that Huntford said, and the first thing the play said. The second thing is let's look at all the evidences, including Scott's own testimony. Let's look at all of it including the 60 pages of journals which had been carefully filleted from the received version that we all know and love. And let's take other testimonies as well, some of which Huntford created himself because he went to Tryggve Gran, the Norwegian who was supposed to teach the British how to ski and was out there in the antarctic with Scott. Let's go to him, he's 92 now but let's go to him before he dies. And let's find out stuff from him, because he's alive and he was there – oral history. And so on and so on and so on . . . But basically let's tell the Scott story as it was rather than as we'd like it to have been, or some people would like it to have been, and let's tell this other story which is germane. It's a very simple proposition and I don't see that on grounds of historiography contestable. The fact is that without contesting it, they subverted that whole notion. This was a knocking job. And the play's reception wasn't helped, the way in which the play was framed by these people – there could have been important work done by radicals and progressives who seek the demythologization of history, in seeing the series, in trying to frame it properly. But a lot of such people in the media wanted to see it as a knocking job . . . that the purpose of it, they thought, is to knock, knock, knock . . . so ultimately I think things were to some extent reduced to the character of Scott, that was the terrain on which you had to fight, the historical authenticity of the characterization of Scott. This really isn't wholly a propos.

Q.   But even on that, it is easy to defend yourself.

A.   I think one could defend oneself very well, but it's like defending a sliver instead of justifying the whole. Now what's great about TV, though we read a great deal of press, a lot of people don't give a shit. A lot of people just go for the thing itself which is the play in production.

Q.   I had the advantage of reading the script before I saw all seven or so hours in one go. I did not see it when it was shown on TV. I read many reviews which were almost entirely negative. This is partly because TV critics are often not terribly good at their job, but it was also partly because the first episode was flawed. They do have some influence.

A.   I'm not entirely sure of that. I can't think of a single programme that I have been dissuaded from watching by reviews which suggest that what I'm watching is rubbish or not worth watching. You and I are a curious sort of people anyway, given the width and depth of a TV audience. We tend to be influenced by other people's impressions and all the rest of it. We inhabit a sort of magnetic field of opinion, and I'm not sure if popular TV watching is like that . . . for example my cousin, who runs a martial arts shop in Manchester. The other day he said, I've been watching that *Berlin Alexanderplatz*, not bad, he said. We talked about it and he said, took me about four and half episodes to get into that. I said yea brilliant, it's taken me thirteen! Why is it doing that? . . . because something inside is working for him, it's working within him, and I think TV is like that . . . it's not like theatre, all you have to do is switch the set on and watch it. You don't have to book, you don't have to park, you don't have to go for a meal beforehand, you don't want to be hit for £12–14 and then find that you've got a dummy. Well let's leave that open as to what effect criticism has.

The one thing you said which is absolutely true, I think, is that the first episode is flawed and that has something to do with the writing. I don't think there's any question about that. It was painfully overlong in the original text. But remember too that three directors worked with this episode, and therefore three directors worked with the cast and gave them different senses of what they were doing. You can see performance change from scene to scene in a quite alarming and hysterical way. And if there's one law that is invariable, it is that if you begin a series with a flawed episode, then you are in trouble. Recovery from that is very, very difficult. I fought for a completely different edit of episode 1 and lost in the scramble to get the fucking thing on the air: which was a scramble, as it turned out, to get the thing ready to show to the Scott/Kennet axis, three weeks, four weeks, six weeks before the bloody thing went out, because of some chairman of the board's private, gentlemen's arrangement with these people. That was the thing which made it impossible to argue, to struggle more for the first episode. I broke myself doing that and I still have editing sheets that I worked out myself on the video for the first episode which were largely discounted in the scramble to get the thing mounted. But yes, more than any other single thing, the first episode's lack of bite, lack of grip diminished the chances of this series being hugely successful, in a way that maybe it deserved, because it is an original piece of work, it is an original production. It's curious because exactly the same thing could be said to some exent about *Sons And Lovers*, and yet the reputation of *Sons And Lovers* is very high now. It's curious when you get out of the fumes and the diesel, the crap and the noise of transmissions and pre-transmission, people take a quite different, settled view of the thing in its entirety, which sees the first episode as flawed, but not so flawed that the others aren't great.

Q. I was speaking to a radio producer talking about *The Last Place on Earth,* and he said, although he had not seen it, he gathered that the parallel was so obvious and dogmatic that he couldn't be bothered to see it, and he was referring to the Falklands. When you started work on this the Falklands had not yet happened. Although the parallels should not be ignored, particularly the sense of an imperial nation in decline, what interested me about the play more was the debunking of the Scott myth. The Falklands parallel in a way merely confirmed the central aim of the project as I perceived it, which was the nature and genesis of historical distortion. In a way the Falklands parallel deflected people's attention from its core.

A. What is interesting is what was in the air and what came home to roost during the writing. I don't know what it was but I know that since 1979 and Thatcher coming to power, I know that there's been a deliberate attempt by government and state to foster the notion that we are still a great British people, no question about that. The whole emphasis on the militarization of society, the enormous budget being expended on military personnel, technology, supplies and so on. To travel through Europe on a train is to risk encountering for longish periods British soldiery on the move. I've had several experiences of British soldiery abusing inhabitants of other countries, French, Dutch etc. I've written a passage in *Fatherland* about it. This was there before and after the Falklands, but it was being deliberately fostered. I called the final episode *Rejoice,* because it was so neat it had to be true almost, because here we were on another crazed, impossible, vainglorious venture, and we were being invited to approve, nay we were being instructed to approve. Our whole Britishness, our status as Britons, depended on our approval. I know that John Wyver and Mike Poole have argued that there is a lack of fit between the Falklands and the race to the pole, because in the one we transparently lost and in the other we transparently won. In the one we were underprepared, stupid and so on, in the other we were massively prepared, effective and all the rest of it. I think this is a deep misreading of what actually went on out there, what went on in the campaign and so on. I mean how long is it going to take us before we recognize that this was a complete con, that the story we have of the Falklands is not what happened at all. We know enough now. We know about the failure of the French exocets to explode inside the bows of ships with hundreds and hundreds of men on board. We know that with a tiny accidental lever one way or another that there could have been a totally different outcome. Don't we? I mean thousands and thousands and thousands of lives could have been lost in that venture with no more shots than were fired. But had those lives been lost, the war would have been bloodier and more bitter. Is anybody seriously suggesting that the war would not have spread to the mainland, had there had not been a decisive victory? It's bull-shit, it's bullshit. What Scott did was emblematize something, what we were doing was acting it out in the Falklands war.

Q. This ties up with the creation of the myth. The idea that we have the right to impose our empire on others, an empire which to all intents and purposes doesn't exist.

A. It's as Anthony Barnett said in that brilliant piece in the NLR, *Iron Brittania*. It's at the ideational level that the problem must be located, it's who we think we are. That leads back to who we think we were. That's the point – not who we thought we were, but who we think we were in 1910–1912. I don't think, I mean I wasn't asking people to view 1912 in direct terms of the book at all. It's bizarre that when the Falklands came up and I was writing the piece, I was still a long way away from the end, but somehow it seemed that everything fitted into place, and the reason for doing it seemed clearer and clearer and clearer. It didn't alter the project, it confirmed the project for me. And Falklands, let's face it, was confirmatory of a great deal of one's differential reading of British history anyway.

Q. There's been a number of important plays and films to come out of Britain in the past fifteen years or so dealing with the notion of the Establishment lie, and when you mentioned Richard Eyre I thought of *The Ploughman's Lunch*, which I think is a very good film although many people disagreed with that. I saw it as an updating and restating of certain things that Hare talked about in *Licking Hitler* and *Plenty*. And yet none of these plays, none of these authors have dealt concretely with this. There is a sense of a congenital, pervasive lie of the British Establishment as though it were outside of history. What I liked about *The Last Place On Earth* is that it grabbed the nettle of where this lie was coming from and why. Were you conscious of that at all, about actually seeking the roots of this duplicity of the British Establishment?

A. I've never been worried about lying. It seems to me that this is quite often couched in a – yes congenital is a good word – congenitally ethical view of power and its employment. I would expect ruling elites to lie. From where I am now, and from what I understand their function to be, I would say not just *de rigeur*, which is like a style of doing things, but absolutely necessary. So that's never been my problem. That they lie to us is in a sense the least of our troubles. The problem is to nail the lie, and to get the people who are being lied to to see that these are lies and not truths. Because it is basically a power struggle. Truth is what loses out.

Why was this terrain more important than other terrains? What is it about the Scott myth, the mythography that surrounds that? Why is that so important? I've known this for many years now, but I've never quite seen the essential adjacency, a contingency of the one with the other – a contingent relationship of one with the other. The myth had to be created to justify the war that followed. And it's because we live in times that are themselves not very different that I wanted to write this piece. Because myths are being conceived and constructed almost departmentally inside government, inside the organs of the state. Scott's was a luck myth. It rooted in what people felt that they had been said to need. So powerful was that feeding of the notion of the greatest club on earth, the British Empire, that it goes on to this day. It's there. And we saw it in that vast and dangerous recrudescence during the Falkland crisis. I mean I have never seen so many Union Jacks and flagwaving and bullshit talking in my life. And I have lived for fifty years. So war and peace, the major issues of war and peace, will we all live or will we all destroy our hope. This is what the Scott myth and its proximity to the Great War, the Great European War, the European Civil War as the Chinese call it, it was that that seized my imagination. But there's a whole garden laid out there in 1912–14 and every single plant is growing now inside Britain, British consciousness and the subconscious of this society. It's not the only thing growing there. There are plants to do with democracy, to do with equality, to do with commoness and fratenity, that are also there. Some of those other things are weeds in my view and they need rooting out.

Q. To what extent is the Scott myth a cover up of a gradual process of imperial decay?

A. It's possible to see it as imperial decay from here, or from post-1918, and the decay was a moral decay, that was part of the mythology and ideology, it was like this great breed of ours, among whom we can number Shakespeare, Raleigh, or Wellington, you know any sort of ragbag collection of great or near-great. Some of them were great at butchery, some of them were great in exploration, but you know everything is collapsed into Englishness or Britishness. It was like we were losing our contact with the breed, with the race, that was the problem. The race wasn't throwing up the great, spectacular stars, who secured the empire in the first place, put us where we are, top of the league of nations, champions of the first division. That's a whole thing which is still pervasive, it still pervades in con-temporary Britain in a contemporary world on the edge of thermo-nuclear annihilation. If it was inappropriate in 1912, how much more inappropriate is it now? Just recently I received some material from The Royal Society of Literature, including the opening remarks given by C. M. Woodhouse at their AGM of 1982. It reads:

> Ladies and Gentlemen, we meet on the morrow of a national triumph in the South Atlantic. It recalls a former fellow of this society, Sir Arthur Quiller-Couch, on another memorable episode in the same area of the world, exactly seventy years ago. Let us keep our language noble for we still have heroes to celebrate.

That is the *locus classicus* of all the cant, hypocrisy, mendacity, iconography of power. Frightening. And do you know, this person is a public person. Hon. C. M. Woodhouse, DSO, OBE. It is clear this person has believed this all his life. But what was his ground? This ground had been prepared, this was written on 16 June 1982, this ground had been prepared for this man to make such a public declaration of value and belief at the Royal Society of Literature, which is of course an apolitical body devoted to fostering an apolitical literature. If a man can get up and speak that garbage to a gathering of allegedly intelligent people, things have not changed as much as they might have. And anything that a small piece like *The Last Place On Earth* can do to redress that balance is important. I didn't know about this statement when I wrote the piece, but I knew about it in another way, you know, I knew it in the behaviour of that British drunken soldiery on those trains and boats which I had travelled on since 1971. And by just looking at defence estimates, and by listening to the language of the people in power. I mean do you remember how we all laughed when Wilson sent in 7 or 8 airstrikes to sink the Torrey Canyon and we all thought it was hilarious. And I don't just mean you and me, I mean a lot of people, it was great we used to watch it on TV, trying to sink this bloody oil tanker and we couldn't hit the bugger! But we didn't feel, fuck we're definitely a second-class nation now. This thing has simply resurfaced, it has never gone, it's always there. And that's how deep the burial is, that's how planted these notions are. This was a small attempt to confront them and to show them the frailty of their historical underpinning. When you actually get to the facts of the situation, it was totally otherwise. As indeed the Falklands was otherwise.

Q. Both on reading Huntford's book and watching *The Last Place On Earth*, I became very drawn towards the Norwegians, who were to some extent experiencing the same process. Nansen for example became mythologized in his own life in that he was used as the model for St. Olav. Was this nationalism justifiable in that they were saying, "we may not have unlimited naval power, but we have intelligence, we are shrewd, and we can achieve things"? I felt rather ambiguous about the Norwegian nationalism.

A. These are the sharp distinctions which the text draws between the British and the Norwegians. First of all the British did for country and empire, that was their goal and their aspiration, and they sought to be at one with the purposes of their nation. There's a long history of that. It doesn't start with Scott obviously. When you look at Amundsen, Nansen and all that crowd, there had been Norwegians for a long time, but there had not been a nation for a long time. Norway became a nation while Amundsen was up finding the north-west passage, 1905 or something. They were in a different historical conjuncture as a nation, an extremely young nation, relatively powerless. There was a power game being played between Germany, France and Britain as to who will rule the roost, and Norway needed allies. And Nansen's role in this as Ambassador is to smooth the way, is not to tweak the lion's tail. That's why Amundsen couldn't disclose that he was taking on the British in the South, because Nansen would have said, forget it. Because the Germans wanted Norway reconflated into Sweden again. It didn't serve their grand design for Europe to have a free Norway, to have an independent state there. So there's that and also I think you can see it, the flag isn't the heart of that journey in any way. It's like a formality, it has to be done properly, but it's not what that journey is about. That journey is about getting it right, doing it properly, doing it well. And I never lost sight of the fact that Amundsen didn't even want to do it. In no sense was it madcap or piratical. It was thought out to the last moment.

Q.   Yes, the execution of the journey was justification in itself.

A.   Absolutely extraordinary. I mean if you want to win the world cup, you've got to have a lot of really good footballers. It's no use having great rhetoric. Rhetoric takes care of nothing.
    What was great about the production was that it actually dared to cast Norwegians as Norwegians, so what one simply couldn't do in the text, which was the Norwegianess of Norwegians, was supplied by the actors. This was an important ideological and historical inscription. The most powerful single enhancement that occurred collectively was involved in that. The boldness of casting Norwegians to speak English but in a Norwegian way.

Q.   It was beautiful. My mind has retained so many images of exchanges between the Norwegians, particularly during the journey. There was a sense of liberation during the whole journey.

A.   For too long any view of Amundsen and the Norwegians was one of banal professional hacks. Spoilsports, liars, cheats, freebooters. Nothing could be further from the truth. These people believed in doing things well, and not losing their minds in vainglorious, rhetorical gestures. Take the way they turned back, for instance, which was a democratically arrived at decision because they had started too early, because it was too cold and because it was no fun anymore. Compare that with the absolutely autocratic power wielded by the Leader over everybody, and people will take a break when Scott decides when the break shall be taken. There is not the slightest fragment of even relative autonomy for these people. So hierarchical.

Q. Oates knows full well that he's not going to make it.

A. He knows he's marching to his death. I think that's clear but not overstated in the piece. And Birdy Bowers doesn't know at all, and that's another kind of Englishness, another kind of subordination.

There's a great moment when the Norwegians see the mountains for the first time and that that is now part of the journey. Now they have to solve this problem, 12,000 ft. of transantarctic mountains. They're trying to work out how many dogs they are going to need, how long it's going to take and so on. And they stand in this kind of misty hollow base of the mountain, little wisps of questions and answers just dotting around these people, it's quite magical. It's like how craftsmen tackle problems. Compared with which nothing about Scott's journey is of any value at all.

We haven't talked about the spaces afforded by the text for these people, these characters to fill themselves out. I mean there was a suggestion that these are cartoon two-dimensional people. And yet when you follow the British from base camp to the Pole and half-way back again, you live their dying, moment by moment in what I believe to be a wholly proper way. And you see their contradictions and you see them seeing their contradictions, like Oates, like Wilson. Nobody can respond to that by feeling that these people are being brutally shovelled out of the way in order for some schematic, political agitprop notion to be inserted into contemporary consciousness. It's bullshit, it's bullshit. That's what I mean by taking the whole thing on, by taking the death on as well as the maladroitness and incompetence, stupidity, hierarchy . . . it's going all the way. You've read that death, those deaths a thousand times, you've read deaths like them, vainglorious, heroic rhetoricized death in British imperial legend. But I have never been down that path with those people before in such an intense, caring way. Caring is not quite the word, but allowing the play of feelings inside it. They are not savage caricatures that we can laugh at, if we share the pain, the desperation, the ugliness.

Q. We talked about certain things growing, the strength of nationalism. The proof of that strength is that one has experienced it in oneself at times. And that's the really frightening thing. One is able to rationalize and explain away this phenomenon, but one is also still prone.

A. I want to say something about the audience, because one writes in the language of one's society for the people of one's society. But objectively the situation is, that when you write for TV, you now increasingly write for quite different societies, quite different cultures, and in the course of the last few months I've experienced totally different responses to this piece from Americans, Germans, French. Americans are interesting, they don't know anything about this, they don't know that Scott didn't win. My structural problem about this piece, which is also a formal problem about the genre, is that you couldn't build any suspense at all around the outcome. The outcome is a received outcome, a known outcome. So any thought that the real interest is in who's going to win is out of the question. But you put an American in front of the series and he says, this guy's crazy, they can't do this without ski, and then that becomes part of the point. Well maybe they can, maybe these fuckers actually can. So then it becomes interesting . . .

Q. And of course because they are seeing a lavish British production and they are so fond of the British . . .

A. Exactly and it's British capital, it's got to be a celebration! I would hazard a guess that that would be differently true for Japanese, who will also be seeing it this year, and Italians. So we are talking about another audience which is not privy, which starts somewhere else.

Q. I remember when I first started engaging myself with this project and read the script, I know that at the beginning I could not remember what the fuck had happened at the South Pole.

A. That's why myth is potent, it wipes out incident, event, reality – it's gone, it's somewhere else.

Q. I remember seeing an adult quiz programme when I was about 12 or 13, fairly crass questions, but one was 'Who was the first to the Antarctic?', and the competitor replied 'Scott'. The quiz master came back in and replied 'Wrong, it was a trick question, it was the Norwegian Amundsen!' There's even that thing in the consciousness that Scott did make it.

A. You've got it! Because why would you celebrate a failure! That kind of basic logic supervenes at a certain point in the reception of the myth.

Q. So reality is subverted, so that in 100 years time . . .

A. Scott will have won it! Who knows, maybe Shakespeare *was* German!

Q. If anyone hasn't seen the production, what tools do they need coming to a screenplay for the first time. In what way is it different from reading a stage play?

A. The first thing to say is that there is little if any *training* in play reading. We think we train people when we teach them how to criticize Shakespeare. But I wouldn't put too much value on that when people come to this text. I won't speak for all screenplays, I'll just try and confine it to how I write. I think the tendency is to skip that which is not dialogue, and I think that has to be resisted. Dialogue in my work emerges from the context, and the context you will often find not in the dialogue, but in the intervening directions or what have you. And the direction is not or very rarely about how actors should be or where they should go or whatever. It's written in impressionistic, novelistic ways. Almost for the reader, in a sense; for the first screenplay of anything is for a reader. The reader may be the director or the producer but it has to be read. And in the reading the piece will be imaged, and that what you're about, that's what the text seeks to do in the mind of the reader. The reader has got to go all the way with the text, and that means as with a novel – you read the whole thing, you don't simply read the dialogue. And I think that's the first and probably the only crucial difference between reading this and reading anything else.

I love reading plays and enjoy reading plays probably more than anything else. I read them precisely because they need something doing to them. They need completing, they need producing. And even a solitary reader can produce the play as it were, in the act of responding to it, if it's well written and if it's well read. It's really how to define what a good reading is – it doesn't mean that you approve or find yourself favourably disposed to it or what ever. It simply means that you go all the way with the text – you give it space in your imagination and your understanding. So that bead by bead a whole thing is constructed, a whole scene. But the moments are joined together in a very particular way, and information comes at you in a very particular way. What people may find reading the screenplay is that there is a very large number of characters, and it's rather like reading a Russian 19th Century novel when the names of the characters don't stick, but unlike in a great bourgeois realist novel, there aren't pages and pages of exterior description, interior description, psychological moods, states of mind, histories and so on. And so it may seem to new readers of screenplay that there is an insufficiency of data on which their minds can feed. But in my case this is perhaps less true than of others. Because in a way I need to know as much as the reader does about these people.

The mode in contemporary playwriting derides the direction, the intervening material that is not dialogue, and that's absolutely right, absolutely proper, given that post-Brecht what is found by *actors* is probably going to be decisive in creating the meaning, just using dialogue. And in that confrontation with modernity in text writing, there has been a growth in the actor. The actor has come to expect to be a determining force in key areas of the text. I remember an actor playing Kabak in *Occupations* who, as part of his own shaping and experience, had learnt to totally distrust the author's indications which were not dialogue – all direction. And on the second or third day of rehearsals he scored out every line of direction, so he was simply left with dialogue. It was interesting because he persisted with this for two or three weeks and then finally came back to the directions, because the dialogues on their own – it wasn't that they didn't add up or make sense or give you a story, it's just that they didn't give you enough. It's just that so much more was needed. The dialogues are the bit which sticks out of the water. It is possible to construct the submarine size of the iceberg from what you can see, but it's difficult, and you might get it hopelessly wrong.

LIST OF CHARACTERS

MEMBERS OF THE NORWEGIAN ANTARCTIC EXPEDITION

Roald Amundsen	*Leader*
Andreas Beck	*Ice Pilot*
Olav Bjaaland	
Lt. Frederick Gjertsen	
Helmer Hanssen	*Dog-driver*
Sverre Hassel	*Dog-driver*
Hjalmar Johansen	
Adolf Lindstrom	*Cook*
Lt. Thorvald Nilsen	*Fram Second-in-command*
Jacob Nodtvedt	*Fram Second Engineer*
Lt. Krystian Prestrud	
Ronne	*Sailmaker*
Jorgen Stubberud	*Carpenter*
Knut Sundbeck	*Fram Engineer*
Oscar Wisting	*Dog-driver*

MEMBERS OF THE BRITISH
ANTARCTIC EXPEDITION

E. L. Atkinson	*Surgeon*
Henry 'Birdy' Bowers	*Storekeeper*
Lt. Victor Campbell	*Engineering Officer*
Apsley Cherry-Garrard	*Paying Volunteer*
Thomas Clissold	
P. O. Crean	
Frank Debenham	*Geologist*
Sub-Lt. Edward Evans	*Second-in-command*
P. O. Evans	
Forde	
Dimitri Girov	*Russian Dog-handler*
Tryggve Gran	*Norwegian Ski Instructor*
Griffith-Taylor	
P. O. Keohane	
William Lashley	*Stoker*
Levick	*Surgeon*
Cecil Meares	*Dog-handler*
Captain Lawrence Oates	*Army Representative*
Anton Omolchenko	*Russian Dog-handler*
Lt. Pennel	
Raymond Priestly	
Captain Robert F. Scott	*Leader*
Dr. George Simpson	*Meteorologist*
Williams	
P. O. Williamson	
Dr. Edward Wilson	*1st Scientific Officer*
Charles Wright	

OTHER CHARACTERS IN THE UNITED KINGDOM, NORWAY, AUSTRALIA AND THE UNITED STATES

Leon Amundsen	*Amundsen's brother*
Lt. Michael Barne	*Engineer*
Mabel Beardsley	*Club Owner*
Admiral Sir Lewis Beaumont	*Publishing Committee*
Betty Gustavson	*Amundsen's housekeeper*
Kathleen Bruce	*Later Scott's wife*
Dr. Frederick Cook	*Explorer (American)*
Lord Curzon	*Publishing Committee*
Sir Leonard Darwin	*President RGS*
Jens Daugaard-Jensen	*Amundsen's supplier (Danish)*
Bernard Day	*Engineer*
De Walden	*Financier of Scott*
Lord Derby	*Scott supporter*
Alfred Eriksen	*Socialist MP (Norwegian)*
Hilda Evans	*Evans's wife*
Sir John Fisher	*1st Sea Lord*
Girl	*Prostitute (American)*
Scott Keltie	*Secretary, RGS*
King George V	
Joseph Kinsey	*Politician (Australian)*
Sir Clements Markham	*RGS: Scott's Patron*
Fridtjof Nansen	*Norwegian Ambassador to Lon*
Liv Nansen	*Nansen's daughter*
Grace Scott	*Scott's sister*
Hannah Scott	*Scott's mother*
Peter Scott	*Scott's son*
Ernest Shackleton	*Leader 1907 Expedition*
Commander Reginald Skelton	*Original 1st Eng. Officer*
Sir Reginald Smith	*Publishing Committee*
Lt. Wallingford	*Naval Lieutenant*
Warder	*Prison guard (American)*
Ory Wilson	*Wilson's wife*
Fritz Zappfe	*Newspaper editor (Norwegian)*

I

POLES APART

Pretitle: Ross Ice Barrier. Fog on ice. Title: THE LAST PLACE ON EARTH. Rasping and sucking of iced lungs, rhythmic, awful, close to, but the fog hides the source. Elongated figures appear — Scott, Wilson, Shackleton — hauling 200 lbs a man. Wilson's eyes are bandaged: a leather trace fastens him to Scott's leading sledge. The men are gaunt, blackened, bitten, all but beaten; they barely move their loads.

Caption: Ross Ice Barrier, British Antarctic Expedition, January 1902.

Scott calls a halt ('Spell ho!'). The three stand in their separate traces, deadened by effort. There is tension, no ease, among the three. Scott checks a notebook of calculations, searches the fog desperately, sees nothing; calls 'On.'

Tent on ice. Fog. Sledges. Loose dogs.

Inside. Light lurid, unreal. Scott bathes Wilson's blind paining eyes. Away from both, Shackleton broods, glancing bitterly at Scott. Shackleton, grim, exhausted, clears ice from a small looking-glass; fingers and breath.

The glass clears. We see Shackleton's face clearly in it for the first time. He bares his teeth. The gums are black, swollen, bloody. Fade.

*Gjoahavn, King William Land, December 1903. Lightless winter day.
The* Gjoa *stands frozen in ice. Some metres from her, an ice igloo.
From within, sound of stone age singing. Caption: Norwegian Arctic
Expedition, December 1903. Cut to:*

*Amundsen, head and shoulders, a European Eskimo, grave, formal,
respectful, listening, observing. An Eskimo man sings. Another
fashions stone with stone. A woman unravels a sock for thread to
sew fur garments. The song stops.*

*Scan interior. Helmer Hanssen and Adolf Lindstrom, in Eskimo furs,
smoke and watch, at ease.*

*The man's sculpture is finished. He hands it very plainly to
Amundsen, who bows acceptance and squints shortsightedly at it,
searching for blubber-light to admire it. The sculptor clucks, shakes
his head, takes back the stone, holds it in his two hands, closes his
eyes, begins to* feel *the piece.*

*Amundsen takes the stone. Closes eyes. Feels. He nods, eyes closed
still. The sculptor smiles. Amundsen opens his eyes. Nods, smiling.
Fade.*

I. Poles Apart.

Naval barracks, Portsmouth, swathed in fog. Caption: February 1907.

*1. Scott sits at desk, trying to write a letter by lamplight. Stares at
the window; fog gives back his own image. On the desk, a framed
portrait of his mother, Hannah, inscribed: 'To my son, who has
greatness in him.' He stares at it, lost for words.*

Knock on door. It's opened by a young naval lieutenant.

LIEUTENANT The Admiral's compliments, Captain Scott. He
expects to be ready for you in five minutes.

SCOTT (NOT TURNING) Thank you, Mr Wallingford. (AS HE'S
LEAVING) Wallingford.

Wallingford's almost gone; is forced back in.

LIEUTENANT   Sir?

SCOTT   In future, you will knock and *wait*, when approaching a
senior officer's quarters, is that understood?

LIEUTENANT   (UNCERTAIN) Yes, I think so, sir . . . I'm terribly
sorry, sir.

SCOTT   (PEREMPTORY) That will be all, thank you.

*Wallingford leaves, unhappy. Scott stands, begins to tidy appear-
ance in a wall mirror, some casual vanity in the self-scrutiny.
Returns eventually to the unfinished letter on the desk. Reads it over
in silence.*

SCOTT   (VO) Dearest mother, I ask forgiveness in advance for
this letter — I'm afraid yet another Black Time is upon me
and you know what that means. I'm sorry I haven't come
up to London as promised, for the Amundsen do; matters
here weigh too heavily. If I did not have you, my dearest, to
watch over and care for me . . .

*A knock again. Scott places letter on desk, turns to face door, calls
'Come.' Wallingford in.*

WALLINGFORD   Sorry sir. There was a message from Sir Clements
Markham, asks if you would call him later this evening at
his home.

*Scott nods, dark, ungiving. Wallingford retreats. The clock on the
mantel strikes seven. Scott returns to the letter, but he's read as far
as he's got with it.*

SCOTT   (VO) If I did not have you, my dearest, to watch over and
care for me . . .

He screws the paper into nothing, a quite violent tiny gesture, throws it on fire, leaves room.

2. *Royal Geographical Society, London. Entrance Hall. Sounds of reception in upper gallery. Sir Clements Markham enters in basket chair, foot swathed, propelled by two butch-handsome midshipmen around eighteen. A uniformed doorman salutes him.*

MARKHAM   Good evening, Walters. Have you seen the Secretary?

WALTERS   Upper Gallery, Sir Clements, Norwegian Reception.

MARKHAM   (STARING AT MARBLE STAIRS A MOMENT) William . . . (THE BLOND MIDSHIPMAN PRESENTS HIMSELF) Present my compliments to Mr Scott Keltie, ask if I might have an urgent word with him down here . . . (THE BOY'S WORRIED) Cut along, you silly goose, he won't bite you.

The boy leaves for the stairs. Markham stares bleakly at the black-board and easel in the middle of the hall, bearing the neat chalk legend: Capt. R. Amundsen: The Discovery of the North West Passage. Reception, Upper Gallery, 7 p.m. Lecture, Lecture Theatre, 8 p.m. Black tie.

3. *Upper Gallery, crammed with guests and members. Images of power, confidence, ease. Glimpses of Sir John Fisher, First Sea Lord, and retinue; old Arctic admirals, faces cracked in the struggle to hear; others. Trail, over this, drifts of Amundsen's informal press conference down the gallery.*

QUESTIONER   (VOICE) . . . I know my readers will be keenly interested to learn of your future polar plans, Mr Amundsen.

AMUNDSEN   (VOICE) (AWKWARD) Well, when I know them myself, your readers shall be the first to hear.

ANOTHER   (VOICE) Oh come, sir. Will you say anything about the . . . rumour that you propose an early attempt on one of the Poles?

AMUNDSEN (VOICE) I can say nothing about rumours.

NANSEN (VOICE) Gentlemen, Captain Amundsen will communicate his plans for future expeditions in the time-honoured way; that is to say, not before they have been formulated . . .

We arrive at the group on their laughter. Amundsen, in evening dress, amidst his display equipment (ski, bindings, fur suits, provisions, poles, tents) looks out of place. Nansen, older, more beautiful, splendid in cape and ambassadorial insignia, is very much at his ease. The press love him.

SCOTT KELTIE Gentlemen, a last question, if you would. I'd like to introduce Mr Amundsen to members before he speaks . . .

JOURNALIST I'm sure we'd all like to know Mr Amundsen's own view of his discovery of a seaway around the top of the world. Would he care to compare it with other polar feats, Dr Nansen's for example, or Scott's work in the south?

AMUNDSEN (TAKING NANSEN'S LOOK, AS JACKIE FISHER JOINS THE GROUP) Fridtjof Nansen's contribution to polar research is not measurable by lesser men. He is the father of all modern exploration, North or South. Scott, Sverdrup, Borchgrevink, Charcot, Peary, Cook, myself — we are all, in a sense, his sons: we follow the master.

FISHER Hear hear.

AMUNDSEN For myself I claim nothing. There is a poem a Viking ancestor wrote a thousand years ago I would like to recite you, but my English is lacking. (TO NANSEN) Havamal . . .

NANSEN (NODDING) Let me see:
Cattle die
Friends die

Thou thyself shalt die,
I know a thing
That never dies,
Judgement over the dead.
(HANDS BACK TO AMUNDSEN WITH ANOTHER LOOK)

AMUNDSEN   I can wait.

The midshipman arrives, as the journalists peel away with Nansen for technical copy.

MIDSHIPMAN   (NERVOUS, AWARE OF FISHER'S PRESENCE) Beg pardon, sir. (SCOTT KELTIE TURNS) Sir Clements Markham's compliments, sir, he would be most grateful if you could spare him a minute in the Great Hall . . . (SCOTT KELTIE'S DISPLEASED) Sir Clements is chair-bound again, sir.

FISHER   Better see what the old devil wants, Keltie, find out what madcap scheme he's dreaming up now . . . (HAND OUT TO AMUNDSEN, WHO TAKES IT) Fisher, First Sea Lord, honoured to meet you. (SCOTT KELTIE LEAVES WITH THE BOY) Liked your answer to those newspaper people. (NANSEN RETURNING) Very diplomatic. (TO NANSEN) Just telling Amundsen here, the Ambassador's done a fine job on him. Personally, I see no comparison between Amundsen's historic achievement — the discovery of a seaway round the world's roof that sailors have sought for four hundred years and more . . . and Scott's Antarctic escapade.

NANSEN   (SMILING) Sir John, I'm sure Captain Amundsen appreciates . . .

FISHER   Coulda bought a whole new battleship with what that little lot cost us. Pah! And for what? A flag in a patch of snow on a chunk of ice. No sensible fellow would want to do that if there was a chance of getting to Monte Carlo.

He nods to Amundsen, ambles on with his aides. Nansen and Amundsen alone for a moment. Amundsen tries to ease the tight

6

collar, the hired suit.

NANSEN You'll grow used to it.

4. Hall and stairs. Scott Keltie arriving with midshipman. Sir Clements's chair is now discreetly parked.

SCOTT KELTIE (ON THE WALK, VOICE ECHOING) Sir Clements, it's very good to see you, Lord Curzon will be delighted you're well enough to be with us again. (ARRIVED) You must forgive me if I hurry back, I have our guest to attend to.

MARKHAM What's this about Shackleton, Keltie?

SCOTT KELTIE Shackleton?

MARKHAM I have it from an impeccable source that Shackleton is about to announce an attempt on the South Pole, with the full backing of this Society . . .

SCOTT KELTIE (SEEKING QUIET) Sir Clements, Mr Shackleton has our good wishes and nothing more.

MARKHAM So he's going. And you know about it. Ha. You've seen the plan? (KELTIE NODS) Am I right in thinking that he proposes using Scott's base down there? (SCOTT KELTIE DOES NOT ANSWER) I see. Have you at least had the courtesy to inform Scott?

SCOTT KELTIE Mr Shackleton laid his plans in confidence before the Committee some months ago. I would no more dream of divulging Mr Shackleton's plans than I would Captain Scott's.

MARKHAM Scott's plans are advanced and well-known . . . And Scott has priority: the work down there is his, if he wants it. Everyone agrees.

SCOTT KELTIE If everyone agrees, I see no problem, Sir Clements. (FORMAL BOW) Excuse me, would you, I have important matters to attend to. My regards to Lady Markham.

He walks back up the stairs to the reception, still audible beyond. Markham watches him a moment.

MARKHAM   (SHOUTING) Damn your eyes, Keltie. How can you support a black sheep like *Shackleton*? The man's a liar, a cheat and a *failure* ... Scott had to send him home, last time, have you forgotten? (WALTERS, THE DOORMAN, SITS ON HIS CHAIR READING A PAPER, HIS LIPS TWITCHING AT THE SHOW) I'll get an inquiry into this, you see, and it will take your *hide* off, Mr Secretary.

Scott Keltie stiffly evaporates at the top of the stairs without turning.

MARKHAM   (NORMAL VOICE) Philip, dear boy, order the carriage, will you. We will not remain here in this perfidious house.

The other midshipman detaches to speak to Walters. Sir Clements fumes inwardly; senses a lifetime's subtlety coarsening into rant and bluster. William blows his nose, embarrassed and alarmed. An ancient Arctic Admiral — Sir Leopold McLintock, late eighties — hobbles towards Markham's bathchair.

ADMIRAL   (FRAIL, DEAF, SCATTERED) Ah, Pimlico, Pimlico. (STOPS, FROWNS) Seen anything of Sir John Franklin? Just talking to him a minute ago, in the thing ... in the thing ...

MARKHAM   Dead, Sir Leopold.

ADMIRAL   Where? (FROWNS, SCANS THE HALL WITH RHEUMY EYES)

MARKHAM   Fifty-six years ago. One hundred and fifty men died with him, Arctic sea.

The Admiral totters off, hearing little, understanding nothing. CU Markham, grave suddenly. William's hand touches his shoulder.

WILLIAM   The carriage, Sir Clements.

Markham gently covers William's hand with his own.

MARKHAM   (OOS) Thank you.

5. *Scott stands in Admiral's study, confronting his image in the porthole wall mirror inset among books. Off, next door, the sound of after-dinner clinking and chat. Some laughter. Scott turns towards fireplace. The mantel clock ticks: 8.25. Scott grits his teeth, working to disperse the dark patches of anger on his cheeks.*

The door opens behind him on a splash of noise. He turns, stiffens to confront the Admiral.

ADMIRAL   Scott, sorry you've had to wait, take a seat. (POINTS TO AN ARMCHAIR. SCOTT TAKES A PADDED UPRIGHT. THE ADMIRAL SITS, BALANCES BRANDY ON HIS CHAIR-ARM) Drink?

SCOTT   No thank you, Sir William.

Silence. The Admiral re-lights his cigar.

ADMIRAL   (UNLEASHING SLOWLY, BUT PICKING UP SPEED) I'll be plain with you, Scott. I've studied all the evidence at my disposal and I can't say things look at all good for you . . . (SCOTT MAKES TO SPEAK) Let me finish. You know perfectly well that the captain of a battleship in collision is technically responsible for that collision. It is no defence to claim that he was not on the bridge at the material time; particularly if the fleet is engaged, as it was, in delicate exercises that demand the executive presence of the executive officer. (SILENCE) Repairs to the *Commonwealth* are estimated at between four and six thousand pounds; to your own ship at around eight hundred; so there can be no question of keeping the matter under covers; the only question is whether we can stave off a court-martial. (SCOTT BLINKS) I shall, of course, do everything in my power to see a court-martial is not constituted . . .

SCOTT   Thank you, sir.

ADMIRAL   Not to save *your* skin, Scott — I've thought you an unlucky officer since the day I clapped eyes on you — but my own. It's my command and Jackie Fisher at the Admiralty would eat my guts for breakfast, given half a chance. (PAUSE) Whatever the outcome, I must tell you that, in my considered opinion, there is no career for you in battleships. Do you take my meaning? (SCOTT NODS STIFFLY) Good. I think that's all I need to say for the present. (STANDS, WITH SCOTT) Good night, Captain.

He returns to the next room. Their chat picks up. Scott is ashamed of his showing. The clock strikes 8.30. He leaves.

6. Nansen's rooms, Norwegian Embassy. Amundsen stares at a framed photograph on the wall: Nansen and Johansen in Greenland, Fram *ice-locked behind them.*

NANSEN   (OOS) Johansen. Ever meet him? (AMUNDSEN SHAKES HEAD) Sad case. Cracked completely. (MAKES DRINKING MOTION) I try to help, from time to time. I owe him much.

AMUNDSEN   I was studying the boat. (THEY STUDY IT TOGETHER)

NANSEN   (GENTLY) *Fram.*

AMUNDSEN   (GRAVE) *Fram.*

They take their drinks to the armchairs. Nansen goes deep into his; Amundsen leans forward.

AMUNDSEN   Herr Doctor Nansen. I have the honour to make an important request of you.

NANSEN   Proceed.

AMUNDSEN   My work in the north remains unfinished. It is my aim to reach the North Magnetic Pole and the Great Nail itself. As soon as possible. (PAUSE) If, after you have studied my concrete plans, you consider I am indeed the man for this undertaking, I request that you relinquish the boat of

Norway for use by me on that work. (HE SITS BACK, A HARD BIT OVER, A HARDER BIT APPROACHING) Because without *Fram*, perhaps that work cannot be done.

Their looks hold across the firelit rug for some moments. The telephone burrs down the room. Nansen crosses lithely to answer. Amundsen watches him, not listening, uninterested, fascinated by Nansen's grace and beauty; while with his free hand he carefully unfastens his collar button.

Nansen returns after half a dozen sentences.

NANSEN When you ask for a man's dreams, you ask for everything. (AMUNDSEN DOESN'T UNDERSTAND) Surprising as it may seem, Captain Amundsen, I have not as yet thrown off entirely the haunting idea that I may still have within me the resources for one final expedition of my own. (AMUNDSEN BLINKS, SURPRISED, THEN NODS) For now, I best serve my country here. But I have long cherished the thought of the South Pole. (PAUSE) I will make you a promise. Should the time come when that possibility is . . . beyond me, you may ask again.

AMUNDSEN Thank you, sir. I am honoured by your trust.

An aide enters, on the knock.

AIDE Mrs Simmons has arrived, sir. I've put her in the study.

Nansen looks briefly at Amundsen, who is wholly incurious.

NANSEN Thank you. See there's a fire.

The aide leaves. The men stand. Shake hands formally.

NANSEN For what it's worth, the telephone call just now was from our man in Edinburgh — Apparently Shackleton's on the point of declaring a bid for the South. (BEGINS LEADING AMUNDSEN INTO THE HALLWAY) There. It's possible he'll spike my dream and deliver *Fram* to you for the North.

AMUNDSEN (RATIONAL) If your dream dies, I think it unlikely it will be Shackleton's doing, Herr Doctor, brave though he may be.

Hall. Nansen glances once at closed study door, but is intrigued by Amundsen's response.

NANSEN I've always found it unwise to underestimate the British.

AMUNDSEN (IN DOORWAY NOW) Shackleton is a romantic. He has a better chance of perishing than of reaching the South Pole. And, like his countrymen, will be as happy with one as with the other. (PAUSE) How else explain his absence from my lecture tonight? Experience teaches them only one thing: that they are British and therefore pre-eminent. (PAUSE) But Nature is deaf to such things: she cannot hear the tunes of glory.

He shakes Nansen's hand again, as close to warmth as he can achieve.

AMUNDSEN Thank you. My regards to your wife.

He bows, leaves. Nansen closes door. Muses. Crosses to the study. Pushes door open, enters, closes it with hands behind him, his head against a pinned map of Antarctica on the door. His POV, across the half bright, half dark room. A young woman, brocade blouse, skirt, ankle boots, thick dark auburn hair freed to the waist, kneels before the fire. She's turned her head to look at him over her shoulder. Her fire-thrown shadow rests on his shirt-front. Trail Scott's voice: 'It's Captain Scott, returning Sir Clement's call . . .'

7. *The servant places the receiver on the marble hall table, passes out of view into the adjoining large drawing-room. Piano, rhythmic, simple. The servant, an old sailor with a bluebird tattoo on his hand, returns, pushing Sir Clements to the table. The music stops. A few low giggles.*

MARKHAM   Scott, thank God, is that you? How soon can you get up to town? (LISTENS, CUTS IN) Wait, wait a moment . . .

He angles his chair backwards, to look into the drawing-room. The giggles close off, the piano starts up. Markham returns to the table; the shot passes him, rounding the corner and revealing the room. William and Philip are in naval PE kit. Philip plays the piano, William does exercises with a pair of Indian Clubs. Over this, we hear Markham in the hall.

MARKHAM   Scott, I can perfectly understand your reluctance to leave Portsmouth with your naval affairs in such a delicate state, but when you have heard my appalling news you may feel you have reason to reconsider the matter . . .

Cut to

8. A train thuds into a tunnel.

9. Scott stares at his civilian reflection in the inky window. Bleak fear in the eyes. Misted daylight wipes the image. He glances down at the folded Daily Mail *on his lap. Headlines declaim:* SHACKLETON FOR THE POLE.

GUARD   Bushey. Bushey.

Scott stands, spilling the paper on to the floor as he reaches for a small leather bag on the rack opposite. When he's gone, we see the fractured headline:

SHACKLE
THE POLE

10. Long POV track in to the lone figure down the platform. Through the darkening mist we see it's WILSON, in old country clothes, shy-faced; saintly, in an English way. He offers his hand to Scott.

WILSON   Captain Scott, how are you, sir?

SCOTT   Happier for seeing you, dear friend. How are you, Bill?

WILSON   Grossly overworked and rather happy, but by the size of your bag I'd say you weren't proposing to stay overnight, and you have not arrived only hours after your telegram to talk about *me*. We have a mile to walk and a lunch to eat, will we talk on the way?

He's guiding Scott through the gates. Wilson, behind Scott, indicates him with a nod of the head to the ticket collector.

WILSON   Here you are, Alfred.

TICKET COLLECTOR   Captain Scott, sir? (SCOTT SHRINKS, THEN SWELLS) Dr Wilson said he was expecting you. I was sure 'e was pulling my leg. I wonder if you'd sign me your autograph, sir, for my boy. 'E's read your book three times, sir, once in Sunday School. Here would do, sir. (HE HANDS SCOTT A NEWSPAPER HE'S FISHED OUT)

SCOTT   Certainly. (SCOTT SCRAWLS HIS NAME WITH HIS OWN FOUNTAIN PEN)

TICKET COLLECTOR   God bless you, sir. Two 'eroes together, quite inspiring.

Scott hands him the paper.

WILSON   (TO SCOTT) Spell ho?

SCOTT   Spell ho.

11. Shots of them walking the Hertfordshire mile, the mist thickening. Scott talks, gesturing tensely from time to time, walking cane up or out. Wilson strides like a priest, arms clasped behind back, nods, listens, unreluctantly sage for the asking. Scott's voice turns to wool on the mist. 'Tynecote' looms; an old retriever runs from the cottage to greet them.

12. Mid-afternoon, the room already quite dark. They sit at table, lunch over, filling pipes from a pouch, Ory Wilson replacing pans on a shelf at the sink. There's a lull around Ory's work. Scott senses the disapproval in her. She eases herself behind Wilson's chair to get through: touches him lovingly on the neck. He takes her hand lightly, kisses it.

ORY (UNAPOLOGETIC) I have some work.

She plants a log on the fire, leaves through an open arch into the next room, sits at her potter's wheel. Scott has awkwardly half-risen, as she's left; resumes his chair.

WILSON (LOOKING AT WINDOW, FORMULATING RESPONSE) We had mist like this, our first day out on the Barrier, remember?

SCOTT (NOT LOOKING) Mmm.

The clock strikes two-thirty. Scott checks his watch methodically, pats it, puts it away. Wilson feels it as pressure.

SCOTT (SOMBRE) I need your advice, old chap. You're the wisest man in all the world and a true friend. (PAUSE) I need your help.

Wilson relights his pipe with a taper at the fire. Ory's wheel hums in the next room. He sits in his old armchair, waves Scott to join him in the chair opposite.

WILSON There are old sores at work here. It is important not to let them infect one's judgement, Con.

SCOTT (BITTER, DESPERATE) It is *Shackleton* has the grudge, not me, Bill. This whole escapade is his way of taking revenge for the slight he imagines I did him in sending him home, don't you see. He had scurvy, dammit. He was a liability. (CALMS, GATHERS) It's so ironic: Shackleton owes me everything and this is how he repays me. (A TEMPO UP) Scott, let

WILSON (A TEMPO UP) Scott, let me tell you quite plainly. Shackleton can have had no idea that you were planning another expedition. Of that you may be quite certain.

SCOTT (SENSING THIS OUT) Bill, you're a saint, you think the best of everyone.

WILSON (PUSHING ON) I'm not telling you what I believe, I'm telling you what I know.

Scott weighs this, working for understanding, not liking it. Ory's POV of his untenanted chair through the arch. Scott sits back in it, entering the frame. Ory stops the wheel, wets it, cleans it.

SCOTT Know? How?

WILSON (INTO FRAME, SEARCHING BEHIND MANTEL CLOCK) Here. (HE HOLDS A WAD OF LETTERS, TELEGRAMS) Shackles wrote to me of his plans almost a fortnight ago. A week or so back he sat in that very chair, filling out the details — boat, crew, expeditionary goals, scientific work, finance, everything. (INDICATING THE SHEAF OF CORRESPONDENCE) Since then, letters, telegrams . . . His talk throughout is of provisions and recruitment and the boat and the paramount need to beat the Belgians, the French. Norwegians, Japanese, Americans . . . (BEAT) Nowhere here (TAPS THE LETTERS) And at no time during our talk was there the slightest hint that he was not alone in the field with full rights of access to sovereign territory. (PAUSE. PUTS LETTERS BACK, RETURNS TO CHAIR, CLEARING FRAME. CUT BACK INTO ROOM.) It may be that he's guilty of a gravely discourteous oversight, in not informing you of his intention to use McMurdo and inquiring whether it might inconvenience any plan of your own: but he is not a cad; on that I will stake my life and reputation. Had Shackleton been aware, I should have known it. (SCOTT SITS QUITE UPRIGHT, WORKING

ON ALL OF THIS) So. You must tell me what you think I can do, to help the matter. (SCOTT BROODS, UNCERTAIN WILSON'S HIS FULL ALLY)

SCOTT   (EVENTUALLY) What did he want? (WILSON FROWNS) Shackleton.

WILSON   He wanted me to join him.

SCOTT   I see.

WILSON   Set his heart on it. (AT HIS PIPE AGAIN, LEAVING SCOTT TO STEW) Scientific Officer. Pretty much my own terms. (LEAVES IT)

Scott needs to know.

SCOTT   What did you say?

WILSON   (UNHURRIED) I said no.

Scott lays his head back on the chair, studies the ceiling, silencing his relief. Silence, save for clock, wheel and fire. Wilson stares at flame, thinking ice. The eyes grow ironic, bitter.

WILSON   (LOW VOICE, FLECKED WITH SELF-CONTEMPT, HARDLY AUDIBLE IN ORY'S ROOM) Couldn't spare myself, you see. From the important work I'm engaged in for the Grouse Commission. Helping Lord Lovat and his friends discover the causes of disease in Capercaillie and Red Grouse. (PAUSE) Ten years ago I was conducting medical research among the poor of Battersea. But then ten years ago I had not learned the value of clean sheets, and good hotel beds, dear Ory. Try to persuade myself it's part of God's purpose, this ease, but all I see is that since I left the Barrier my life has not had a moment's real *suffering* to offer Him.

Scott has watched him very carefully, dimly sensing purchase. Ory watches Scott, wheel stilling.

SCOTT (CAREFULLY INTIMATE) I've never much believed in God, Bill, never hidden it from you, but there are moments in a life when events seem to bear the unmistakable print of a providential hand. I sense this to be such a moment. (WILSON'S DRAWN TO THE GRAVITAS) Shackleton's offer stirred desire in you, for service and self-sacrifice, but something impelled you to say no. Bill, for three months I have had in my desk a list of key personnel to man the next expedition. At its head, as Second-in-Command and Senior Scientific Officer is Dr Edward Adrian Wilson. And in brackets after it: *sine qua non.* I have always known that . . . if I ever get back to the South . . . and see the Pole . . . I would have you by my side, Bill.

Long silence. The dog trembles in its basket, dreaming.

WILSON That's very gratifying to know, Captain Scott. I'm obliged.

SCOTT We make a good team.

WILSON You know I have to tell you what I told Shackles: I couldn't be free until next year at the earliest?

SCOTT I can wait. If Shackleton cannot be stopped, I shall have no option but to wait, at least until the outcome of his efforts is known . . . (BEAT) But even if he were to do the honourable thing and withdraw, I should still not leave until you were properly free to join me. (PAUSE) There's a . . . rightness in things, you know, Bill: the work in the

18

South is mine; just as the scientific endeavour is yours.
(DELIBERATE PAUSE) It may be enough that he be made to
agree not to use my base at McMurdo.

*Ory quietly passes through the room, calling the dog, Punch,
to follow her. They hear her leave the house and walk along
the window path and away. Scott checks Wilson's reaction, needing the mood to hold. Wilson appears barely to have taken
her in.*

WILSON It's very peculiar, you know. You fill me with that
same certainty: I *know* you're right. (BEAT) It's like . . . an
ordinance . . . an ordination. Yes.

A lamp blubbers, smokes a little, settles.

SCOTT (OOS) Yes.

13. Thames dockland, waterfront. Drizzle, haze.

SHACKLETON (CU. FAINTLY IRISH SOMEWHERE) Keep 'em shut.
Nice and tight. (WILSON'S FACE, CU, EYES CLOSED, SHACKLE-
TON'S AGAIN, WIDENING TO REVEAL HIM POSING WITH A
SKINNY PONY ON EACH HAND, JUST PRODUCED FROM A NEAR-
BY LOT) All right, you can look. (WILSON SEES THE PONIES,
BLINKS) From Siberia. Don't you see, *we* know *horses* . . .
Leave dogs to them as know 'em . . . With these little mutts,
I shall see the Pole, Billy boy. Thanks, Mr Marsden. (A
YOUNG MAN COMES OUT OF A SHED, REMOVES THE PONIES.
SHACKLETON SHAKES WILSON'S HAND, CLASPS HIM WARMLY
TO HIM) Well, Billy, I've been agog since I got your note.
You'd better put me out of my misery. Have you changed
your mind about coming?

WILSON No. Shackle, I haven't.

Shackleton nods, the disappointment sharp for a moment.

SHACKLETON   Well. That's a shame. (PAUSE) What can I do for
you, Billy? Ask away.

WILSON   Scott has asked me to speak with you.

SHACKLETON   (FACE CLOSING) Scott? What about?

WILSON   Could we walk, do you think? (HE WAVES AT THE
WHARF, ACTIVE WITH WORKERS, SOME OF THEM SHACKLETON'S
WITH PONIES, CRATES, FODDER.)

SHACKLETON   (DELIBERATING) I have some interviews for crew
at Waterloo Place, walk me over.

*He buckles his cape securely, twigs his artist's floppy hat, calls his
projected whereabouts to a passing colleague, turns back finally to
where Wilson waits.*

SHACKLETON   Right, say on.

*14. Shots of gull screaming over the river; a second; two discrete
sounds. They fight over items of ship's refuse.*

*15. Overhead shots of Wilson and Shackleton, through wharves and
side roads. Wilson talks, quiet, insistent. Shackleton listens grimly,
big arms behind broad back.*

*16. Sudden shot of Shackleton, from close up, halting the walk and
Wilson's sentence.*

SHACKLETON   (WHITE) Billy, let us have one thing clear between
us before you go on. If indeed Scott *has* plans, they were *at
no time* made known to me. There can therefore be no
question of my withdrawing. To suggest otherwise impugns
my honour and integrity.

WILSON   (SIMPLE, IMPLACABLE) Agreed. Equally, I would ask

20

you to accept without qualification Scott's word on the prior existence of his own intentions.

Shackleton feels the weight and the coldness of the logic he's invited.

SHACKLETON (MOVING ON) There is more, I suppose?

17. A tug funnel, CU, shrills petulant warnings. A second, CU, gives calm tenor response. Down the dark water a ship's horn moans at fog.

18. They walk in LS as before. Abrupt cut to

19. City graveyard on river. Shackleton, foregrounded, facing river, reviewing Scott's McMurdo paper; his face is bleak, angry, distressed as he confonts the enormity. Wilson stands some paces behind him, church-fringed, an impassive pressure at the back of the shot.

WILSON (GENTLY, NOT LIKING SHACKLETON'S DISTRESS) . . . No success, Shackles, not even the Pole itself, could morally justify forestalling Scott's prior claim to the use of that base. Certainly the gilt would be off the gingerbread . . .

SHACKLETON (AS IF TO HIMSELF) He dogs my days, this . . . little careerist, this . . . mediocrity. Man I will not call him. Too small. Too mean. He will not rest until I am dead and my mouth stopped. (TURNS ABRUPTLY TO FACE WILSON) He nearly killed the pair of us out on the Barrier, Bill, with his antics . . . And home he comes, to take the glory, and write me into history as a burdensome liability to the enterprise. My God, Billy, we *all* had scurvy, you're a doctor, you know that! I have said in public only enough to clear my name of this vile, self-serving slander, and carned his undying hatred. I *will* not sign to this! This virtually guarantees I shall not reach the goal of the expedition. This he must not, cannot ask. (THEY LOOK AT EACH OTHER FOR SOME TIME. SHACKLETON SEARCHES FOR MORAL SUPPORT, FINDS ONLY IMPLACABLE SYMPATHY. HE TURNS AWAY AGAIN TOWARDS THE RIVER. BLEAK, RESOLUTION SUDDENLY EBBING)

Shall I say it for you, Billy? If I refuse to sign, he will have no recourse but to put the facts before the public etc. etc. The scandal scares off my backers and the expedition evaporates. (LOOKS AT MEMORANDUM. MISERY GREASES HIS FACE) O Billy, Billy, Billy. These are scoundrel days, when honest men do the work of blackguards. I pray you have sound reasons, Billy. I do. I do.

CU Wilson, guiltless, doing his duty. The church bell begins to toll.

Ship's horn.

20. Amundsen on deck, Christiania Fjord, gazing at a single castle-like house lifted up above the far shore.

SMALL BOY'S VOICE   (OOS) That's Fridtjof Nansen's house. It's called Polar Heights, my father told me.

AMUNDSEN   (KNOWING) Is it?

SMALL BOY   Great men live in great houses.

The house floats gently by.

21. Quayside, Christiania. Leon Amundsen greets his brother undemonstratively; business first.

LEON   There are press in the Passenger Hall. (POINTS THE DIRECTION) They want to talk with you. There's a rumour the Americans are heading North.

AMUNDSEN   Rumour. Mmm.

LEON   I thought you might be able to tell them we had the boat.

Amundsen looks at him impassively for a moment, then shakes his head.

LEON   No announcement, then.

AMUNDSEN   Can we get this way?

Leon nods, phlegmatic, takes up his brother's case, ducks under the rope, holds it up for the tall man.

AMUNDSEN   How is the house coming along? Is it finished yet?

LEON   The house? It's costing us a fortune.

AMUNDSEN   Great men must live in great houses, Leon.

22. Scott's study, 56 Oakley Street, SW3, recently acquired. His hands lift the last books from a tea chest, place them on a shelf.

SCOTT   (OOS, CALLING) Mother, I've finished in here, come and look.

He looks at the room. It glistens with mounted medals and framed scrolls around the walls: RGS, Philadelphia GS, Royal Scottish GS, Royal Danish GS, American GS, the King's special Antarctic Decoration; his CVO; printed resolution of thanks from the Royal Society; Honorary D Sc from Cambridge; others. The bookshelves are modest and lightly filled with verse and general reading; no maps, atlases. On the desk, a picture of his mother holding him on her knee in the garden at Outlands; above it, the picture of Scott and Wilson at their Furthest South, signed 'In admiration, Bill.' Dank weather beyond the slim window.

Hannah Scott in, late sixties, frail but tough, carrying envelopes and a book.

HANNAH   You have mail. (PLACES IT ON DESK) And Mr Love asks if you would kindly sign his copy of your book. (SHE HANDS IT TO HIM) The tenant at Outlands, you remember. (HE NODS) (SHE INSPECTS THE ROOM) It looks very nice. I do hope we'll be happy here.

SCOTT   You're not to worry, I won't be on half-pay for ever, mother, and it will be a capital base while I'm mooching.

HANNAH   It's not for myself I worry, Con. (BEAT) It hurts so to see you . . . becalmed like this.

He sits down at the desk, chews the inside of his lips, reaches for Mr Love's book and a pen.

HANNAH   Go to Mr Barrie's luncheon party, it will do you so much good to be with others and feel their regard.

He smiles wanly, hands her the book, takes her hand, kisses it.

SCOTT   You're the only one to really *matter*, mother. (SHE TOUCHES HIS THINNING HAIR ONCE, REMOVES HER HAND) We'll see.

HANNAH   I'm old and tired. You should be making plans . . .

She leaves the room. He sits a moment, quite black; runs a slow pencil through the mail, restless, stops the rummage; removes an addressographed envelope; opens it, removes two sheets of paper clipped together. He reads the top one-liner, turns nervously to the second. Over his changing face, we hear Shackleton's voice:

> 'Dear Captain Scott, I undertake to leave the McMurdo Sound base to you, and land either at the place known as the Barrier Inlet or at King Edward VII Land, whichever is the most suitable. I will not work to the Westward of the 170th meridian west and shall not make any sledge journeys going west . . . I hope this letter meets you on the points you desire . . .'

Scott turns back to read the covering note, then lays them on the desk, begins to straighten his dress and smooths his hair in a wall-mirror.

SCOTT   (CALLING) I believe I'll go to Mr Barrie's after all, mother.

He leaves the room. We hear him whistling in the passage. Close in on the top letter, until we can read:

'Dear Scott, I think this is fair. Cordially, Bill.'

23. *Images of Shackleton and* Nimrod *setting out for the South. Crowds, flags, King Edward VII and Queen, pole fever, patriotism, fervour, singing. Over this, binding it, a schoolboy's essay fragment, voiced:*

'Today, 7 August 1907, will live proud in the history of our country. For on this day, the intrepid explorer Captain Shackleton and his doughty crew turned their backs on the comforts of civilization and fearlessly set sail for the *terra incognita* of Antarctica. Our hearts, though they beat a little faster, journey with them on their dangerous enterprise, knowing that they go not for material gain nor personal advancement, but to show the world and their countrymen that British pluck can still triumph over all adversity. Thee we salute, brave Shackleton, the envy of our race . . .'

24. *Scott appears in CU, somewhere along the sequence above. Gradually establish Mabel Beardsley's salon, Artillery Row, evening. Scott stands in hallway, discreetly observing a young woman in the quite busy drawing-room. The woman is lively, direct, rather singularly dressed, very tanned, healthy-looking; twenty-nine.*

MABEL BEARDSLEY (OOS; CONSPIRATORIAL) Your wish is my command, Captain Scott. It wasn't easy. Doesn't she look wonderful?

Scott turns, surprised.

SCOTT   Mabel. I'm most grateful. Yes, yes. Very lovely.

MABEL   Come, I'll take you over.

SCOTT   No, I'll . . . there's no hurry.

Mabel smiles, happy procuring for the famous.

MABEL   I wish it were me, darling, but you know that, don't you, you, cruel man you . . .

25. *Develop wheeling images, over time, of Scott studying the woman and her gradual awareness of him. Once, their eyes meet: he smiles rather formally, bows from across the room. She smiles, looks away. A young man (Howard de Walden) hovers by her chair. Henry James, Max Beerbohm, Ernest Thesiger and J.M. Barrie add a certain weight to the rather raffish gathering. Fragments: James:* 'It doesn't much matter what you do in particular, so long as you have had your life. If you haven't had that what **have** you had? The right time, my dear Miss Bruce, is any time that one is still so lucky as to have. Live!'; *Barrie:* 'Ah, the tragedy of a man who has found himself out'; *Beerbohm:* 'What have you done, Kathleen? You've set them both to self-quotation, they will go on all night long . . .' *In the last image, the woman leaves the drawing-room, enters a back parlour. Scott watches.*

26. *Back parlour. She sits alone in the room, pinning a fallen hem, her calves and ankle boots generously revealed.*

SCOTT   (OOS) Do I disturb you, Miss Bruce?

She looks at him very frankly, unalarmed.

KATHLEEN   Not at all, captain. I'll just finish this.

He looks pointedly at a wall painting, but it's a Beardsley and offers no refuge. She watches out of corner of eye; is amused.

KATHLEEN   There, that should hold it. Won't you sit down?

He smiles, takes a chair opposite.

KATHLEEN   You remembered my name. I'm flattered.

SCOTT   And you mine.

KATHLEEN   (LAUGHING) Yes, quite a feat that, I meet so many great and famous explorers it's a job sorting you all out.

26

Scott laughs with her; an unfamiliar sound. They stare at each other for some moments.

SCOTT You've been abroad?

KATHLEEN Greece. Vagabonding.

SCOTT I tried to reach you, after . . . Thin air . . .

KATHLEEN Why?

SCOTT I can't say. I felt I'd like to know you better.

She glows at him across the shaded parlour. He looks for more words; they don't come.

MABEL (IN DOORWAY) Isadora's *not* coming after all, Kiddie, stuck in Brussels of all places, Arabella has the story. I hope you're keeping the good captain amused. (SHE'S GONE)

KATHLEEN Well? (SCOTT MAKES NO ANSWER, STRETCHED TAUT BETWEEN FASCINATION AND FEAR) What time is it? (HE CHECKS WATCH, TELLS HER) I have a supper engagement in Soho at nine. (BEAT)

SCOTT Ah. (TEETH WORRY HIS UPPER LIP) I had hoped to have the pleasure of escorting you home. (HE STANDS, UNCERTAIN NOW)

KATHLEEN (STANDING) Really? That sounds fun. In that case, why don't you call a cab? (SCOTT FROWNS) What's the matter?

SCOTT Are you sure?

KATHLEEN (MATTER-OF-FACT) Of course.

27. Interior, third-floor studio apartment, Chelsea, overlooking river. Busts, canvases, works in progress; divan below open window; an active, decisive room, sparse but alive. The stair door opens inwards, revealing Kathleen Bruce in doorway, Scott a pace or so behind. She lights a small lamp, rakes the fire to a glow, removes her topcoat and hat, fills a kettle with water, calm, matter-of-fact, talking all the time (rent four shillings a week, the landlady, the view of the river, the light for her work). He stands, irresolute yet drawn, in doorway, hat in hand.

KATHLEEN (SEEING HIM) Well, Captain?

SCOTT Miss Bruce, it was wrong of me to ask to see your room. I fear I only jeopardize your reputation.

KATHLEEN Captain, I lived for five years in Paris, as a student, I have fended for myself since the age of seventeen, and I am absolutely my own woman. I would like you to see my room.

He enters slowly, closes the door behind him.

SCOTT You are . . . an extraordinary woman, Miss Bruce.

KATHLEEN Because I know my own mind? If I were a man, I'd be very ordinary indeed. I have no alcohol, I don't drink it, will you have tea? (HE NODS) Sit by the fire where I can see you. Are you hungry, have an orange. Call me Kathleen, will you?

28. She stands at the stove for the tea to brew, watching Scott study her busts and canvases; removes the two pins that hold her hair, which floods her shoulders.

KATHLEEN That's Isadora Duncan, the dancer, my deepest friend. She has the most beautiful body I have ever seen, I love it, sometimes I think I love it better than my own. (HE LOOKS AT HER, SEES THE HAIR) When she dances. (SILENCE, THE LOOK HOLDING. LOW VOICE) Will you get there, Captain? (BEAT) The Pole?

SCOTT Kathleen.

KATHLEEN (LOW, FIERCE) You *will*. I knew it from the first moment I met you.

He stares mutely at her, roused and frozen.

KATHLEEN (SOFTER NOW) I don't believe sleeping together would be a particularly good idea for either of us. I know for myself I am reluctant to risk any major complications to an already complicated life.

She carries the brown enamel mugs of tea to the fireside, kneels on the rug before the chair he eventually occupies.

KATHLEEN I love your modesty. You're so English you're like a foreigner. I want to call you Con but I can't, it won't come. (SHE TURNS HER BACK ON HIM, CLOSE, BEGINS TO BRUSH THE RICH HAIR)

SCOTT Kathleen. I *asked* Mabel Beardsley to invite you today.

KATHLEEN (BRUSHING, BRUSHING) I know.

He absorbs this like a drug, sucked by the rhythmed hair.

KATHLEEN Here.

She hands him the brush. The hair gleams at him.

29. Sequence of images of the developing relationship, scored by fragments of their letters. The principal visual and epistolatory theme is Kathleen Bruce leading him her dance.

Fragments: Scott: 'I've tried to telephone you without result, so now this is to ask you if I may take you out to dinner tonight? It seems so long till Friday — give me all the time you can. I've been worrying about you, imagining I may have hurt you in word or deed. Dear if you only knew, I'm half frightened of you. I've so little, so very little to offer. Dear blue eyes, they haunt me . . . One thing, dearest, there must be no sadness in that sweet face — never — that is the only fixed thought in me now . . . What a world you are opening to me. It's like a dream . . . Do you realise that you will have to change me, change me? . . . In the end I'm half fearful. Shall I satisfy you, girl of my heart? You'll have to inspire a dull person indeed.' *etc.*

Kathleen: 'It makes me *mad* to read "All serious thoughts go when I see that sweet face." You are a busy and important man with a career to attend to and an historic mission to accomplish and if you were not I don't imagine I would have given you a second glance, so please don't be silly (though it's very nice!) Bless you, bless you, bless you. The sun is shining, I am as happy as can be. I do find your love for me so precious, so very precious . . . There could only be one reason in life for me to want to get married; but bearing your son now, given our financial circumstance, would only be an encumbrance we could scarcely cope with . . . Don't let's get married . . .' *etc.*

Towards close of sequence, cut in unexplained image of Amundsen, face on, in large reception hall of Nansen's house, Polhogda, Lysaker.

30. Amundsen stands, hat in hand, before the large, theatrical staircase, listening to the house. A dog barks outside, quite close. Cut to

31. Shot of the house from headland garden. The barking dog crosses frame, after rabbit. Cut to

32. Amundsen again. Barking recedes. We hear the house with him: creaks of magnificent wood; footsteps in upstairs room; voices, low, raised, all remote in the big house. Amundsen stands stock-still, impassive, masking the churning well. Click of a door, Liv Nansen, fifteen-year-old daughter, appears, tall, quite lovely, very grave. She stares at Amundsen for some time, caught in her tracks. Voices upstairs lift and fall, Nansen's, Eva's, then silence. Liv knows he's Amundsen; understands upstairs.

AMUNDSEN Good day.

LIV NANSEN Good day.

She walks on, soundless, passes into another room. The house is still. Amundsen waits, staring at stairs. A door slams upstairs, a woman calls 'No!' in pain. Slow steps round the upper gallery. On the stairs themselves. Nansen appears, tall, pale, beautiful, face masked to stillness. He stops two steps from the floor. Amundsen looks up at him.

NANSEN   You shall have *Fram*.

AMUNDSEN   I thank you, sir.

NANSEN   You're younger, you have a great life's work ahead of you, going South first would delay that work too long. I will draft a letter to Parliament for you.

AMUNDSEN   I'm in your debt.

NANSEN   You'll excuse me, will you — I think I have caught a slight chill. (HE TURNS TO WALK BACK UP THE STAIRS)

AMUNDSEN   Dr Nansen, I will not betray this trust. My work *will* have meaning.

NANSEN   There is nothing called meaning in Nature. Meaning is a purely human concept which we put into existence. Life has no meaning.

He walks on and up and out of sight. Amundsen puts on his hat, a servant has appeared to show him out. In Liv's room, a piano strikes up, with a bizarrely cheerful tune.

33. Svartskog, Bundefjord. Cork, cheers, bubbles; glasses reach for the spill. A dozen or so housewarming guests stand or sit in geniul clusters between house and fjord, as the wine is passed. Old Betty shuffles in and out, loving the work. Leon is in charge of drink. Lindstrom appears at the top of the front steps, a tray of his superb cakes in hands. Betty fusses them from him, takes them to the long table. Amundsen shakes hands with guests, friendly and remote. he stares up at the roof, where Stubberud, twenty-two, is replacing tiles. Stubberud sees him watching, waves with his hammer. Amundsen gestures with his glass that he should join the party. Stubberud nods, works on. Greetings, laughter, somewhere behind Amundsen. He turns; sees Lindstrom hugging a new arrival, Helmer Hanssen. The man, thirty-seven, has a small seaman's pack with him. Sees Amundsen. Walks towards him, taking in the house on the way.

HANSSEN   Fine house, chief.

AMUNDSEN   It will be. When the young man's finished with it. (STUBBERUD WORKS ON) Thank you for coming, Helmer.

They shake hands warmly.

HANSSEN   You know me, chief. (BEAT) Just waiting for the call.

AMUNDSEN   Have some wine, I have a speech to make and then I'll show you your room.

Hanssen nods. Amundsen takes his bag, hands it to Betty, crosses to the long table, where the guests are gathered.

Long shot of the scene, Amundsen's words and the ensuing toast adrift in the soft air.

34. Night. The lit house happy with music, talk, laughter. Some people are already leaving.

35. Late. Drawing-room, as yet sparsely furnished. The core remains, drinking schnapps: Leon, Zappfe, Hanssen, Lindstrom, Amundsen. Betty shuffles around, clearing things, muttering to herself in Swedish.

LINDSTROM   Ah, the *Gjoa*. She was a beauty.

HANSSEN   You didn't think so up North that night the Chief said we'd have to abandon her. (TO AMUNDSEN) Remember, you gave us an hour to pack our necessaries? I walked into

Lindstrom's cabin, he's sitting on the floor with an empty case in front of him and all his belongings all over the room . . . Said he'd brought along so much he didn't want the misery of picking what to leave, and cursing the boat in five languages . . . I counted forty-three pairs of socks.

LINDSTROM   A man can't cook if his feet are cold.

AMUNDSEN   (GENTLY) Betty, it's late, won't you go to your bed?

BETTY   Bed, is it? (SOMETHING IN SWEDISH) Hunh. (POCKETS HER DUSTER) Will I be cooking tomorrow or is it your guest again? (GLANCE AT LINDSTROM)

AMUNDSEN   You cook, Betty.

BETTY   Time you were in your bed too, Master Roald. Hunh.

She stumps off. Passes Stubberud on the stairs. He carries a tool bag, though he's in best suit. He's open-faced, moustached, simple. Stands in doorway.

STUBBERUD   All done. One or two little things for the morning but . . . I'm sorry it wasn't quite perfect for the warming, Mr Amundsen.

AMUNDSEN   (WHO'S POURED HIM SCHNAPPS) Here, come and sit down. Jorgen Stubberud, our carpenter in Bundefjord, responsible for everything you see. Come on, sit there. Damn best carpenter in Norway.

Stubberud smiles shyly at the company.

AMUNDSEN   He's in his best suit because he was invited as a guest. He brought his tools because he's in love with perfectness. Your health, friend. (DRINKAGE AND INTRODUC-TIONS) Helmer Hanssen, Adolf Lindstrom, both with me on the North West Passage. Fritz Zappfe, old friend; my brother Leon.

STUBBERUD   It's an honour, gentlemen.

LEON   (CHECKING WATCH) Roald, I have to be getting back quite
soon. I don't know whether . . . (HE LEAVES IT, THE MEANING
CLEAR)

AMUNDSEN   (NODS; THINKS; GETS UP AND WALKS A LITTLE) Yes.
Yes. (FINALLY) Gentlemen, it won't surprise anyone here to
learn that I have . . . plans. This is in confidence, of course,
(WITH A SMILE AT ZAPPFE) not for your morning paper . . . (A
SMILE AT STUBBERUD) and certainly not for Bundefjord.
Some work has been done already — my brother Leon has
been acting as business manager for half a year — but there
are difficult waters ahead for some months. I want you,
Adolf, and you, Helmer, in particular to know them now
because the longer the notice, the greater the chance that
you'll agree to accompany me.

HANSSEN   The Great Nail.

AMUNDSEN   Exactly.

It's absorbed, phlegmatically.

LINDSTROM   When?

AMUNDSEN   Two years. Perhaps less.

LINDSTROM   In the *Gjoa?*

AMUNDSEN   *Gjoa's* sold. To pay debts on the North West
Passage.

LINDSTROM   What then?

AMUNDSEN   The *Fram.*

LINDSTROM   You have the *Fram*? (AMUNDSEN NODS. LEON BLINKS
AT THE CALM OVERSTATEMENT) So. Where's the crown?

AMUNDSEN (SMILING) The crown is where it belongs. Well? (HE LOOKS AT LINDSTROM, HANSSEN, LINDSTROM AGAIN)

LINDSTROM I'm in.

Amundsen looks to Hanssen.

HANSSEN As what, Chief?

AMUNDSEN Ice-pilot. Driver.

HANSSEN I get eighty a month at the Customs House.

AMUNDSEN A hundred and twenty.

HANSSEN A hundred.

AMUNDSEN Done.

HANSSEN Good. I'll speak with my wife.

They laugh, raise glasses, clink them, drink.

AMUNDSEN I'll say more tomorrow. And I'll need to ask you for some help, when the time comes, Fritz, in the matter of publicity. But I can tell you, gentlemen, after tonight we are most definitely on the way. More schnapps, Jorgen?

Stubberud's rising, collecting his bag.

STUBBERUD I must get to my home. Thank you. I'm er . . . I'm honoured by your trust.

He says his goodnights, Amundsen accompanies him to the front door.

36. *Front steps. Amundsen watches Stubberud down the steps.*

STUBBERUD Mr Amundsen, if you find you have need of a

young lad with a bit of use in his hands and happy using
'em, I'd be at the head of the queue, packed and ready to go.

AMUNDSEN (TOUCHED) I'll remember it.

*Stubberud leaves. Amundsen stands for a moment on the step, stares
at a sky crammed with stars.*

The star-sky bleaches into whiteness. Heated pop-pop of engine.

*37. Lauteret. Snowscape. Pop-pop closer. A weird early motorized
sledge edges slowly into frame, inches forward, coughs to a stop on
the far edge. Two men move awkwardly on ski towards it, slipping
and floundering: Scott, Skelton, in anoraks. Scott is particularly bad
on ski: eventually takes them off altogether and mires his way over.
Barne fiddles at the hot engine as they arrive.*

BARNE Couple more snags, I'm afraid, sir. One or two fairly
major modifications.

SCOTT No matter, Barne. This is good work, good work Skelton,
both of you. Gentlemen, I caught a glimpse of the future
there; with luck, it will be our future. This will be our
passage to the Pole. I feel it.

SKELTON I'd counsel a *little* caution, sir. There are some pretty
hefty technical problems . . .

SCOTT We'll solve them, Commander Skelton. In the best
traditions of the Service. Right, Barne?

BARNE It's going to cost a fair old packet, sir.

SCOTT Just see it's patched up for the morning. I'll try to see de
Walden does the rest. He arrives this evening. (HE BEGINS
TO WALK OFF TOWARDS THE CHALET HOTEL BELOW, COLLECTS
HIS SKI ON THE WAY) Damned things. (TURNS) I should say
that if things go well tomorrow, I shall in due course be
writing to the Admiralty to secure your loan to my Southern

expedition. Reggie, you'll be my Engineering Officer, second-in-command. Michael, you'll be motor specialist, in charge of those . . . But we have to impress de Walden . . .

He stumbles off, ski over shoulder, down the slope. Barne and Skelton watch him, exchange a look.

38. Lauteret. Evening. Hotel dining-room. Scott sits waiting at table, in captain's uniform. He glances from menu to entrance and back again. Stands as a tall young man approaches the table. They shake hands. The man carries a newspaper, which he puts down by his place.

DE WALDEN (SITTING DOWN) I've kept you waiting, I needed to rest after that dreadful journey. (BRIEF LOOK AT MENU. TO WAITER) Escargots, de veau, epinard.

Waiter passes to Scott. Wine waiter takes his place at de Walden's elbow. He orders Bourgogne, Grand Cru)

DE WALDEN Miss Bruce is not dining with us?

SCOTT Miss Bruce did not come, sir.

DE WALDEN (A FLECK OF DISAPPOINTMENT IN THE UPPER-CLASS CONTROL) Really? She told me only last week she was certain to come.

SCOTT I thought so too.

De Walden falls silent, out-of-sorts, though not obviously. Scott makes no reading of it, wanting to get on.

SCOTT The . . . er tests so far have been very satisfactory. I think you'll be amazed how well she performs.

DE WALDEN (UNDELIGHTED) Good.

Silence. Scott is sensing the diffidence without understanding its origin.

SCOTT I have some confidence it could prove the key to the journey. And you may be assured that your benefaction would be amply attested to in my subsequent account of the expedition. (DE WALDEN GIVES LITTLE BACK) Even so, in fairness I feel I ought to warn you that the original estimate for development and manufacture may well need further revision upwards — by perhaps a considerable sum — I know the cost of the work to date has been burdensome enough . . .

The wine arrives.

DE WALDEN (COLD, RUTHLESS, MATTER OF FACT) Captain Scott, I do not know what would constitute a 'considerable sum' in your scale of things, but I'm informed by the gutter press that I earn, from ground rent alone in the City of London, more than a quarter of a million pounds per annum, or, as they quaintly put it, £685 a day. In my scale of things, the cost of your whole expedition would not remotely constitute a 'considerable sum'. Perhaps we should wait until the tests before talking finance.

SCOTT (STIFF) By all means. (THE SNAILS ARRIVE. AND SCOTT'S MELON)

DE WALDEN Good. (BEGINS TO EAT AT ONCE; EYES SCOTT A LITTLE) Did you hear about Shackleton? (SEES HE HASN'T) Reported landed at McMurdo, all going well and according to plan. The *Nimrod's* back in New Zealand. Here, see for yourself.

Scott stares at the Continental Daily Mail *for a long moment.*

SCOTT (EVENTUALLY; IN CONTROL) No. I hadn't heard.

DE WALDEN (CASUAL) Didn't I hear somewhere that he'd agreed with you not to use McMurdo?

SCOTT (TIGHT) I don't see how, Lord de Walden. It was a purely private agreement.

DE WALDEN   But it's true?

Scott's silence is unequivocal.

DE WALDEN   Well, what a rogue! I'm damned. (WIPES LIPS, SNAILS GONE) With nerve like that, he should be in Business. (HE CHUCKLES, AMUSING HIMSELF. SCOTT PUSHES HIS PLATE AWAY, SICK WITH FEAR, SMARTING UNDER DE WALDEN'S ARROGANT CONDESCENSIONS)

Mix to long shot of the two at table.

Bring up first lines of Scott's letter to Kathleen Bruce and mix to

39. Kathleen, CU, in front parlour of Oakley Road house.

SCOTT   (VO) . . . It was a perfectly plain distinct statement binding in an honourable sense — he definitely agreed not to approach our old quarters.

Kathleen stands, examining various family photographs and memorabilia, reads the suffocatingly Victorian petit-bourgeois room. There's Scott at eighteen, a midshipman; Scott and Wilson on the Barrier; Scott the infant in Hannah's arms at Outlands.

SCOTT   (VO) This has dealt my hopes of success a sickening blow. It makes it definitely impossible to do *anything* until he is heard of again. I feel a shock at the terrible vulgarity which Shackleton has introduced to the Southern field of enterprise, hitherto so clean and wholesome. Again and again I ask myself: what does it all mean? If I did not have you, my dearest, to take my corner and care for me . . .

She turns suddenly, though there's no sound. Grace Scott (Monsie) stands in the doorway, pleasant but cool.

GRACE   Mother will be down directly, Miss Bruce. These days, she rests a good deal. Won't you sit down?

KATHLEEN   Thank you. Are you Grace or Kitty?

GRACE   Grace.

KATHLEEN   I hope we'll be friends, Grace. Perhaps you will call
me Kathleen.

*Grace makes no answer, fiddles pins from a dressed dummy, spillage
from the Scott daughters' dressmaking business.*

GRACE   (EYEING KATHLEEN'S FASHIONLESS GARB) This is to be
Lady Wortley's wedding dress . . .

KATHLEEN   It's very handsome.

Grace registers the choice of word.

GRACE   She's been engaged to be married for almost five years,
but the order for the trousseau comes barely a month
before the ceremony. Still, beggars can't be choosers.

*Kathleen says nothing, stays cool under Grace's disapproval.
Hannah's voice calls her daughter from upstairs. Grace starts at
once, the obedience a reflex, stops by the door.*

GRACE   Miss Bruce, mother has always had a very special place
in Con's life. She's sixty-seven now and growing frail.
Whatever you decide to do in the future, I hope you will
respect the bond between them, not seek to snap it.

KATHLEEN   Miss Scott, I am principally here to give your mother
that very assurance. I am not even sure I can cope with
being his wife; I certainly have no desire to become his
mother.

*Another call from upstairs ('Grace, I cannot find my spectacles . . .')
Grace nods to Kathleen; leaves. Kathleen sits a moment, then stands
rather violently; stares at a picture of Scott (in morning suit) and
Hannah outside the gates of Buckingham Palace. CU Kathleen, eyes*

fierce with will. Over this, her letter of reply:

KATHLEEN (VO) Write and tell me — at once, please — that you *shall* go to the Pole. What's the use of having energy and enterprise if a little thing like *that* can't be done. So hurry up, don't leave a stone unturned — and love me more and more because I need it . . .

40. Tatler *cameo pictures of Scott and Kathleen (ref. 26 August 1908) with their actual captions. Church bells peal.*

41. *Brief graphic treatment of the Hampton Court wedding, reception (for one hundred and fifty guests) and departure; a progressive sequence that leads to*

42. *Channel boat to Dieppe, in fog, and*

43. *Overhead shot of Kathleen swimming naked in the sea. (Etretat, by Le Havre) Hot September day, towards evening. Scott watches her a moment, from rocks above the water. She sees him, waves, he waves; lies down; stares at the sky. His POV of the sky. Overhead shot of Scott's face. He closes his eyes quite tight, shutting out the images of doom; finds them behind the eyelids; opens them again.*

Drops of water spray him. Kathleen stands over him, the blood-orange sun at her back. He sees her dark shimmering mass as if in a vision.

KATHLEEN (QUIET) With this body. I thee wed. (BEAT) You mustn't be sad.

He turns away from her, a slightly uncontrolled movement. She picks up her towel, begins to dry herself.

KATHLEEN Is it last night? (HE MAKES NO ANSWER) You're not on trial, Con. (KNEELS BEHIND HIM) What is it?

SCOTT (NOT TURNING) Everything. (FACES HER) Nothing. Here, let me dry you.

KATHLEEN Tell me.

SCOTT Teach me things. Teach me how to be like you, free and bold, your own self. Our lives are so different. I have never found the world . . . trustworthy. To me it has always been implacable, hostile, against me at every step. (SHE TAKES HIS FACE IN HER HANDS, KISSES HIS FOREHEAD GENTLY. HE LIES DOWN. STARES AT THE SKY AGAIN) Life . . . drives me ahead of it, I seem to have no say in the matter; and whatever I do, whatever direction I take, there's never any shortage of those who would frustrate me first and then attack and criticize me later. The Navy humiliates me, keeps me a captain, one of the oldest in the service. I reach the furthest south and my reception dinner is in a disused warehouse in Greenwich. Shackleton vilifies me for years and then receives the Society's benediction for an expedition that should have been mine. As if that weren't enough, they attack my scientific findings. Damn them, damn them, damn them.

KATHLEEN Con, don't.

She watches him. He stares at the sky. She slips on her simple loose-fitting dress and sandals.

SCOTT (SITTING UP) Well, it doesn't matter. I have you now and you show me a way to be happy. Let some other poor mutt feel the lash of their ingratitude a little. Perhaps I'll retire. Write books. Learn from you how to live.

Kathleen listens carefully, leaning against a rock to fix her sandals. She notices blood on her hand, traces it to an oozing cut between her toes, somewhere down his words.

KATHLEEN Ah. Look.

He walks over, kneels to look.

SCOTT You must have grazed a rock. (HE BEGINS TO CLEAN IT

42

WITH THE TOWEL) Shall I kiss it better?

Their eyes meet. She raises the foot. He kisses the cut between the toes. She arches slightly, stares at the sky.

SCOTT   I love you. I fear you will not be happy. Tell me how I'm to make you happy.

KATHLEEN   I want your son. Nothing else will make me happy. Nothing.

She kneels down to join him. Takes his head on her breast. Holds him tight for a moment, then more loosely as he settles there.

KATHLEEN   Oh Con. (SHE KISSES HIS BROW, A MOTHER WITH HER CHILD) My destiny — I have known it since the age of fifteen — is to bear a special son, of a special father. Just as yours is to prove yourself to this hostile world a man above men. (BEAT) If you feel you cannot *be* that great sire, you should say so now, it's not too late. Think carefully. It means shaking off all this talk of retiring and leaving the field open, and writing books. If I'd wanted a mere husband, do you think I'd've chosen *you*? I chose you because you have a greatness in you . . . and I want some of it in me.

She lies him down on the rock; lies raised beside him, over him.

KATHLEEN   Speak.

SCOTT   You fill me with such strength, such belief. Don't tire of me, will you, I couldn't bear it.

KATHLEEN   (INTENSE) While you go forward, I will never take my eyes off you. (BEAT) Do you know Sir Edgar de Speyer? The banker. He's given a firm promise of assistance on the day you make your announcement. Which must not be a day later than Shackleton returns — assuming he returns empty-handed. Do you know Bridgeman?

SCOTT   The Second Sea Lord? Hardly.

KATHLEEN   He tells me he's appointing a Naval Assistant to work with him at the Admiralty, early next year. I made quite a hit with him. You can't mount an expedition from Devonport, you need to be in London for that . . .

SCOTT   You're extraordinary.

KATHLEEN   (SMILING) In the meantime, you must concentrate on helping me achieve *my* end. And since we'll be living apart for much of the time, it will call for some ingenuity. So I'm making up a calendar for you to take with you, showing my most fertile days for each month . . . Of course I'd like you home whenever you can be there, but I'll be especially delighted if you come on the best days . . . (SHE KISSES HIM GENTLY, THEN MORE SENSUALLY) Will you make me happy? Will you?

They kiss on, in long shot. The enormous sun fills the horizon.

Over this image, Amundsen's voice: 'Are you French, m'mselle?'

44. Chicago. A girl, perhaps sixteen, washes and towels her body behind a screen.

GIRL   (PUTTING ON LACE UNDERWEAR, KIMONO) What did you say?

Cut to Amundsen, in winged-back chair.

AMUNDSEN   (STARING AT SCREEN) I asked if you were French, m'mselle.

GIRL   (EMERGING) French?

AMUNDSEN   (SLOW: CLOCKING HER YEARS) Fifi . . . Isn't that a French name?

GIRL   Ah. No. I'm not French. (AFTER THOUGHT) I *give* French.

Amundsen frowns, not understanding. Studies the girl-child.

GIRL   Welcome to Chicago. Miss Carrie says you're to have a
good time on the house. You a celebrity, mister? (AMUNDSEN
SAYS NOTHING) You having trouble with the language?
Clean. (SHE INDICATES) Have a check every Friday. Clean.
(BEAT) Something the matter, mister?

AMUNDSEN   (GATHERING) No. Do you have other clothes?

GIRL   Sure. (SHE CROSSES BACK BEHIND THE SCREEN) I got peach,
I got black . . .

AMUNDSEN   Whichever.

*The girl talks on as she changes. He's taken a five-dollar note from
his wallet. Lays it on the pillow, leaves silently.*

*45. Lübeck. Railway Station. Amundsen, with luggage, awaits a
connection. A group of lively men carrying ski and baggage arrive
on the platform, headed for the station restaurant. They observe
Amundsen, discuss him from a distance; one detaches, sending the
others into the restaurant; approaches Amundsen, ski on shoulder.
He's tall, lithe, moustached, mid-thirties. Amundsen becomes aware
of the watching man, looks at him. Senses he should know him.*

MAN   (DISTINCTIVE COUNTRY ACCENT) Roald Amundsen. Olav
Bjaaland. It's an honour to meet you.

AMUNDSEN   You're Bjaaland? I watched you win the World
Cross Country at Nordmarka . . .

BJAALAND   Really. I enjoyed that day.

They shake hands formally but with some warmth.

BJAALAND   We're on our way to Chamonix, the whole team.

We'd very much like you to eat with us, if you have the time.

AMUNDSEN   That would be a pleasure. I have an hour.

BJAALAND   You've been away?

AMUNDSEN   America. Fund-raising.

BJAALAND   I hear you're going North again. This time for the Pole.

AMUNDSEN   (SMILING) I have some plans.

BJAALAND   You know, I think I'd find that great fun. Being with Amundsen at the North Pole. Shall we eat?

They begin to walk towards the restaurant. A boy is shouting headlines in German down the platform.

AMUNDSEN   (EYEING HIM) It won't only be fun.

BJAALAND   Like a huge ski-race. What could be better. (HE LAUGHS, FULL, ALIVE)

AMUNDSEN   (SIMPLE) If you really mean it, it could be arranged.

BJAALAND   (NO DRAMATICS) Good. That's what I thought you'd say. Here's my hand.

They shake hands solemnly. Then grin, like kids.

AMUNDSEN   I think it will be fun.

They move on towards the buffet. In long shot, we see Amundsen buy a paper from the boy, read the headline. Bjaaland waits, his hand on the restaurant door. Amundsen indicates he'll follow him, turns back up the platform, enters the telegraph office.

46. *A stenographer types out a cable in English. Amundsen stands*

by a grille, counting marks onto the counter, the paper on the counter by his right hand. The stenographer reads the message in broken English as he types:

> ... must congratulate you on this wonderful achievement. The English nation has by this deed won a victory in the Antarctic which can never be surpassed ...

We see the German newspaper headline: it is impenetrable, save for 'Shackleton' *and* 'Sudpolen'.

Bring up 'Three cheers for Mr Shackleton!' *and street-singing march* Rule Britannia.

47. *Ext. The Scott's cab, Royal Geographical Society. Evening.*

Shot of the Scotts descending from their cab and approaching the steps to the building through respectful but not delirious applause. Scott in dress uniform, Kathleen in cloak over evening dress.

They enter the large doors and join the throng of guests within.

48. *Int. The entrance hall, Royal Geographical Society evening.*

Hall, packed and alive. Flags and pennants everywhere. A small orchestra plays British music at the far end by the lecture theatre. The Scotts stand for some moments, ignored, out of it. Kathleen is calm, indifferent; but these are always Scott's worst moments.

Kathleen looks at him steadily for a moment.

KATHLEEN You will go through with this?

He nods tersely. She greets Lady Markham, moves to join her. Markham limps floridly forward to collar Scott.

MARKHAM You're wrong even to *be* here, do you know that?

SCOTT Sir Clements ...

47

MARKHAM   Take the word of an old man who has walked the
rogues' gallery all his life and knows the cut of things. Hold
your tongue. Announce your plans in your own time and
on your own ground. Here, with this scoundrel — whose
latitudes, I may say, draw a large bill on one's credulity —
you'll merely . . . vulgarize the business into . . . pole-
seeking . . .

Scott sees Kathleen approaching, Lady Markham on her arm.

SCOTT   (IRRESOLUTE) The iron will not stay hot for ever . . .

*A liveried sergeant at the top of the stairway bangs his stick for
silence and begs the company to proceed to the Great Hall forthwith.
Sir Clements limps grumpily with his wife. Kathleen studies Scott's
taut face.*

*Scott gives her his arm, runs almost at once into a swirl of Admirals
and luminaries in the confluence of staircase and hall. Sees the
laughing Shackleton. Shackleton sees him. A moment. Tiny deflec-
tions of heads. And on.*

49. Int. Great Hall, The Royal Geographical Society evening.

*Dinner Reception. Shackleton, guest of honour, Scott presiding,
at opposite ends of the high table. Shackleton has his wife,
Keltie, Curzon and the RGS hierarchy for company. Scott has
Kathleen and the Markhams. Waiters in and out; claret flowing,
smoke rising.*

*Scott watches everything, judging the moment. His wife talks rather
intimately with de Walden, who sits by her. She turns; gives him a
firm stare; nods.*

*Scott bangs the table with his gavel, stands abruptly. The room
drones into hush. Scott pauses, wordless. Sees Markham's upturned
face; Shackleton's; Kathleen's.*

SCOTT   Ladies and gentlemen, I am proud and privileged to

propose the toast to our honoured guest.

He takes a piece of paper from his pocket, looks at it. Shot of Shackleton, eyes tensing.

SCOTT A leader in the *Daily Telegraph* on the subject of Mr Shackleton reads as follows: 'In our age, filled with vain babbling about the decadence of the race, he has upheld the old fame of our breed . . .' (HEAR HEARS, KNUCKLES ON TABLE ETC.) For once, the *Daily Telegraph* has it right. For it is an Englishman who has journeyed to within ninety-seven miles of the South Pole. Just as it will be an Englishman who eventually achieves it. (BEAT; DELIBERATELY) Let me say then, straight out, as the call goes out, that I am ready, able and eager to take it up, and to go forth in search of that object . . .

Some spontaneous chauvinist applause from the hall, less from the high table. Scott uses it for his build.

SCOTT And let me thank Mr Shackleton for so nobly and so bravely showing the way . . .

Applause swells from the hall, more knuckles rap the high table.

SCOTT (GLASS RAISED) My lords, ladies, gentlemen: Mr Shackleton and his deeds.

The company rises to complete the toast; remains standing to applaud the honoured guest. Shackleton and Scott exchange a look. Markham's happy Scott's pulled it off. Kathleen's standing applauding, showing around six months pregnant. She takes Scott's look: indicates with her eyes that her applause is for him.

50. *Ext. Svartskog, day.*

Leon Amundsen on the approach to Svartskog. He walks quite quickly, worried by his news.

51. Int. Hallway, Svartskog, day.

Leon stands at the foot of the stairs, checking the direction of the voice. He takes the stairs quickly, two at a time. We follow him through the extraordinary house (fitments, furnishings, glass transfers of Eskimos etc.) as he approaches the source of the talk and slows.

Through the glass panel of a door he watches his brother demonstrating a morass of equipment — sledges, ski, sticks, clothing, skins, furs, boots, goggles, socks, sextants, maps, theodolites, burners, cans of provisions, maps, books, tents, hydrometers, on and on — to Betty, who sits morose and uncomfortable in the chair provided.

Leon watches the mime sombrely. In the middle of demonstrating the superiority of the Telemark ski Amundsen catches sight of his brother. Breaks off at once, approaches the door, opens it, pleased to see him and in fair high spirits.

AMUNDSEN (LEADING HIM IN TO THE MORASS OF THE ROOM) Leon, you're back, excellent. I'm just putting the finishing touches to my presentation to the Parliamentary Committee . . . (WATCHES BETTY'S HUGE YAWN) I've been trying it on Betty but I suspect she's made her mind up already — if you've had enough, Betty — we'll have some cider.

BETTY (STANDING) Enough? Hunh. Madness. Look at it. (SHE SURVEYS IT) Madness. I wouldn't give you a kroner for it, north pole, great nail, pack ice, ski bindings, *Fram* . . . (TO LEON) And you should be ashamed, encouraging him . . . grown men . . .

AMUNDSEN Betty . . .

BETTY You want cider. I'll fetch cider. Don't ask me to listen, I don't want my head filled with such nonsense . . .

She's gone. Amundsen smiles, waves Leon to a chair stacked with boots and socks. Amundsen stands by the window looking out at the fjord. Leon clears the chair, sits, watches his brother, notes the keenness, the life in him, the pleasure of the work.

AMUNDSEN It's coming together, Leon. I feel it. See if you can arrange another mortgage on the house. And see if you can find a convenient way of buying me out of the business: I'm going to need a good deal more than this committee will offer.

LEON Roald . . .

BETTY (OOS) (RETURNING) Cider.

She places the tray on a table between them, hobbles out on a mutter. Amundsen crosses to pour. Hands a glass to Leon.

AMUNDSEN (HAPPY; SIMPLE) I'm going *north* again. It's the best feeling in the world. (HE CLINKS HIS GLASS ON LEON'S, SAUNTERS OFF THROUGH THE DEBRIS, FULL OF IT) Well, how was Copenhagen, you saw Daugaard-Jensen?

LEON (AT LAST) Roald, I saw Cook in Copenhagen.

Amundsen turns, frowning a little. Scans Leon's face for signs.

LEON He's back. Arrived two days ago.

AMUNDSEN (SOFTLY) Good old Fred.

LEON He's claiming the Big Nail.

Amundsen puts his glass down, crosses to a window, stares out a moment.

AMUNDSEN I must cable congratulations.

LEON You think it's true?

51

AMUNDSEN   If Cook claims it, I believe it. (SILENCE) Did you order the dogs?

LEON   Provisionally; where, date and number to be confirmed. Daugaard-Jensen will be in Copenhagen till Thursday, I said I'd go back when I'd talked to you . . . (AMUNDSEN STARES ON AT THE FJORD) Do you still want me to, Roald? (PAUSE)

AMUNDSEN   (QUIETLY) No. I'll do it.

52. Reception, Hotel Phoenix, Copenhagen. A moil of photographers and pressmen wait around in the hope that Cook might appear. Amundsen threads his way to the desk, gets Cook's room number. Over this, Cook's voice at top of next scene.

53. Cook's suite. Signs of their late dinner on a table or trolley. Cook pours Bourbon into two glasses on a dressing-table, talking to the seated Amundsen through the mirror. Cook is amazing: two years hair-growth on head and face, the black hair two feet long. He's older than Amundsen, small, tough.

COOK   (CULTURED AMERICAN) Goddam, Amundsen, I can't think of a soul I'd prefer to have met me than you, old friend. I think of you often, always with affection. You've come a long way since the *Belgica* days, my God you have . . . (HANDS AMUNDSEN THE DRINK) To success. (THEY DRINK; COOK CHECKS HIMSELF IN THE MIRROR) I look like the wild man of Borneo, I can't take it off for another two days, had to make a deal with the syndicated press to stay native till they'd taken all their pictures, try and defray some of the costs of this damned trip.

AMUNDSEN   Did you see Peary?

COOK   Not a sign.

AMUNDSEN   I didn't know you were up there.

COOK Two years. Snuck in.

AMUNDSEN You were alone?

COOK Couple of eskimos.

AMUNDSEN Netsilik?

COOK (SHAKING HEAD) Greenlanders.

Amundsen nods. Pause.

AMUNDSEN And did you get the Big Nail?

COOK Yep. I believe I did.

AMUNDSEN How did it feel?

COOK Cold.

AMUNDSEN (SMILING) But fun, hunh?

COOK Fun? A little.

AMUNDSEN (SIMPLE, GLASS UP) I salute you.

Amundsen drinks. Cook empties his glass, crosses to bring the bourbon back to where they sit. Refills the glasses.

COOK *You* have plans?

AMUNDSEN I have the *Fram* now. (COOK NODS) Going north. Three year drift. I plan to pay the Nail another visit on the way.

Long silence. Cook thinks.

COOK Sounds to me as if the drift won't do more than repeat Nansen's work . . . and frankly, the Nail seems right out of the picture, because I can't see why anybody should want to go to a place where somebody else has been. (PAUSE) If you want a *Pole*, I'd suggest you turn round and head south. That'd be my advice.

Amundsen drinks carefully, impassive.

AMUNDSEN   I think I must go ahead as planned, Dr Cook. The preparation is much too far advanced — I head North in January.

54. Hotel Phoenix, scantly lit corridor. Amundsen knocks once, twice on a door. A voice calls him in.

55. Bedroom. Jens Daugaard-Jensen writes up a ledger in his bed, by the light of small bedside lamp.

DAUGAARD-JENSEN   Captain Amundsen, come in. Have a chair.

AMUNDSEN   I'm sorry it's so late. We had much to talk about. (SITS ON A CHAIR OUTSIDE THE POOL OF LAMPLIGHT. LEANS FORWARD INTO IT) Jens, I have some small changes to my order.

DAUGAARD-JENSEN   Wait. (HE PUTS THE LEDGER ASIDE, TAKES UP NOTEBOOK AND PENCIL)

AMUNDSEN   Fourteen complete Eskimo suits, sealskin, not ten. Twenty prepared sealskins for repairs, not twelve. Twenty dogwhips, sealskin straps, ditto. Dogs. They have to be the best. The very best. I'll pay whatever they cost.

DAUGAARD-JENSEN   (REPEATING LEON'S ORDER, WRITING IT DOWN) Fifty Arctic dogs.

AMUNDSEN   No. One hundred. (DAUGAARD-JENSEN BLINKS, LOOKS AT HIM. AMUNDSEN'S IMPASSIVE) And I want them from Greenland. (PAUSE) To take with me.

Daugaard-Jensen writes it down carefully. Stares curiously at Amundsen.

DAUGAARD-JENSEN A hundred Greenland dogs.

AMUNDSEN When do you leave?

DAUGAARD-JENSEN First boat tomorrow.

AMUNDSEN (STANDING, HAND OUT) I'll leave you to your sleep. Thank you. You're a good friend.

Amundsen walks towards the door, pauses half-way, turns, face in shadow.

AMUNDSEN Jens. I trust you to keep your private thoughts to yourself until . . . matters explain themselves. Go well.

He leaves. Daugaard-Jensen studies the list in the notebook.

56. Bedroom. Amundsen lies clothed on the bed in half-darkness. He stares at the ceiling; white and cracked, like a glacier. Very slowly, mistily, it becomes the Great Ross Ice Barrier.

II

A DREAM THAT IS DYING

Title: *THE LAST PLACE ON EARTH*

II. A Dream That is Dying

1. Long shot of Edward VII knighting Shackleton at Balmoral. Over this, an impersonal voice speaks the Shaughnessy lines:

> Each age is a dream that is dying
> Or one that is coming to birth

2. Kathleen Scott, in CU, pushing, on all fours. A midwife watches, lips tight with disapproval. Kathleen repeats 'Boy boy boy boy' over and over, on the push.

3. Brass plate: British Antarctic Expedition. Registered Office. (Victoria Street). Magnesium flashes of Scott inserting key into front-door lock, amid moil of onlookers and pressmen. Scott is persuaded to address them impromptu from the top step.

SCOTT . . . Gentlemen, the main object of this expedition is to reach the South Pole, and to secure for the British Empire the honour of this achievement. Subsidiary to this — but no less important — will be the extensive scientific research I have projected. By August next, I shall need to have raised in excess of £40,000, if I am to be successful in these endeavours. I have pleasure in declaring the Appeal Fund open (WAVES A BANK CHEQUE IN THE AIR, FOR PICS) . . . and am happy to place this personal cheque for £3,200 — my life-savings — into the kitty.

Cheers. Applause. Snaps.

VOICE (CALLING) What's it going to be, boy or a girl, sir?

SCOTT (SMILING) I believe my wife has decreed a boy. We'll know soon enough.

Three cheers go up. Scott waves to the crowd. More shots. He goes inside.

4. *CU hours old infant. Kathleen, herself. Scott, adoring, moved.*

KATHLEEN Name him.

SCOTT Peter.

KATHLEEN Peter?

SCOTT Pan. He will live for ever.

She watches him watch the child; finds she loves him.

KATHLEEN Thank you. (HE DOESN'T UNDERSTAND) For my dream . . . Hold him.

Scott takes the child with great, gentle care. Carries him to the window, the day bright gold beyond the glass.

KATHLEEN (ARRANGING HIS FLOWERS) Markham. Peter Markham. What do you think, Con? We shall need to bind Sir Clements to your expedition with hoops of steel . . . Peter Markham, it's good. Con?

He holds the child still at the golden window, his back to her. Does not turn. In CU we see him surprised and embarrassed by tears. Bring up voice of Eriksen from scene 5.

5. *Norwegian Storting (Parliament); Chamber. Alfred Eriksen, Socialist MP, on his feet. Nansen watches from an upper visitors'*

gallery, Leon Amundsen at his side.

ERIKSEN (TO CONSIDERABLE VOCAL SUPPORT) . . . there are people dying of cold and of hunger in our capital city here and now and we say we haven't the resources to offer them relief. Thousands living in squalid and miserable shacks and we say there is nothing we can do to help. Sick people wanting for medical care, the needs of the old and the impaired ignored . . . Yet here we are again being asked to put a further 25,000 kroner into the pocket of the brave but impudent Mr Amundsen for what he calls 'extra scientific work' but what is actually more of the old baloney. And this in spite of the quite binding assurances we were given in last year's debate that it would be the final grant. In my view, we are being asked to throw good money after bad. The question of the Pole has been settled and there is nothing left for Mr Amundsen to do that could possibly justify a further grant. I oppose . . .

Cheers, stamping. Nansen leaves grimly; Leon follows.

6. Storting. Large entrance hall. Nansen and Leon in huddle by pillar.

NANSEN   Well, we'll know soon enough. Though I believe we've lost. It's a pity your brother couldn't be here.

LEON   He wanted to be here, he's been held up in Copenhagen.

NANSEN   It would have helped the case to hear from him first hand about this . . . extended programme. Dogs, men, time, money. Well, he'll learn. (PAUSE) At least the budget for the basic work in the Polar basin remains untouched, I suppose that's something.

Liveried ushers begin posting the results of the division. Members and others cluster idly round the boards. Eriksen passes, pleased, in an angry way.

ERIKSEN   Sorry, Nansen. For once it its miserable life the House

59

has decided to listen to reason.

NANSEN (COOL, IN CONTROL) You stopped the grant, Herr Eriksen. You will not stop the work.

Eriksen passes on.

LEON I'm due at the harbour.

They shake hands.

NANSEN Ask your brother to call me. I need to know his plans. The North Pole's a big blow to his prospects of success, but I can't afford to let him do anything . . . reckless.

A moment. Leon searches for meanings.

LEON I'll tell him.

Leon leaves. Nansen crosses to a division board. Reads the figures (66–32).

7. Docks. Amundsen's ferry at quayside. Leon waits, frowning, as the last passengers alight and disperse. Some crew begin debarking. Bags trundle by on trolleys. Leon perplexed; a little concern showing. A tall seaman, in cap and dark glasses and choker, passes him, a roll-bag on his shoulder. He stops some paces beyond Leon, begins re-tying the bag.

AMUNDSEN Leon.

Leon starts, recognizes his brother. Looks away.

AMUNDSEN Do you have a carriage?

LEON By the gates. You specifically asked before you left for a press-conference, I've got a dozen press waiting . . .

AMUNDSEN That was before I left. Tell them I missed the boat.

I'll wait by the gates.

He shoulders his bag, mingles with other crew, disappears into the customs halls.

8. Carriage, Christiania. Amundsen exchanges clothes with a merchant seaman. Leon watches, unamused.

9. Street corner. The carriage halts, the seaman alights, swings bag over shoulder. The carriage draws away.

10. Interior, carriage.

LEON Would you mind telling me what's happening?

AMUNDSEN (CALM; ALMOST HAPPY) We're going to talk to Zappfe.

LEON (TIRED IRONY) The journalist.

AMUNDSEN The journalist. I've asked him to meet me.

LEON (DISTINCT, PATIENT, SERIOUS) Roald. We've lost the best part of one hundred thousand kroner since the North Pole went. Our funding is in ruins. Yesterday I had a letter from Lord Northcliffe cancelling the contract for exclusive rights to your North Pole story, today Parliament emphatically turned down your request for further subsidy. Matters are grave. I say this as a businessman, without exaggeration: you will spend the rest of your days repaying the debt you incur on this voyage. The rest of your days, Roald. I believe you should give that some thought.

The carriage clicks on, out of town now.

AMUNDSEN What? You think we should abandon the project altogether?

LEON At least cut back, Roald. Nansen says the same; he wants to speak with you. We can't afford the published programme, let alone the additional work you're . . .

Amundsen looks out of the window, calls the driver to drive through the gates.

AMUNDSEN   I need your *trust*, Leon.

Leon nods, in difficulties.

11. *Long shot of Amundsen, Leon and Zappfe enisled amid grassy gravestones. Amundsen stands, talking; Leon listens, Zappfe makes notes in a book, sharing a bench. Two carriages wait on the distant path beyond.*

AMUNDSEN   So. The question is being asked: will Amundsen press on, in spite of this catastrophic loss of support, or will he abandon his work in the north. With all the emphasis at my disposal I give you my answer: Amundsen *will* carry out not only the basic work of the published programme but at least a further fifteen months scientific work in and around the polar basin. For this, I shall require an additional eight men, fifty dogs, a dozen sledges, extra fuel and provisions. (LEON'S EYES WINCE AT THE NEWS) Add this: I cannot believe that when my countrymen have had the opportunity to study my revised plan they will deny me the means to carry it out. (HE HANDS ZAPPFE A DOZEN OR SO TYPED SHEETS OF PAPER) Here it is, print as much as you can, Fritz. And that's exclusive.

Zappfe scans the sheets, checks his notes.

ZAPPFE   Well, this is bold. I'll do what I can.

AMUNDSEN   (AS IF REMEMBERING, CASUAL) Dates. I have decided to delay departure by around six months. (ZAPPFE PURSES LIPS AS HE WRITES. LEON CAN SCARCELY BELIEVE IT) Say, July, August next year. As you know I'm having *Fram* fitted with a diesel in Stockholm. That work has been seriously delayed by the strike of Swedish engineers.

ZAPPFE   That's going to stretch funds even further, isn't it? (HE
LOOKS AT LEON, WHO SHRUGS)

Amundsen turns away, quite deliberately. The interview's over.
Zappfe pockets his book, stands, shivers a little at the surroundings.

ZAPPFE   Can I say we met in a graveyard?

AMUNDSEN   (SLOWLY) Say what you like. So long as it helps our
cause.

Zappfe shakes hands with the brothers in turn, walks off to his
carriage. Amundsen begins plucking wild flowers and tall stems of
wild oats. Leon stands, stretches in the heat.

AMUNDSEN   (CALLING) Fritz. (ZAPPFE TURNS) Thank you.

Zappfe waves, shy. Goes on.

LEON   Roald. We must talk, you and I. This is beginning to
sound like . . . madness.

AMUNDSEN   (OCCUPIED) Is it? Remember Tollefsen? Did I ever
tell you about Tollefsen? (IT RINGS NO BELLS) Come.

He leads Leon through a wilderness of paupers' graves, the wild
posy in his hands. Collects a cracked earthenware pot en route.
Searches. Arrives.

AMUNDSEN   See.

They look at the plot. Name (Hans Tollefsen) and dates (1870–1902)
in unadorned stone, barely seen through the weed growth.

AMUNDSEN   Tollefsen was on the *Belgica* on the Southern Journey. Ordinary seaman. A good man. The second winter in
the ice he went mad. (SNAPS HIS FINGERS) Tried to kill the captain with a meat-axe. There was barely a man on board who
would not have cheered himself hoarse if he'd succeeded —

de Gerlache was a bastard and largely responsible for Tollefsen's condition. But still we called him mad and tied him to his bunk for weeks on end until he subsided. On the way back de Gerlache ordered me to arrange Tollefsen's discharge. In Punta Arenas. Twelve thousand miles from home. I handed in my notice on the spot, took Tollefsen and brought him back to Christiania. In the main he was fine. Except that he cried. Wept. The whole time. I took him to his mother's home when we got back and promised him I'd take him North with me when he recovered. (HE STUBS THE PLOT-EARTH WITH HIS BOOT) He killed himself three days later. He dipped his head in a bowl of kerosene — his mother thought he was washing his hair — and set fire to it. (PAUSE. TURNS TO FACE LEON. PICKS UP THE REFERENCE DELIBERATELY) There are forms of madness, Leon. Tollefsen's rage for justice is one. Human creativity's another. They're all different, but they all lie together, like the colours on a trout's belly. (PAUSE) The whole line of my life has led me to this work in the North. I do not pretend that I would not have liked the Great Nail, call it a vanity, but strategically it was always only the bauble, to underwrite the real work of the expedition. (PAUSE) If I abandon that work now, I abandon my whole meaning.

LEON   (UPSET) Roald, I know, I'm not asking it . . .

AMUNDSEN   (ALMOST FIERCE) But we can't run up further bills for an expanded programme. What if I told you that an expanded programme was the *only* way to get the money for *all* of it? Hmmm?

LEON   I don't know what you mean.

AMUNDSEN   (FIERCER, RATIONAL, BITTER) Then *think*, for God's sake, think, man. The press barons and the industrialists and the politicians want a coup before they'll fund the serious work, so we'll give them one. It so happens the voyage takes us south by the Horn. We take dogs *with*

us, instead of collecting them in Alaska. On the way, we
make a minor diversion and take the South Pole. (PAUSE.
MILD SUDDENLY) Wouldn't that be a coup of sorts?

*Leon sits slowly down against a tree and removes his hat, trying to
deal with it.*

AMUNDSEN   We have funds enough to set out. What we bring
back will ensure our solvency. And we will have explored
the North Polar basin on the strength of it.

LEON   (RATHER DULLY) The South Pole. It's brilliant.

AMUNDSEN   It'll do. God knows I have little enough interest in
the thing, to me it's just a patch of ground left behind by
Shackleton; but if that's the price I have to pay for *serious*
work, I'll have to pay it.

LEON   Can it be done?

AMUNDSEN   Just. So long as we keep it to ourselves. Until the
right moment.

LEON   Which is when?

AMUNDSEN   Let's say until we're beyond recall.

LEON   Tell nobody?

AMUNDSEN   Mmm.

LEON   My God.

*Amundsen grins. Leon laughs in shock. Something's released in him,
an energy, love for his brother.*

LEON   We'll go to gaol!

AMUNDSEN Yes!

They stand in the wilderness.

LEON It might even be treason or something. Their boat, their money, given for one purpose, used for another.

AMUNDSEN (SOFT) Only if we fail.

Silence. Leon considers failure.

LEON (THOUGHTFUL) We *could* go to gaol.

AMUNDSEN There are worse places. (HE STUBS HIS TOE INTO THE GRAVE-EARTH) Here's one. (PAUSE) The South Pole is probably another. (SMILES) We'll see.

They walk back through the brush to the pathway. After a moment, Amundsen puts his hand on Leon's shoulder. The carriage comes to meet them.

Mix to

12. *Images of Amundsen's recruitment and preparation; all mute (cf. 13). The* Fram, *in dry dock, being honed for work.*

Daugaard-Jensen and an assistant bartering for Eskimo dogs in Greenland. The Danes drawing the twelve dogs behind the sledge down a slope, towards a Danish Government dog-pen, already half-full.

Close shot of ski-bindings, flexing and slackening, on the move. Bjaaland approaching Amundsen on ski. Amundsen stoops to examine the bindings. Bjaaland indicates a possible modification, with sweeps of the finger. Amundsen nods, after thought.

A laboratory. A food scientist working with Amundsen on pemmican. Amundsen adds vegetables and wholemeal flour. The scientist shrugs his 'perhaps'; then nods, after thought.

*LS of Amundsen, on deck of boat in harbour, deep in conversation
with a Norwegian naval officer. In close shot, the man is about 30,
slim, clean-eyed. Amundsen says something, turns away to squint at
a whale being landed. Nilsen says something. Gives Amundsen his
hand. Amundsen is pleased. Smiles. For a second it warms the eyes.*

*A whalers' bar. Amundsen asking for someone. A man is pointed out
to him. Amundsen approaches the fairly crowded table across smoky
oaken room. Introduces himself to the giant seaman. Beck blinks,
stands slowly, draws his hat from his head, respectful, a little awed.
His mates pass the name around, lip to ear. Several more hats are
slid from heads. Amundsen offers his hand to Beck. The giant takes
it. Amundsen sits at the table; takes a beer.*

*CU Hassel, urging dogs on with low growls and barks. Amundsen
waiting by the Tromsö Customs Shed for the sledge to approach.
Hassel secures the sledge and dogs. Approaches Amundsen diffi-
dently, removing gloves. Amundsen holds a sheet of paper in his
fingers. Hassel takes it; reads it. He's impressed, surprised, finally
satisfied. Shakes his head, smiling thinly, eyes calm and cold. He says
something to Amundsen. Amundsen laughs; points to the dogs. Hassel
strokes his incongruously waxed moustaches, indicates agreement.*

13. *Intercut, montaged with 12, are images of Scott; public, voiced.*

*Bags clink along rows, a fund-raising collection. Union Jacks drape
the platform, 'British Antarctic Expedition' above. The burghers of
Manchester applaud the appearance of Scott, in naval uniform. Lord
Derby welcoming him:* '. . . I am not being unduly insular when I
say what I know a great many of my fellow countrymen feel —
that *every* uninhabited part of this globe belongs by *right* to
England. *(Applause)* Ladies and gentlemen, so long as we have
in our midst the likes of Captain Scott and his men, prepared
and eager to go out and face the Great Unknown, no one in
England need lie awake at night in dread of those . . . boys of
the dachsund breed.' *Flags are waved, applause raised. Scott
smiles tightly.*

Outside the (Free Trade) Hall, a large picket of militant trade unionists blocks the exit. Banners proclaim their cause: Jobs not Glory; Why go to the South Pole, there's a wasteland on your doorstep called Lancashire; Not a Penny for the Pole; Send an expedition to Manchester and discover Poverty.

Scott and dignitaries being wedged through the jostling crowd by police towards waiting cabs. Placards thrown; truncheons out.

Scott's address to the manufacturers of Liverpool, over shots of port passing at table and cheque books being flattened for the pen. The guest of honour, on his feet, presses on with half-promises of precious industrial ore discoveries (pitchblende for radium) which would restore British industrial pre-eminence. A half-inch of cigar ash flops soundlessly into a glass of wine.

Three cheers called for and lifted, over shots of public school buildings. Scott (vo) thanks the school for the donation and promises to name the four ponies it will afford in accordance with the school's wishes: Christopher, Victor, Bones and Weary Willie.

14. Outhouse, Svartskog. Indian ink plan drawings, in two projections, of Amundsen's winter hut. A hand pencils in bunk areas, space for equipment, provisions.

STUBBERUD (OVER) Eleven men . . . provisions . . . equipment . . . but still small enough to pack on board and reassemble on the ice. Mmm. (AMUNDSEN GRUNTS, WATCHING STUBBERUD'S PENCIL. STUBBERUD COMPUTES MATERIAL REQUIREMENTS, CONVERTS WORK INTO HOURS AND PEOPLE) How long do I have, Captain?

AMUNDSEN How long will it take?

STUBBERUD My brother Hans could probably . . .

AMUNDSEN I want you to build it yourself. (STUBBERUD NODS, UNQUESTIONING) Here, preferably. (STUBBERUD SCANS THE PLACE: ASSENTS) Midsummer, how does that sound?

STUBBERUD   (READING LIST OF SPECIFICATIONS AT TOP RIGHT OF PLANS) If that's when it's needed, that's when it'll be ready.

AMUNDSEN   (RELAXING) Good. (SEES LEON APPROACHING FROM THE HOUSE, MOVES A FEW PACES TOWARDS THE DOORS) If anyone should ask, you're working on the house.

STUBBERUD   It says 'Observation Hut'. Is that what it's for?

AMUNDSEN   (SLOWLY) Yes, that's right.

STUBBERUD   (STUDYING DRAWINGS AGAIN) It's just that there aren't any windows, Captain . . .

Leon in. Amundsen and Stubberud examine meanings a moment.

LEON   A word? (AMUNDSEN FROWNS) It's important.

Amundsen joins his brother outside the outhouse. Leon leads him out of earshot, hands him a cablegram. Amundsen studies it.

AMUNDSEN   Nansen. (SHOWS IT TO LEON) Wants a meeting.

LEON   I know. He's getting nervous. He thinks you're up to something.

AMUNDSEN   (RESTATING THE STORY AGREED) Tell him I'm still away, I haven't been in touch . . .

LEON   Speak with him. Tell him *something*.

AMUNDSEN   Lie? Lie to Nansen? I can't.

Silence. Amundsen stares at the fjord through trees. Thinks, resenting this pressure.

AMUNDSEN   (FINALLY; AN EFFORT) Send a cable. Tell him . . . (RECONSIDERS, DECIDES) Tell him I'll see his man Johansen, if it would please him.

LEON   That might help. (CAREFUL) What, you'll take him?

AMUNDSEN   (FLINTY) If I must.

LEON   (THINKING THROUGH) We need *something* to keep him easy. Can you work with Johansen?

AMUNDSEN   (BLEAK) I don't know. We shall have to see.

LEON   (LEAVING) I'll send the cable. (TURNING) Here's the copy of the standard contract you wanted. (THIN SMILE) Maybe you'll scare Johansen off with it.

AMUNDSEN   (SCANNING IT) This is for Stubberud (SEES LEON'S INCOMPREHENSION. SOFTLY:) No use taking Winter Quarters if no one knows how to put them up.

Amundsen returns to the outhouse. Leon blinks again at the news. Approaches the outhouse, watches Amundsen and Stubberud within, leaning over the plans again. Suddenly the younger man freezes at something said, turns to look up at Amundsen's face, excitement crescent below the disbelief.

15. Ext. Victoria Street Expedition Offices. We follow a postman in a slow track back along a long line of men, towards the entrance to No. 36, where a placard on a stand, positioning the queue, announces: 'British Antarctic Expedition: Volunteers'. Gaunt faces, shabby clothes, a sense of soup kitchen. The postman climbs the stairs to the upstairs offices, past more queuing men; and into the main office, the queue cramming in along one wall until arrested at a temporary counter, where a clerk takes down essential particulars. The postman empties the contents of his bag on the counter, calls 'Mails' to anyone who will hear, and leaves. The track continues, establishing the room's and adjoining rooms' many and confused processes. Beyond the counter, three bluecoats (PO Evans, Lashly and Williamson) work stolidly at shortening a new sledge, using a battered 'Discovery sledge as model. Fragments of their common-sense chat suggest they don't fully understand the task they've been set. Evans leaves the others to check the assignment with the

Owner. On the move, a glimpse of a man (George Simpson, meteorologist) in a small room bulging with scientific paraphernalia, whirling a sling-thermometer round and round his head; and two young men, red-faced, seated in a corridor, shoes off, massaging their feet. Evans looks through the glass door of the Owner's inner sanctum, sees Scott, seated at desk, in rather sticky discussion with the standing Meares. Evans knocks, adjusting to formal as Scott looks up and waves the big man in.

SCOTT   What is it, PO?

EVANS   (THICK RHOSSILY VOICE) I'm starting on that sledge-shortening, sir. Would you 'appen to know what the *maximum* load'll be, sir? Don't wanter take too much off.

SCOTT   *Maximum* load? Erm. What was it last time, PO, two hundred pounds, was it?

EVANS   Think it was a bit more than that, sir. Not to worry, I'll press on and experiment.

SCOTT   Good man. Any sign of Dr Wilson yet?

EVANS   On his way, I do believe sir. Two of his young hopefuls have arrived, walked all the way from Cambridge, they say, to show us they can march to the Pole if necessary. That's the spirit, eh, sir?

He leaves. Scott relights his pipe, taking his time. Meares (late twenties) scans the office, a chaos of patent foods, burners, fuels, items of clothing and equipment, mounded one on another.

SCOTT   (FONDLY) Petty Officer Evans. A finer man never walked the polar wastes. (MEARES, QUITE TENSE STILL, SAYS NOTHING) All right, Mr Meares, I'll see if I can't re-route my brother-in-law to meet you out there and give a hand.

MEARES   (TIGHT) With respect, sir, unless he has some expertise in horses he'll be surplus to requirements. I can collect all the handlers I need when I get there.

Scott studies the framed pics on his desk: the Discovery *in the ice; his mother at Outlands; his wife and child; Wilson outside the* Discovery *hut, smiling.*

SCOTT (LEVELLY) Mr Meares, you come to me highly recommended by those whose judgement I have come on the whole to trust, but it must be clearly understood between us that it is not my practice or indeed the Navy's to have one's orders questioned. Yours are to go to Siberia and buy the thirty-two ponies and thirty-five dogs I have decided we shall need for our work in the South. If you feel you cannot do that, you must say so.

MEARES (FINDING THE CONTROL) Of course I shall do as you instruct, sir. I simply wanted you to be aware of the limits of my qualifications. Dogs I know. Horses I don't. If you tell me to buy horses I will buy them and do the best I can.

SCOTT Excellent. I ask no more. It's my considered view that a man who knows, really knows, *any* animal, knows all animals to some extent. (STANDS. HANDS MEARES A DOSSIER OF INSTRUCTIONS. OPENS DRAWER. COUNTS OUT MEARES'S EXPENSES ON THE DESK. MEARES COUNTS AND POCKETS THEM) Bon voyage. I'll expect you in New Zealand in early October with full complement . . . Cable if there are problems. Good hunting. (HE SHAKES HIS HAND. MEARES IS DISMISSED; QUITE GRIM. LEAVES)

Track Meares out into main office, where Edgar Evans is gingerly testing the place to cut. Meares watches, as he puts on overcoat and hat for the street.

EVANS I reckon 'ere'd be about good, or maybe yere. What'd you think, Bill? (LASHLY SNIFFS, UNCONCERNED) Yere, maybe?

LASHLY (HAMPSHIRE, FORTY-FOUR, COUNTRY) I'd say it depends, Taff.

EVANS   Whadder you say, Williamson?

WILLIAMSON   Don't know, Mr Evans.

Evans rests the vacillating saw a moment.

EVANS   Thing is, if we plan the same loads on shorter sledges
. . . (WORKS IT OUT) Them loads'll be 'igher, won't they?

LASHLY   Aye. Right.

EVANS   Now then. Wharrabout the wind?

Lashly and Williamson look at each other.

LASHLY   I said that half an hour ago, Taff.

*Meares walks by the counter, still covered in the spilled mails, goes
against the queuing tide to the top of the stairway, steps back to let
Bill Wilson through.*

WILSON   Cecil Meares, is it?

MEARES   That's right.

WILSON   Wilson. I/C Science. (THEY SHAKE HANDS) Recognized
you from your application photograph. When do you leave?

MEARES   Tuesday week.

WILSON   Got everything you need, old chap?

MEARES   (GLANCE AT SCOTT'S DOOR) In this show, it would
appear the only thing you need is your orders. (HOLDS UP
HIS DOSSIER) Siberia here I come. See you in New Zealand.

*He pushes briskly off down the stairs. Wilson reflects a moment,
then moves round the counter towards the two barefoot men,
waving to the whirling Simpson as he avoids personnel scurrying*

here and there on important errands. The men drink cocoa from chipped mugs, exhausted.

WILSON (SHAKING HANDS) Griff, Charlie, how are you, my boys? Seen the Captain yet?

GRIFFITH TAYLOR (BEARDED, AUSTRALIAN, LATE TWENTIES) No, he's busy, sir.

WILSON What happened, did you fall in the river?

SCOTT (OOS, APPROACHING) Bill! Thank the Lord, you're here at last. Come, I need to talk.

WILSON Captain Scott, I'd like you to meet Griffith Taylor, geologist, and Charles Wright, who's a physicist, both on my short list to go South with us.

SCOTT Gentlemen. (STUDIES THEM) I understand you marched here from Cambridge.

WRIGHT (GLASSES, CANADIAN, MID-TWENTIES) We did indeed, sir. Fifty-five miles.

GRIFFITH TAYLOR On lemonade and hard-boiled eggs.

SCOTT (TO WILSON) I like their spirit, Bill. Are they good scientists?

WILSON Both highly recommended.

SCOTT Then we'll take them. (HE SHAKES THEM BY THE HAND, THE MAN OF DECISION) Welcome aboard, gentlemen. (TO WILSON) Come, we must talk.

WILSON (FOLLOWING, WINKING TO THE YOUNG MEN) Go and play with Dr Simpson there. (SIMPSON WHIRLS ON) I'll be with you presently and we can talk.

Scott waits for Wilson by the group of sledge-shorteners, who are no further on. They stand respectfully in Scott's presence.

SCOTT Here's a sight to gladden the heart, Dr Wilson. Three old *Discovery* men . . .

WILSON (SHAKING THEIR HANDS IN TURN) How right you are, how right you are. How are you, Lashly?

LASHLY Very well sir thank you sir.

WILSON Good to see you, Evans. Williamson.

EVANS (SMARTLY) Pleased to be back, sir.

WILSON Do or die, eh?

EVANS Absolutely sir.

SCOTT Carry on, PO.

He leads Wilson off into the sanctum. Evans sinks down below the table to retrieve the uncapped flask he'd placed there on Scott's approach. Draws hard on the neck. Corks it. Puts it in his pocket. The fat piles up around his neck as he squats.

EVANS You never drink, Bill?

LASHLY Never did. Nor smoked.

EVANS 'Ow about the other?

Lashly sniffs. No answer. Evans winks at Williamson.

EVANS I like a drink. S'matter of fact, I'm on this lark for one thing and one thing only. A couple of years out there's gonna buy me a nice little pub in Rhossily for my retirement. Aye. Been my life's dream, a pub.

He takes the flask out, uncaps it, dreaming the dream.

LASHLY   Watch you the Owner don't catch you, he'll blow you to Christmas and back . . .

EVANS   (EASY) I can 'andle the Owner, don't you worry boy. (DRINKS) Likes big strong men, you see. (RIPPLES UPPER ARMS THROUGH TUNIC) Don't worry, I know how to keep my nose tidy . . .

SCOTT   (OOS) PO Evans.

EVANS   (RISING FAST, HAMMER IN HAND, FROM BEHIND SLEDGE) Sir.

SCOTT   See if there's some tea going, would you.

EVANS   Tea it is, sir. (SCOTT WITHDRAWS; TO WILLIAMSON, SOTTO) Tea, boyo.

Scott retires to the office. We follow him in. Wilson's browsing the contents of a box file marked 'Recruitment'.

WILSON   (TAPPING FILE) Like the look of it. You must have worked like a nigger to gather this little crowd.

Scott resumes his desk-chair, searches for something, glum suddenly. Wilson sees the pic of Kathleen and child on the desk.

WILSON   Bonny boy.

SCOTT   Mmm. You must bring Ory over and have tea, now you're in town again. Here.

He hands Wilson a handwritten letter he's been searching for. Wilson reads it, hands it back, comfortable, unhurried.

WILSON   Yes, I remember him. Came out with the rescue ship, didn't he. Bright young chap. Is there a problem?

SCOTT   (RATHER GRIM) I'm informed by Sir Clements that he's tired of waiting and is currently engaged in raising funds for an expedition of his own.

WILSON   Really. (BEAT) That's awkward.

SCOTT   Fact is, Bill, he's a very persuasive young man and he's picking up money that by rights should be mine.

WILSON   Mmm. Can't Markham talk to him?

SCOTT   He has. And apparently he has a price.

WILSON   Ah.

SCOTT   It seems he's prepared to make over all he's raised to me, provided I agree to take him on as my Number One.

Long silence. Wilson studies his pipe.

WILSON   (QUIET) What does Markham advise?

SCOTT   He's urging me to take him.

WILSON   And Reg Skelton? I thought you'd promised him Number One.

SCOTT   Not promised exactly. Intimated. (LONG PAUSE) I'd value your opinion, Bill. It's wearing me down, I can tell you. As if I hadn't enough on my hands . . .

WILSON   (IN ROLE) Well, as I see it, old Skelton's pretty indis-pensible, nobody can handle the motor sledges the way he can. And he's a pretty seasoned Antarctic campaigner . . .

Knock on glass door. PO Evans in, mugs of tea in his beefy mitts.

EVANS   (PLACING IT) Tea, sir. You'll excuse me, sir, I want to get

77

this sledge work done and out of the way.

He's gone. The mugs steam on the desk between them.

WILSON   (EVENTUALLY) On the other hand . . .

Evans arrives back at the sledgework table. Three steaming mugs of tea lie on the sledge. The volunteers' line is unending down the room.

EVANS   By God, am I glad old Wilson's coming, calm the Owner down a bit. (HE POURS RUM FROM THE FLASK INTO HIS MUG) Two foot, that's what I reckon, and we'll call it a three-man sledge. What do you say?

Williamson sups his tea. Lashly measures two feet with a rule, attacks the sledge with a saw, takes two feet off in no time at all. Evans stares at it.

EVANS   Jesus, man, it was only a suggestion . . .

LASHLY   Aye, well, now it's a fact. Where's the other?

They stare at the shortened sledge. Behind them the smoke rises over their leaders.

16. *Markham's drawing-room. Afternoon. Kathleen and Lady Markham sit, almost wordless, on a window-seat at one end of the room. At the other, Markham plays with the child on his knee. Scott's standing, staring out of a window, quite bleak.*

MARKHAM   Fine chap. Dependable. Enterprising. Had my eye on him for this kind of work since he was a middie on the *Worcester.* (SCOTT SAYS NOTHING) Be assured he will not let you down, Con.

SCOTT   (STIFF) You made the terms quite clear, I presume, Sir Clements?

MARKHAM   Quite. (HE PLAYS WITH THE CHILD A MOMENT. SCOTT

EXCHANGES AN ANGUISHED GLANCE WITH KATHLEEN, WHOSE FACE URGES CALM) He makes one further stipulation himself. (SCOTT LOOKS AT MARKHAM QUICKLY) He's adamant he cannot work as second-in-command if there are senior men below him . . . (SCOTT CHEWS HIS LIPS, TEMPER FLUSHING HIS CHEEKS) For what it's worth, I believe he has a point, a clear chain of command is never more vital than in work at the ends of the earth. Of course, it's hard on old Skelton, but . . . he's a little long in the tooth, you know . . .

Scott fumes darkly; doesn't dare to speak. The doorbell has rung; the ancient butler shuffles to answer.

MARKHAM   I know you'll place the interest of the expedition above all else . . .

BUTLER   Lieutenant and Mrs Evans, sir.

Evans and his wife stand in the archway, a handsome pair. Markham hands the child to Scott, hobbles over to greet them. Scott's eyes meet Evans's. Evans gleams in his uniform, broad, strong, twenty-six, eyes bright with ambition.

Over this, top of Nansen's voiced letter from below (scene 17).

17. Int. Tromsö seamen's hotel, docks area. Amundsen at recessed table, reading a letter spread before him. He eyes a curtained stairway from time to time.

NANSEN   (VO) I am, I must say, quite sad you have not had the time, or thought it necessary, to keep me informed of your progress, if only in general terms. As your patron, as you know, I stand responsible for what you do before both our parliament and our people. (A CHURCH CLOCK IS BANGING TEN: AMUNDSEN CHECKS HIS WATCH, EYES THE STAIRWAY AGAIN, SCANS ON DOWN THE LETTER) I'm to help Captain Scott at Fefor at his final motor sledge trials there in March. He's asked if I will sound you out on the possibility of organizing joint research on some simultaneous magnetic observations at North and South Pole. Would you kindly let him or me know whether you are agreeable. It's important we Norwegians should be seen co-operating with the British — a great power's goodwill must be kept at all costs, when you're a small, emerging nation.

A man steps through the stairway curtain and shuffles stiffly to the bar. Amundsen watches him carefully from his recess. The man is reaching fifty, shortish, powerful; but there's a hurt, dead look about him. He wears a seaman's serge jacket and trousers, peaked hat and carpet slippers. He checks his appearance rather edgily in the bar-mirror as he waits for his drink. When it comes, he sips it, seven or eight sips, replacing the glass on the counter after each sip, an act of control. Finished, he straightens his cap and returns through the curtains and up the stairs.

Amundsen counts out coins for his coffee, turns the letter over, scans to the end.

NANSEN'S LETTER (VO) I was delighted to learn from your brother that you intend to see Hjalmar Johansen for your work in the North. Johansen's a good man and a fine explorer and will not let you down, though times have been hard with him since the last journey. I cannot stress too much what this matter means to me. Through him, I would be able to join my spirit with yours in the work that lies ahead . . .

Amundsen pockets the letter, checks his watch again; crosses to the curtained stairway. His face is gaunt, stressed by the long deceit he is forced to practise.

18. Int. Johansen's room, old, small and dingy but bearing recent signs of broom and duster. Artefacts from his Arctic work cover walls and surfaces, an almost conscious display of his past achievement: photographs of him with Sverdrup, with Nansen, with Eskimo, with seal and bear, on the Fram, *on ski, with dog and sledge; seal tusks; Eskimo fur-skins; a Nansen burner; competition cups and plaques for skiing; maps and memorabilia. Amundsen reads it all from just inside the door, as Johansen closes it behind him and shows him to the table, where the room's good chair has been prepared for him. Amundsen studies the books there — Johansen's own; and a popular edition of the Norse Sagas with an intricate illustration of St Olav on the cover — while Johansen gathers coffee and mugs at the stove.*

Johansen comes to table, pours coffee.

JOHANSEN   (INDICATING THE ST OLAV AMUNDSEN GAZES AT) Dr Nansen. Hero to saint in one year flat. The artist used Nansen as his model. The year we came back heroes, both of us, from 86° 17', the Furthest North. The year I saved his life in the ice. (HE'S SEATED BY THE WINDOW NOW, SOME BRIEF BITTERNESS SHARPENING HIS LIPS) No one will blame the artist, Nansen was always the handsome one. (HE GIVES AMUNDSEN HIS PROFILE, TRACES HIS BOXER'S NOSE WITH HIS FINGER, SMILES) Excuse me, Captain, I don't have too many callers now, I'm rattling a little. I'm honoured you came to Tromsö to see me. I believe my record speaks for itself; but if you have questions please ask them.

Amundsen puts his mug on the table, takes a foolscap envelope from his pocket, removes a typed two-page document from it, places it on the table between himself and Johansen.

AMUNDSEN   I have only one question, Herr Johansen. That's a copy of the contract I ask those who serve with me to sign. The first page is standard stuff, wages, conditions, duration, terminal point. I'd like you to read the final paragraph, over the page there. (JOHANSEN BEGINS TO STUDY IT) I'd be obliged if you would read it aloud. (JOHANSEN'S EYES FLICK TO AMUNDSEN, A QUICK PROBE FOR MEANING, THEN BACK TO HIS TEXT)

JOHANSEN   "In promising to work for a successful outcome with unflagging resolution, I affirm on my honour that I will obey the leader of the expedition in everything at any time."

Another look at Amundsen, whose eyes are steady.

AMUNDSEN On the saloon wall of the *Gjoa* I hung the words: 'On this ship we are all captains, we are all crew.' Not a man went with me but knew the truth of it a hundred times by the time we were through. Yet all gave that promise, each made that affirmation. (PAUSE FOR COFFEE, THE NERVE HYP-NOTIC. TAKES OUT A SWAN FOUNTAIN PEN. UNCAPS IT. LAYS IT ON THE TABLE) My question is: can the man who sailed with Otto Sverdrup and Fridtjof Nansen and once held the record for Furthest North and wasn't invited to model for St Olav so promise and affirm? (VERY SOFTLY, AFTER THOUGHT) It is a matter of . . . respect.

The pen lies between them. Johansen looks at it, at the clause, control flaking under the pressure. Amundsen watches him with no certainty of the outcome and no clearly resolved sense of his own desires in the matter. The negative particles of an existential moment gather in the air. Very slowly Johansen's eyes swell with tears, a physical distillation of the deep inner friction between pride and need. A heavy blast of a ship's siren weighs dully on the air of the room. Johansen takes the pen.

18. *Ext. Bundefjord ferry. Amundsen stands at the stern, tall, gaunt; watches the wake wash from fury to peace down the grey water.*

AMUNDSEN LETTER (VO) Dear Nansen, I hope you will be pleased to hear that I have included Hjalmar Johansen in the expeditionary party. The die is cast now: my only way is forward . . .

19. *Images of Europe — Caption: March 1910 — establishing the essential character of the continent's historical conjuncture, on the last throb of one revolutionary wave, on the verge of another. (Elgar's Violin Concerto was first performed in this year; and Stravinsky's 'Firebird'.) Militarism, nationalism, chauvinism, industrial militancy, the political mobilization of women by women, all imaged, the essential context from which this particular narrative is abstracted. The last image, on the mix, is a vast expanse of white — empty, ominous with the sound of dull rumbling machinery.*

The empty pan finally locates the source: the final motorsledge trials (March 1910) at Fefor, E. Norway.

20. Frozen lake, at side of good ski-resort hotel. A small crowd of holidaymakers has turned out to watch and cheer the proceedings. Half a dozen or so, on ski, have slung ropes round the caterpillar and are drawn, slowly but perceptibly, behind it in its inch across the lake. Bernard Day drives it. Scott, Skelton and Barne watch together, from some distance, Skelton, (on ski) making careful notes on its progress and marking the defects. Barne moves uneasily, his neck in a broad surgical collar. Skelton calls instructions to Day from time to time.

21. Across the lake, beyond the sledge, two figures approaching along the gravel path that skirts the lake. The figures become Nansen and Kathleen, deep in talk. Kathleen laughs several times, Nansen charms on, taking her elbow gently to help her over bad terrain. Kathleen stops on the hotel approach to watch the sledge bumble remorselessly on. Nansen stands close by, his attention largely on her. She's aware of it, likes it.

KATHLEEN   (A TINGE OF TEASE) You don't seem very interested in my husband's motorsledge, Dr Nansen. I thought you were here to help us.

NANSEN   (QUITE INTENSE) Your husband is . . . not an easy man to help, Mrs Scott. (SHE CHECKS HIS MEANING, LOOKS AWAY AGAIN) Is it true your mother was Greek?

KATHLEEN   (SLIGHTLY STARTLED) Yes.

NANSEN   I think I heard it from Shackleton. (BEAT) It's possible to be too English, you know. The worm of doubt turns the soil of thought.

KATHLEEN   Con spent half the night discussing your advice with me . . .

NANSEN   And rejecting it. It's all right, I don't take it personally, and if he's successful I'll sing his praises until I'm hoarse. But with not nearly enough dogs, nor enough men who know how to feed and handle and care for them, without the right sledges, clothing, equipment and provisioning, any success will be desperately hard-earned and staying alive a considerable achievement in itself. (SHE LOOKS AT HIM QUICKLY. HIS FACE IS TENDER, ATTENTION WHOLLY HERS. SOFTLY) Do you know he has still not ordered ski? I spoke with Hagen's yesterday, they say if he placed the order tomorrow they might still not be able to meet it in time for his departure.

KATHLEEN I know he does not share your view of them, Dr Nansen . . .

NANSEN Not my view, *every*body's. Sverdrup, Borchgrevink, Amundsen, Cook, Peary . . . You cannot *walk* the Antarctic as you walk a country lane in Sussex, Mrs Scott. (A LOUD CRACK, LIKE A RIFLE SHOT, FROM THE MIDDLE OF THE LAKE. SOME SHOUTS, MOVEMENT: PEOPLE GATHER AROUND THE SLEDGE, SCOTT AND SKELTON JOIN THEM. AT THIS DISTANCE, IT IS NOTHING) Come, I want you to meet someone.

He takes her elbow, heads her towards the hotel entrance.

22. Lake. Skelton and Day remove the broken axle. Scott watches, bleak, critical. Holidaymakers fringe them: the audience. Barne stands by, amused.

SCOTT Can it be put right?

SKELTON It's cracked. It'll weld back but . . .

SCOTT Damnation. What's the nearest town?

DAY There's a village down the valley has a garage . . .

SCOTT How far?

DAY   By road? Fifteen miles each way.

SCOTT   (SNAPPING) Right, that's it then, we might as well pack
     in for the day.

*He turns away, plods briskly through the snow towards the hotel.
Barne and Skelton exchange a glance. Day hoists the cracked axle
onto his shoulder.*

*23. Hotel terrace. Scott approaching entrance. Kathleen calls from a
terrace table, walks to meet him.*

KATHLEEN   Con, over here. What is it?

SCOTT   (MOROSE, HARD DONE BY) Damned axle bust and a whole
     day gone. We *must* be in London the day after tomorrow,
     and I still have Amundsen to see.

KATHLEEN   Come. Fridtjof wants to introduce one of his young
     protegées. (HE BEGINS TO RESIST) Con, you can't mope in
     your room, I insist you be sociable. (SHE TAKES HIS HAND,
     SOFTENING IT) Besides, I'm in need of a husband's protection
     in such stunningly attractive company.

*They reach the table, where Nansen and Tryggve Gran stand
waiting. Gran's twenty-one, tall, broadshouldered, blond, rich,
athletic, in ski-clothes, his ski against a chair behind him. Intro-
ductions. Gran's correct, deferential with Scott.*

NANSEN   Young Gran has ambitions to go to the South Pole
     himself.

SCOTT   (NOT GREATLY INTERESTED) Really. I hope he'll have
     better luck than me. She's got a cracked axle. And she was
     doing beautifully, too . . .

NANSEN   Can it not be mended?

SCOTT   Not a chance. It's a thirty-mile round trip to the nearest workshop. We'll be lucky to have it fixed for tomorrow.

Nansen says something to Gran in Norwegian. Gran thinks; answers.

NANSEN   Gran knows the village. He reckons he could have it back in four or five hours.

SCOTT   How? Does he own an aeroplane?

GRAN   (SIMPLY PATTING THEM) No. Just a pair of ski.

SCOTT   (SLIGHT, KNOWING DISDAIN) Ah yes. The magic carpet. (SMILES THINLY AT NANSEN, THE RAT SMELT) Ski again.

NANSEN   (MILD, RATIONAL) But if your work is suspended anyhow, what is there to lose?

Scott smiles his thin, knowing smile, stares out at Skelton and Day bringing the axle across the lake. Nansen looks at Kathleen.

SCOTT   (DRAWING GRAN'S ATTENTION A BIT) See, the thing weighs twenty-five pounds if it weighs an ounce.

Gran shrugs unconcernedly. Scott reads it as arrogance.

KATHLEEN   What does it matter, Con? Mr Gran says it can be done, I think he should go.

SCOTT   (AFTER SOME MOMENTS, NOT LOOKING AT HER) All right. Let him go.

24. *Gran, in MCU, having axle roped across his shoulders, adjusting goggles.*

25. *The group are gathered to watch him set off across the lake, a real skier. Already it's good, qualitatively different from the Brits' work. Nansen seeks Kathleen's eyes: a covert understanding between them, across Scott's blank stare after the disappearing Gran.*

SCOTT (TO SKELTON) I think we should review performance so far, Commander.

SKELTON We'd better blanket the engine.

SCOTT Very well. I suspect we'll have more than enough time. Shall we say my room in an hour.

He returns his gaze to the lake. Fails to pick up the figure he's been following. Nansen smiles thinly.

26. Lake. The caterpillar's engine, heavily blanketed.

27. Hotel. Upper double windows, thrown open. Scott appears, talking, passes from sight.

28. Terrace. Nansen and Kathleen, taking tea in the sun. Nansen consults his watch, walks to the edge of the terrace, scans the horizon.

KATHLEEN Nervous, Dr Nansen.

Nansen turns his head, smiles.

NANSEN No, no. He's here.

Kathleen stands, joins him. Nansen points. She picks it up.

KATHLEEN Amazing.

NANSEN Not to a Norwegian.

KATHLEEN (FINDING HIS EYES; INTIMATE) You planned the whole thing, didn't you?

NANSEN (SMILING) The axle was a godsend, I must admit.

Scott calls his wife from the upper windows to look at the advancing Gran. He's excited, waves his watch. She waves back. She's seen.

KATHLEEN (CASUAL, AS TO A FRIEND) You don't imagine
Mr Gran could be persuaded to abandon his own project
and join our expedition as ski-instructor, do you, Dr Nansen?

NANSEN (A PERFECT IRONIC PONDER) He might be, Mrs Scott. If
he's asked.

KATHLEEN Good. Excuse me, I must have a word with my
husband.

*He bows elegantly, enjoying the complicity and her ironic entry into
the game. Walks out to the lake to greet the skier.*

*29. Hotel. Dark upper corridor. Kathleen listens outside the door to
the sound of raised voices inside, Skelton's, Scott's. Skelton's anger
at being jettisoned at Evans's behest is considerable and crackles
across the gap between ranks. Kathleen moves to one side as
someone approaches the door from within. Skelton stands in it for
his parting thrust, his back and profile visible.*

SKELTON . . . If the dispensing with my services is so easy, I
think it might have been put so three years ago when you
first asked me about a motorsledge. There was no hint then
of using me up and then shunting me out of the way. You
can go to hell, Scott.

*He slams the door, marches off down the corridor. The door re-
bounds, opening slowly to reveal Scott by the window, aghast at the
stress of difficult decisions. Kathleen fills the doorway.*

SCOTT Well. That's Skelton out of the way. This damned Evans
has a lot to answer for.

*He turns to look through the window. Day unstraps the axle
from Gran's shoulders, the weld bright in the mid-afternoon sun.
Kathleen closes the door, crosses to the window to stand with her
husband.*

SCOTT Who is this fellow?

KATHLEEN   Just a young boy who wants to go south. Competent skier, Fridtjof says, no more. And a great admirer of yours.

SCOTT   I had no idea ski could make such a difference.

KATHLEEN   But it's too late, isn't it, what could you possibly do?

SCOTT   (THINKING) I don't know. (THINKS ON) Perhaps I could invite him to go with me.

KATHLEEN   What a good idea. Ha. And he could instruct the men on skiing technique.

SCOTT   Exactly.

He's pleased with himself, the issue settled.

KATHLEEN   What a good idea, my clever, clever man.

She kisses him on the neck. He smiles.

30. Hotel. Christiania. Lobby desk. The concierge in MCU placing a telephone call in Norwegian. She looks out of frame briefly at someone on the other side of the desk.

31. Svartskog. Phone shrilling on Amundsen's desk. Amundsen works at an easel, on a large chart of the Antarctic region, with projections in pencil and small three-dimensional black flags for the route. The route itself travels across carta incognita *from sea to pole.*

Amundsen collects the phone eventually, holds it to ear but does not speak.

32. Christiania. The concierge nods, says, 'Hello, hello' in Norwegian, explains her call. Widen to include Scott in the shot.

CONCIERGE   (IN ENGLISH) It's his brother, Gustav. He says he doesn't know where Captain Amundsen is.

SCOTT   Ask if he speaks English. (SHE ASKS. SHAKES HER HEAD)
Ask if he knew anything about my appointment with his
brother. (SHE ASKS. SHAKES HER HEAD)

CONCIERGE   He says he's very sorry.

Scott bites his lip in frustration. Can't decide what to do.

SCOTT   Thank you.

*33. Svartskog. Amundsen rests the receiver. Runs a pen through the
word 'Scott?' in his desk diary.*

*34. Ext. Spring sun. A hand works a pen-knife on the bark of a tree,
fashioning the 'C' in 'R.F. Scott'. Sounds of Kathleen and eight-
month-old Peter Markham practising toddling nearby. Scott pauses
to watch, from the cocoon of tree. Behind mother and child, across
large gentle lawns, the Scott family home 'Outlands', long since
leased to tenants.*

KATHLEEN   When you come home, we'll buy the lease back and
live here. What a wonderful place to spend a childhood,
Con. It explains so much about you. (SHE HUGS THE CHILD
AS HE WAVERS TOWARDS A FALL, GREEDY FOR HIM) Did you
miss me, baby boy? I missed you horribly. (LOOKS) Con?
(SCOTT LEANS AGAINST THE TREE, SAD, BLEAK, WITHOUT
ENERGY, A LOST CHILD) Are you all right, Con?

SCOTT   I can't bear it. The thought of leaving you both.

KATHLEEN   Ssh. Two years and you'll be back and we'll have the
rest of our lives together, the three of us.

SCOTT   (PICKING AGAIN AT THE BARK) I very much want you to
come out to New Zealand with me . . .

Nothing. Some movement at the house neither of them sees.

KATHLEEN   (ABSORBING IT; SEEKING CALM) I don't think it's

practicable, Con. The child would have a miserable time all those months at sea.

SCOTT *You*, Kath.

KATHLEEN *Leave* him? (BLINKS) I'm not sure I could.

Call from down the lawn. Mr Love, the tenant, hurries across it, slightly out of breath.

LOVE (BELFAST DRAPER) Awful news, sir, awful. I just heard it on the station. The King died at 5.30 this morning, God rest his soul.

Kathleen hugs the baby fiercely. Scott slowly removes his hat, awed and oppressed by the news. Peter Markham calls Mamamama quite distinctly.

LOVE I thought you'd like to know, sir.

SCOTT Yes, thank you.

LOVE I'm grateful, sir. For the carving. And proud. The whole country's behind you, sir. Bless you all.

He skirts mother and child and hurries back to the house. Peter Markham whimpers, mewls, as Kathleen places him on a rug and approaches her husband, whose face wheys in the gloom of the tree.

KATHLEEN People die. Even kings. He was old . . .

SCOTT (PEREMPTORY) I'm going to change my plan. Leave earlier.

KATHLEEN How? The boat's not ready, the . . .

SCOTT We'll get the boat ready, we leave in June.

KATHLEEN June? It's impossible. There isn't the time to *do* everything.

Scott returns to his knife-work, the blade fast and crude now, energy running again.

KATHLEEN   This is irrational, Con. (PAUSE) Con, think what it would be like for *me*. I wouldn't be allowed to go on the *Terra Nova*. For most of the time I'd be with the bloody *wives*, away from you *and* my son.

Scott carves on, implacable.

35. Montage sequence of preparation and ceremonies of departure. A motorbike speeds through dockland. An autocar tails it, two men inside. The biker brakes sharply near the ship he's seeking. Parks the bike. Hands the keys to one of the following men, who hands him his battered suitcase, touches his peaked cap, shakes hands and departs for the car.

The young man surveys the ship a moment, its flag still at half mast. Men swarm over and around it, making monstrous din, refitting and stowing in full and chaotic flood. The man wears a long, scruffy Aquascutum raincoat buttoned to the neck, a dented bowler on the back of his head and brown boots. He climbs the walk with a slight but visible limp, stands for some moments on deck, watches a Petty Officer humping crates of champagne, whisky, port, cigars, tobacco, hare soup, across the deck.

PO CREAN   (IRISH; 'THE WILD MAN OF BORNEO') If it's lost and confused you are, son, you've come to the right berth. Can I help you at all?

MAN   (SOFT VOICED, UNASSUMING) Captain Oates, reporting for duty.

Crean blinks, offers a salute of sorts.

CREAN   My God, thought you was a farmer, sir, lookin' for the grain boat. You'll want Mr Campbell, sir, the Mate . . .

OATES   (INDICATING THE RICH FARE) I thought we were leaving civilization behind. Seems we're taking most of it with us . . .

Oates follows Crean's finger towards the thick-set heavy-voiced Victor Campbell, who works the stowers with satanic energy. Oates tips his hat to Kathleen, who's taking inventory with the expedition's store-keeper (Bowers), a short, sturdy Scot, about twenty-seven.

KATHLEEN   Who on earth is that, Mr Bowers?

BOWERS   (WORKING ON) No idea, ma'am.

She watches Oates shake hands with Campbell, who summons Teddy Evans from an upper deck.

KATHLEEN   (RESUMING) What do you have there, Mr Bowers?

Shot of the box Bowers is dealing with, filled with medical supplies.

BOWERS   One tube 'Tabloid' Hypodermic Morphine Sulphate, grain ¼.

She finds it on the sheet. Reads it out as she checks it off.

KATHLEEN   (SUBDUED SUDDENLY) What's that for, do you think?

Bowers looks up at her. A sombre silence.

BOWERS   Blessed if I know, ma'am.

The flag hangs limp, half-masted, over the seething decks.

KATHLEEN   (CALLING SUDDENLY) Over here, PO Evans. We need those over here.

Evans and another toil over with a case of large tins of baked beans in tomato sauce.

KATHLEEN   There should be another sixteen of those somewhere.

BOWERS It's a great pity you're not travelling out with us, Mrs Scott.

KATHLEEN I'm not allowed to. I'd go on this thing any day. Travelling with the wives isn't my cup of tea, I'm afraid.

36. *Teddy Evans leads Oates to his quarters down narrow passages.*

LT EVANS I should clean up before you meet the Captain, Oates. He's a little traditional about these things.

OATES Really. Why the change of departure dates, by the way?

LT EVANS Ours is not to reason why, Captain. In the Navy, the Owner's decision is final.

OATES I thought we were registered as a merchant ship.

Evans looks at Oates from the doorway; smiles cannily. Enters the Nursery. Oates follows Evans into the cramped quarters, where Cherry-Garrard and Tryggve Gran are stowing personal effects in mousehole spaces.

LT EVANS This is Captain Oates of the 6th Inniskilling Dragoons. I/C horses. Mr Cherry-Garrard, Mr. Gran.

They shake hands pleasantly.

OATES Where will the ponies be housed?

EVANS We have to get to New Zealand first, Oates. Then we can start worrying about ponies . . . Make yourself at home. I'll tell Captain Scott you're here.

Evans leaves. Oates finds a bunk, opens his case, looks for his work-clothes; removes an old pair of twill trousers and a shetland pullover.

CHERRY-G. (20, SWEET) I'm the other Paying Guest. Friends call me Cherry.

OATES Titus, Napoleon, Farmer Hayseed. Take your pick.
Lawrence.

Oates takes a chequebook from his case.

*37. Scott's cabin. Oates signs a cheque for £1,000 to the account of
the British Antarctic Expedition: Lawrence E.G. Oates. Hands it to
Scott across the desk. Scott takes it, places it in a drawer. Oates
wears his old work clothes, a knitted balaclava. Scott's in naval
uniform.*

SCOTT I'll send that by messenger to the Treasurer. You'll help
Bowers with stores until we take on your charges in New
Zealand. Any questions?

OATES (PLAIN) Just one, sir. I offered to go along and choose the
ponies myself. Was there some particular reason I wasn't
asked to?

SCOTT Yes there was, Captain Oates. You were in South Africa
at the time and I did not believe it was worth the expense of
shipping you half-way round the world to send you all the
way round the other half. We have to count our pennies.

Oates thinks he might say something. Doesn't.

OATES Thank you, sir.

*38. Overhead shot of full company on deck, drawn up for inspection.
King George V, Scott and Wilson, retinue following, walk the perfect
ranks. Slow POV track of party and crew: seventy-seven in all.*

*39. Three cheers raised for the departing monarch. A band on the
quayside strikes up with the anthem.*

*40. RGS Farewell lunch. Sir Leonard Darwin, President, delivering
fulsome farewell speech, over tracks of the assembled expeditionary*

party, wives, friends and dignitaries.

DARWIN If this expedition has one supreme meaning, it is that
Captain Scott is going to prove once again that the man-
hood of the nation is not dead and that the characteristics
of our ancestors, who won this great empire, still flourish
amongst us (etc. etc.).

*Throughout the proceedings, a silent drama of stares and glances
between Scott and Kathleen across the top table, as they work out
their conflict.*

*Shots of Evans gleaming, his wife; the Markhams; Wilson and Ory
holding hands; Bowers, Campbell; Oates, in ancient and ill-fitting
apparel; Cherry-Garrard, Gran, and a table of POs and other ranks,
Evans prominent, well on the way to oblivion, eyeing uniformed
waitresses as they clear or fetch.*

*Applause for Darwin. Scott studies the notes of his reply. Pressmen
turn a page of their notebooks, keen for copy. Kathleen passes a note
across the table. Scott opens it:* 'I should be with you.'

Scott rises, off a long look at her.

SCOTT My lords, ladies and gentlemen, on behalf of the British
Antarctic Expedition, I thank the Lord President for
his most gracious and flattering remarks concerning our
qualities and aptitudes — matters, in my experience, always
best left to others. (SOME APPRECIATIVE LAUGHTER, HEAR
HEARS) But this I will claim — and claim it without a hint of
boast or self-regard: we are, without doubt, in my conten-
tion, the best-prepared, the best-manned, the best-equipped
— and possibly the best-looking (BOYISH GRIN) — expedition
that ever left these shores for distant parts.

*Hear hears, table slapping; a slight commotion, distantly heard, and
subsiding, from the POs table. Scott sips water; glance at Kathleen.*

SCOTT (ON) It is still not clear, but a few short days from departure, whether I shall in fact be able to go with the *Terra Nova* on the first leg of her voyage. (EVANS BLINKS UPRIGHT, LOOKS AT AN IMPASSIVE WILSON AND A SEARCH-ME CAMPBELL. KATHLEEN'S EYES BRIGHTEN TOWARDS UNDERSTANDING) The decision to leave in June not August all but guarantees a speedy passage through the Southern pack ice, but in the hectic dash to make ready important expeditionary matters have been laid to one side, and it is these I must now attend to, since I am determined that nothing that can be done shall not be done to ensure success. (PAUSE) As to that success itself, I say only: if I am to be remembered at all in time to come, I would prefer it to be as a truth-seeker rather than as a Pole-seeker. We go south to unlock the secrets of Nature, that mankind might profit from the knowledge. We know there will be risks and we are ready for them, proud bearers of the nation's flag and guardians of her honour, members of the greatest club on earth: the British Empire . . .

Scott sits down, to loud hurrahs and hear hears. As the noise subsides, and Scott looks again at Kathleen, a muffled scream from down the room and a crash of dishes on the oak floor. PO Evans lurches to his knees to retrieve the dish of sherry trifle dropped there by the goosed waitress. He slops among the peas and trifle pathetically. The room's attention draws coldly away from him and back to the top table. Teddy Evans stares coldly down the room at the rumpus. Scott hands Kathleen a note. She reads it. Looks at him.

41. Cheering, waving, bunting, hornblowing, fountainshooting departure.

42. Night. Deck, Greenhithe. Farewells (Wilson-Ory; the Evanses; Cherry-Garrard and his father; Bowers and his mother; Lashly and his wife; others. Scott and Kathleen are walking the groups, chatting and shaking hands, ambassadors.

SCOTT   (TO TEDDY EVANS) Well, Lieutenant. I shall expect a full report on boat and crew the moment you reach Simonstown. I'll be there to meet you. I can't imagine there'll be problems, but if there are, you should seek to solve them in accordance with the spirit of the written instructions you've been issued with. I wish you a pleasant voyage.

EVANS Thank you, sir.

Scott shakes hands, moves on to Wilson.

SCOTT Keep an eye on things, will you, Bill? The Number One will almost certainly need . . . guidance.

WILSON I'm sure it will be a pleasant and thoroughly uneventful trip. See you in South Africa. What a pity you don't travel on the same packet as Ory and Mrs Evans . . .

KATHLEEN Yes, *isn't* it a shame.

Visitors have been leaving. Scott reaches gangwalk, turns to wave goodbye. PO Evans lifts three cheers for the Owner.

43. Terra Nova *heading out.*

44. *Scott and Kathleen on quayside, waving in the crowd. Scott's hand finds Kathleen's. Squeezes it.*

45. Terra Nova *at sea. Images of key members of the party: Wilson sketching sea-bird or sleeping on top of ice-house; Cherry-Garrard and Wilson douching each other with buckets of ice-cold sea water on deck at dawn; Oates smoking a corncob, massaging his thigh; Bowers working, etc. Over, newspaper quotes from* Sheffield Daily Telegraph' ('It may be that . . . we are a race of degenerates, living in a flabby age. But at least there can be no degenerates aboard the *Terra Nova* . . . These men are the spiritual sons of the great Elizabethans . . . where a Shackleton fails gloriously, a Scott is found ready . . . to renew the attempt. While England has such men to lead . . . we may thank God and take courage . . . . This is a case in which failure — if failure there must be — is only less glorious than success.'), Morning Post ('[it is] not the selfish hope of honour or a season of fame, but the love of

achievement that drives men to defy Nature. They set the game beyond the prize.') *and* Westminster Gazette ('[all the men] have been specially picked, and not one but what is . . . willing to spend his life, if need be, in the cause.'). *Last image of boat at sunset.*

46. Mix to Fram, *at sunset, moved to Svartskog pier at the bottom of Amundsen's garden. Bjaaland, Hanssen, Lindstrom, Nilsen, Wisting and others in a group — Johansen a little apart — lean over the rail, watching an action in the garden. Sound of hammering and banging, over track of their puzzled, sceptical, disbelieving faces.*

47. Table, lit by lamps. They sit drinking and chatting, villagers on a warm summer's evening. A church clock strikes eleven. Amundsen looks at his watch, smiles at Leon, sees how the men are.

AMUNDSEN   (EASY) Time to go. (MEN DRINK UP CASUALLY) Betty has a gift for each of you before you leave.

The men file round to shake hands with Betty and receive the grey woollen socks she's knitted, then saunter in easy groups down to the Fram, *pipes glowing in the gloom. NILSEN stands by, checking the men down the pathway to the boat. Amundsen stands with his brother by the table. Hands him three envelopes.*

AMUNDSEN   Next stop Madeira. Till then. (STARES AT SKY) Fine night for it. (SHAKES HANDS WITH HIS BROTHER, APPROACHES BETTY, WHO WEEPS STEADILY. HE TAKES HER IN HIS ARMS, SON WITH MOTHER, KISSES HER HAIR LOVINGLY. WHISPERS) Listen. Listen to me. It may be five years before I return. While I'm away, people may say . . . bad things about me. Believe none of it. Wait until I'm home and you can hear the truth from my own lips.

BETTY   Just come back. That's all I ask. Here, take your socks.

He takes them, kisses her, walks down the path towards the waiting Nilsen.

AMUNDSEN   (TURNING, VOICE LIFTED SLIGHTLY) I'll name something after you . . . Mount Betty, how about that?

*He waves, joins Lt Nilsen, ambles on towards the boat. Leon puts his
arm round Betty. They watch together as Captain and First Officer
join the ship.*

48. The Fram *slips silently down the fjord towards the sea. Nansen's
house dominates the far bank. Amundsen looks at it; salutes respectfully.*

49. Nansen stands at his study window, watching the Fram *glide
by. VO: 'watching the* Fram *depart for the North was the most
bitter moment of my life'.*

*50. Nilsen joins Amundsen on deck. They stare ahead in silence for a
while.*

AMUNDSEN   Fine night.

NILSEN   St Olav's day.

AMUNDSEN   Is it? (LOOKS AT NILSEN BRIEFLY)

NILSEN   You said we needed to talk, Captain.

AMUNDSEN   (AFTER THOUGHT) Yes. You need to know one or
   two things.

*51. Screenful of barking and fighting Greenland dogs. Widen to
reveal them in a lighter, being run from island to* Fram. *Hassel
stands in their midst, sorting them out with the stock of his whip. At
the front, another man: huge.*

*52. Deck. Dogs being marshalled, grouped, secured, separated,
Amundsen, Lindstrom and Hanssen in the thick. The slatted false
deck is unfamiliar, makes footing difficult. Already sixty dogs aboard.*

LINDSTROM   (DEEP IN) My God, Andreas Beck as I live and
   breathe . . .

The giant from the lighter has just climbed aboard, a dog under each arm, his roll-bag slung over his shoulder.

Amundsen detaches from the mêlée, relieves the man of the dogs, greets him warmly. Hassel supervises the winching of the remainder.

HANSSEN   (BY LINDSTROM) Who's that?

LINDSTROM   Ice pilot.

HANSSEN   I thought I was ice pilot.

LINDSTROM   Yes, but that's Andreas Beck.

Lindstrom drags a dog to a mast, lashes it there. Hanssen stares on at Beck, startled, perplexed. Nilsen, passing, full of dogs.

NILSEN   Come on, Helmer, it's us or them.

HANSSEN   (CALLING AFTER HIM) You tell me why we're humping coals to Newcastle and I'll behave as though it mattered. Come here, Satan! (HE TACKLES A DOG TO THE DECK, STRUGGLES TO MASTER IT)

53. Moonlit night. Funchal Lanes. Fram *at anchor, half a mile from the island. Dogs howl, perched as silhouettes on every conceivable surface. The crew line the rail, staring at the lights and calling the dogs by name to shut up. Nilsen approaches from below.*

NILSEN   We sail at two tomorrow. Captain wants to see everyone on deck at noon.

LINDSTROM   I thought there was shore leave.

NILSEN   I'm sure the Captain will deal with that tomorrow. (HE'S GONE)

LINDSTROM   The Chief's cooking something up. I've known him like this before. He's barely spoken to a soul since we left. Well, it could be good, it could be crazy.

BJAALAND   Perhaps he's a man who hates lying. I don't like it much myself.

People look at him, reflect a meaning or two.

HANSSEN   (QUIET) It's why I haven't asked about Beck.

WISTING   Maybe he plans a small diversion to the moon. Maybe those dogs know more than we think.

54. Amundsen, CU, studying document in his hand. His brother Leon sits in the cabin with him, smiling as the letter's read. Nilsen sits with them. Noon sun bright beyond. Amundsen looks up at his brother.

AMUNDSEN   I think it's time we told the truth. (HANDING NILSEN A ROLLED MAP) Nail this to the mainmast when the men are assembled, Mr Nilsen, and weigh anchor. (NILSEN LEAVES)

LEON   Are you nervous?

AMUNDSEN   (LIKE A GRAVE ADOLESCENT) Yes. It's only just occurred to me — they may say no. Is it possible?

Sound of men assembling above; anchors being weighed.

LEON   (SLOWLY) (AMUNDSEN PICKS UP HIS HAT) What would *you* say?

AMUNDSEN   (CLEAN, QUICK) I'd go. (A LOOK) There are the letters . . .

Leon takes the unsealed envelopes, checks addressee's names: King Haakon, Professor Nansen, Captain R.F. Scott.

55. Deck. The men gathered, in loose lines. Nilsen has just nailed the map of Antarctica to the mainmast. Dogs, muzzled but free, wander around and between their feet. Their masters boot them fondly away.

BJAALAND   Geography lesson.

HASSEL   Wrong map, Nilsen. And why are we weighing anchor?

LINDSTROM   Part of it's right. There's the Horn.

Nilsen stands quietly, ignoring the ribaldries. Things quieten, grow expectant, when Amundsen and Leon appear. Amundsen puts his hat on, carries a walking cane. Surveys the bunch of them, fringed and interpenetrated by dogs, in the noon sun.

AMUNDSEN   I want to announce a minor change to our plans. I'm sorry it wasn't possible to put this to you sooner, but the matter will explain itself, I hope. I apologize for my recent remoteness, evasiveness. I preferred silence to the lie direct. (PAUSE. LOOKS AT THE MAP) Less than a year ago, when news came in that the North Pole had fallen, this expedition ran into the ground. Money dried, contracts torn up, promises rescinded. To have sought to finance it myself by loans would have left me with ruinous responsibilities for the rest of my days, and effectively ended my life as an explorer. I hope no one will blame me too harshly for considering that option somewhat less than palatable. (A GRIN OF SORTS. GRINS BACK) I resolved at once to work on another, one for which everyone on board has been specifically recruited, and one which, if we're successful, will amply meet the costs of the principal work in the Arctic. I could not *announce* the revised plan, because I was confident that the Government and the powers-that-be would have prevented it, perhaps by simply repossessing the boat. Even now, the world does not know the new plan. Apart from my brother and Lt Nilsen, you're the first to hear of it. Only when we're out of reach of cablegram and wireless will my brother release the news.

LINDSTROM   (A FAT CHUNK) Any chance of you releasing it to us before then, Captain?(LAUGHING.SOMEBODY PUSHES LINDSTROM)

AMUNDSEN (THROUGH THE LAUGHTER) Of course. Instead of sailing north from Cape Horn towards Alaska, there will be a minor diversion for one year in Antarctica and a trip, for some of us, to the South Pole.

Men's laughter slows down a little. Images of key men: Bjaaland, smiling; Stubberud, awed by everything; Leon, searching faces systematically; Lindstrom, pushing his hat back and starting to grin; Johansen; Wisting; Hassel, impassive.

LINDSTROM It'll be good or it'll be crazy, didn't I say it?

A few ragged laughs. Mainly quiet, as men think, weigh.

AMUNDSEN (FACTUAL) You'll have to trust me it can be done. (LONG PAUSE) I'd like your answers one at a time, please.

They look at each other, to see who will start.

AMUNDSEN If you agree to go, you will have extra pay and one hour in which to write your letters. My brother will see they're delivered the day before the news is broken. We have coal, oil, food and water enough to take us to the Ice Barrier in one go. We have two ice-pilots. (A GLANCE AT HANSSEN, WHO NODS UNDERSTANDING) Those who say no will go ashore here with paid passage home. (PAUSE) Who's coming?

Silence again. Boat creaks, anchorless.

JOHANSEN (OUT OF NOWHERE) Johansen comes.

Others join, slowly at first but building, growing excited, at moments slightly giddy, as it all sinks in. They call their names out in the manner of Johansen: Bjaaland, Hanssen, Lindstrom, Wisting, Gjertsen, Beck, Ronne (the cross-eyed sailmaker), Stubberud. Amundsen keeps his eye on Sverre Hassel, who remains detached from the emotion growing around him.

AMUNDSEN (PERSONAL, THE TWO OF THEM) Will you come, Sverre?

He's a key man; a tough moment for Amundsen.

HASSEL (PRECISE) Would you want me for the Pole? (AMUNDSEN NODS ONCE) Can my job back home be protected?

AMUNDSEN My brother will take care of it.

HASSEL Then I'll come.

Amundsen shakes his hand, then on to the others in turn, who are by now quite worked up. The dogs, too, have begun to share the excitement. Somebody fires a flare into the air. The dogs go crazy.

Long shot of the distant boat, drifting gently down the lane, energy releasing itself in waves from the dot-crowded decks.

56. Overhead shot of Leon, in a Funchal bumboat, being rowed towards land. He carries a packet of letters tied in string. His POV reveals the Fram *heading out to sea.*

In closer shot, we see him take Amundsen's three envelopes from an inner pocket, check they're in the right envelopes, seal them up and thread them in with the crews', all the same news now. Over these images, voiced fragments of the two letters (Haakon's; Nansen's: '. . . and when you pass judgement on me, Herr Professor, do not be too harsh. I am no humbug; necessity forced me. I beg your forgiveness for what I have done. May the coming work help to atone . . .')

We see the Scott *envelope, formally addressed poste restante, Melbourne.*

AMUNDSEN (VO) Dear Scott, Beg to inform you, heading South, Amundsen.

Shot of the Fram, *the dash begun.*

III

O PHILOSOPHY!

Title: THE LAST PLACE ON EARTH

III. O Philosophy!

1. Terra Nova, *under plain sail, seen from a distance. Caption: Indian Ocean, Sunday, 4 October 1910. Faintly heard, men's voices singing to pianola accompaniment:*

> Lo the world is ripe to win!
> Up and bring the harvest in!
> Though the reapers still are few,
> Vast the work they have to do.
> Father, great and good, we ask
> Nerve and courage for the task,
> Joyfully thy love to blaze
> O'er the earth's unlighted ways.

(The Message: *Songs of Praise No. 645*)

2. Main deck. Scott reads service to assembled officers, scientists and men. Herbert Ponting, camera artist to the expedition, takes photographs throughout from the fringes.

SCOTT   (PRAYER FOR THE NAVY) Prevent us, O Lord, in all our doings with thy most gracious favour and further us with thy continual help; that in all our works begun, continued and ended in thee we may glorify thy holy name and finally by thy mercy obtain everlasting life through Jesus Christ our Lord.

107

ALL   Amen.

*3. Mess Deck. Men's quarters, cramped, appalling. Scott conduct-
ing regular Sunday inspection, Lts Evans and Campbell in attendance.
Images of Scott adjusting items of personal kit laid out according to
naval regulation. Seamen stand to attention in their spaces.*

SCOTT'S JOURNAL   (vo) Each day furnishes but further confirm-
ation of my decision to relieve Evans of the ship in South
Africa and resume command myself. Not only do I gain a
first-hand knowledge of the men and their capacities, I am
slowly repairing the damage done to morale by Evans's
wayward handling of matters on the way out . . .

*4. Sunset. Crow's Nest. Wilson sits watching the blooded sun,
sketching implements set aside. In CU, his lips move slowly, in deep
silent prayer.*

SCOTT'S JOURNAL   (vo) Wilson is 'Uncle Bill' to one and all . . .
and what a powerful influence he has among the younger
sort, and how wisely and widely it is exerted. Giddy young
bloods in the company vie to mould themselves on his
moral example . . .

Mix to

*5. (Scott's last sentence over) The 'Nursery'. Oates and Bowers on
their bunks, smoking and reading in silence. Oates reads a large* Life
of Napoleon; *Bowers is checking inventory sheets. A slight scuffing
sound outside door. Both hear and ignore it. A bugle shrills and the
door bursts open. Mayhem: a lightning Boy's Own dorm raid by
Nelson, Griffith-Taylor, Wright, Pennell, Rennick, Atkinson and
Cherry-Garrard, in improvised fancy dress, a fair bit of it female.
Public school banter at high pitch: shrieks of* 'Curl top gallant
sails!', 'Titus', 'Birdie', 'Silas', 'Keir Hardie', 'Atch', 'Cherry-
Blaggard', 'Cave', 'The Owner', 'The Wicked Mate'. *Oates,
comically deadpan, attempts to ignore them; Bowers fights
doughtily to drive the raiders out. The romp drifts inexorably
towards nakedness. Young bodies begin to glisten.*

6. Fram, *at sea, in mirror shot of scene 2. Caption: Atlantic Ocean, Equator, 4 October 1910. Faint sounds of dog lap across the water.*

7. *Bridge. Nilsen has watch. All hands on deck as the dogs are gathered and leashed for feeding. Amundsen's fourteen are on the bridge; Bjaaland, Hassel, Hanssen, Johansen, Wisting, Stubberud, Prestrud and Lindstrom, masters of ten apiece, secure their dogs for the stockfish and doenge that Gjertsen, Back, Ronne and Nodtvedt carry from the ice-house. The dogs are active, difficult; sticks and whipstocks prod them into order.*

Over this:

AMUNDSEN'S JOURNAL (VO) Crossed the line in the afternoon, three days later than planned. Lindstrom has promised a celebration meal in the evening, with coffee, liqueurs and cigars on deck afterwards, but the work of the ship and especially the dogs causes us to forego the festive visit of King Neptune with his scissors and jug, but everyone knows why and all agree the work should come first . . .

8. *Decks. Hard work, collaboration, method. Ronne, tiny, cross-eyed, almost drops a box of fish. Johansen catches it, swings it high over his head in an effortless show of great strength, hands it back to Ronne, who sinks once more beneath it.*

9. *Bridge. Nilsen calls out a course reading to Ludvig Hansen at the wheel, then scans the decks. Kutchin conducts oceanographic soundings over the stern. A commotion sets up on the foredeck. Amundsen joins Nilsen, looking for the cause. Furious fighting, several dogs involved.*

10. *Deck. Oscar Wisting, late thirties, short, stocky, moustached, calling the lather of dogs to order. Bjaaland and others rib him. 'Throw the devil overboard, let Shark eat shark' etc. Johansen offers Wisting the loan of his whip. Declined.*

WISTING Give it *up*, Shark. Give it *up*!

Shark is huge, silver white; unimpressed. He knocks a second dog over, steals its food. Uproar.

WISTING Right. That's it.

Wisting launches himself into the midst of the crazed dogs. Laughter and ribbing give way to amazement, and a little concern. Wisting separates Shark from the others: corners and confronts him. The dog stands proud, haul in his mouth, eyes white, dangerous.

WISTING Give it up. Come on, give it up. (HE HOLDS HIS HAND OUT, ADVANCES SLOWLY. THE DOG GROWLS, HARSH, UNAFRAID. COMRADES CALL HIM TO TAKE CARE. LINDSTROM OFFERS HIM A BROOM) All right. You asked for it.

He leaps on the dog, crashing it to the deck, in a totally unexpected attack. Man and dog, fur and cotton, roll across the false deck in almost seamless unity. The rolling stops, man up, the dog's head clamped in one powerful arm, his own face within inches of the teeth. With his free hand Wisting punches the dog on the nose repeatedly until it releases the dogfish. The robbed dog dives in to retrieve it. Wisting holds on to Shark, eye to eye for several moments longer, talking with it in weird squads of sound marshalled some-where in the region of his gullet. Shark has the phlegm to accept the situation. Wisting releases him casually, steps out of the ring, his back to the miscreant. Shark watches, does nothing.

There's blood and slice marks on Wisting's arms and wrists; nothing serious. Men cheer ironically at the victory. Wisting's a touch embarrassed.

JOHANSEN (SOUR) Coulda lost a hand, Wisting.

WISTING (UNREPENTANT) All the dogs have to eat, Hjalmar, not just the bullies. He'll have to learn it.

Amundsen, relaxed, hair longer, watches intently, enjoying it.

11. *Equatorial sunset; fast, spectacular. Slung lamps light an area of*

110

main deck, where the men take coffee and cigars after celebration meal, in among the dogs. Bits of work continue to be done: Hassel stitching a fan-harness; Ronne running up an adapted three-man tent on a Singer sewing machine. Beck and Nodtvedt play violin and mandolin with big men's delicacy. Prestrud sings an old whaler's song through a megaphone. Gentle eddies of it wash across the dark water. Hanssen, Bjaaland and Stubberud casually study a chart of the Antarctic region. Hanssen's whip-stock traces out their line of entry to the Barrier and the Bay of Whales. Their dogs sniff and gallop around them, searching out the fondling hand. Lindstrom carries a jug of coffee and a bottle of cognac around, topping up where he can.

Amundsen sits on deck, making pencil jottings on a pad. He stops as the song ends, joins the general appreciation. Some banter. He writes something else.

Lindstrom climbs to the bridge. Johansen at helm, proud, separate. Lindstrom offers cognac or coffee. Johansen stares at the bottle a moment, then holds his tin mug out for the coffee. Below, Beck and Nodtvedt strike up a spirited version of a cakewalk.

Deck. Wisting appears on cue from a hatchway, in incongruously full Polar kit (reindeer fur etc). Proceeds to cakewalk elegantly around the deck with his dancing partner, the great silver Shark, glittering under the lamps, to the applause of all. Watching dogs set up a chorus. Amundsen watches smilingly, begins to jot something down on the pad. In CU we see: Polar Party *and a list of names beneath:*

Self
Hanssen
Bjaaland
Hassel
Stubberud
Prestrud
Johansen

He adds, 'Wisting?' *Strikes out the question mark.*

111

12. *White screen. Caption in red:* O Philosophy, you leader of life. *Cicero:* 'Tusculanae Disputationes' I. 17

13. *Outlands. High summer. A young boy stands in the middle of a vast lawn. He wears full dress uniform of an admiral of the fleet, many sizes too big for him. An old man, his father, in fawn jacket and straw hat, potters about a flowerbed some distance away. His mother sits at a white table beneath a huge copper beech. She counts small piles of coins, enters her reckoning into a black notebook. Several girls, his sisters, play a tag-game in trees. An older boy, his brother, practises cricket strokes in the middle of the mother's line of vision. She smiles appreciatively.*

The boy in the middle of the lawn goes unnoticed.

CU boy's face. The sounds fade. Wind brisks the trees. The boy has seen something approaching. Apprehension. Fear.

His POV, wide. It's winter. The lawn is dead white, the landscape empty. Something, a dog, lollops towards him. There is something in its mouth.

The dog runs at speed but gets no closer. The boy's fear grows. A whiny whistle sounds. Once. Twice.

The dog is at his feet. Debouches its load.

CU Scott's face, vivid with horror.

Image of Peter Markham, a bloodstained bundle, on the snow between his feet. Whistle whines again.

14. *Scott jerks awake on his bunk, sweating. Reaches for the speaking tube. Uncorks it.*

15. *Bridge. Pennell at speaking tube, Bowers, Atkinson and Gran watching something approach the ship through the murk.*

PENNELL   No, no idea, sir. I suppose it's come from Melbourne harbour. (LOOKS AGAIN) Well, I wouldn't swear to it, sir, but I think I can see a woman . . .

16. Shot of small motor launch in lee of Terra Nova. *A woman, Kathleen, soaked, stands upright and defiant, a leather mail satchel slung over shoulder. Bowers, Atkinson and Gran stare over the side. Oates approaches, stares down at the small careening vessel.*

BOWERS It's the Captain's lady!

OATES (VERY SOFT) More like the Lady Captain, Birdie.

Bowers goes to climb the rope ladder down to the launch.

KATHLEEN (CALLING) Don't bother, Mr Bowers, I'm coming up.

She begins the precarious ascent. Bowers, Gran and Atkinson stand fascinated, paralyzed. Pennell calls something down from the bridge. Some feet from the group, Thomas Crean is abseiling down the ship's side towards the climbing woman, a second length of rope across his shoulder. Bill Lashly undemonstratively takes the strain by a small capstan. Crean secures Kathleen with the rope as Scott arrives on deck in disarray. He looks down into the lanterned murk. Kathleen looks up. Holds up the leather satchel.

KATHLEEN (CALLING) The mails!

17. Scott's cabin. Leather mail satchel on desk, some of its contents disgorged. Kathleen's hands processing Scott's mail. In back of shot, Scott prone on his bunk in post-coital torpor.

KATHLEEN (ALIVE, PURPOSEFUL) . . . That's the Governor-General's garden party in Sydney on the 23rd. Sir Joseph and Lady Kinsey *will* be there — they've offered us their house near Dunedin for the New Zealand tour, isn't that kind? (SHE LAYS SEVERAL LETTERS OUT IN PILES WITHOUT COMMENT, AND ON) Ah yes, Federal Prime Minister Hughes, funny little Welshman, offering a meeting on the 20th; request for £5,000 towards cost of Expedition noted etc. etc.

113

I'll be surprised if they give us anything, though it's a disgrace after what they lavished on Shackleton. I asked Hughes how it would look if the Japanese beat us to the Pole because his government had failed to fund us. He looked thoughtful. (OPENING ANOTHER) Ah, Samuel Horden, now this is a good man, I met him at a soirée in Adelaide, industrialist, very rich, and quite prepared to make a large donation, he tells me, if the Australian government doesn't, provided we'll help with some publicity — he makes bicycles, I believe. (ON AND ON, THE SILVER PAPER DAGGER SLICING CRISPLY) Melbourne, by the way, is a dreadful place. If the ship leaves as planned for Wellington on the 18th, I see no earthly reason for staying here beyond then. (STACKING AGAIN) Showing the flag . . . showing the flag . . . showing the flag . . . New Zealand . . . address at fund-raising garden party . . . I almost lost my mind on the trip from South Africa . . . Hilda Evans is a drivelling hysteric behind the bluff façade, and Ory Wilson a sanctimonious bore. In my ideal world there would be no women, just beautiful husbands and darling sons. (SHE LOOKS AT THE PIC ON SCOTT'S DESK OF HERSELF NURSING PETER MARKHAM; SHE STACKS MORE MAIL IN PILES ON THE DESK) Oh, the rest of your scientists turned up last week, nice boys . . . and Cecil whatsisname, the dog man . . .

SCOTT   Meares . . .

KATHLEEN   He and brother Wilfred came through with the animals, all safe and sound, you'll be pleased to hear. (SHE STUDIES A CABLE IN ITS ENVELOPE, SLITS IT NEATLY WITH THE DAGGER) Cable. (SHE READS IT IN SILENCE) This doesn't make sense.

SCOTT   (PRONE; FOND, DROWSY) Read it. The oracle awaits.

KATHLEEN   'Beg to inform you, heading South, Amundsen.'

Scott sits up slowly, swings his legs to the floor, stares across the cabin at his bathrobed wife. Sounds of sea and ship fret at the space

114

between them. Scott's face white, tight, the blackness ahead just glimpsed.

KATHLEEN Postmark October, Christiania. (SHE OFFERS IT TO HIM. HE SHAKES HIS HEAD.)

Silence.

SCOTT It makes . . . no sense.

Knocking at door. Wilson's raised voice outside.

WILSON (CALLING) Are you young lovers decent in there? The launch is ready to leave for the mainland and Evans and I are off to see our wives . . . Will you come or what?

SCOTT (TENSE) Give us five minutes, Bill, there's a good chap, we're doing the mails.

WILSON Five minutes it is, Captain. How are you, Kathleen?

KATHLEEN Well. I'm very well, thank you.

It's the exact measure of their mutual dislike, the greeting, the response. Wilson's gone. Kathleen shivers, begins preparing herself to leave the boat. Scott's just replacing the speaking tube.

SCOTT I've asked Gran to step down.

KATHLEEN Shouldn't you cable someone? London, Markham?

SCOTT I don't know.

He crosses to the desk, buckles the leather satchel, places a blotter over the opened mail, studies the telegram as he buttons his shirt. Knocking.

SCOTT Come. (GRAN IN DOORWAY) Ah, Gran. Come in, come in.

Scott takes the desk chair. Gran stands, shy and huge; a decent smile at Kathleen. Scott hands him the cable. Gran reads, slow, infuriating. Looks at Scott.

SCOTT Know anything about this, Gran?

GRAN No. Nothing. What should it mean?

SCOTT What do *you* think it means?

GRAN (CHECKING POSTMARK) Amundsen goes North, everyone knows . . .

Scott has fallen silent. Gran looks at Kathleen.

GRAN Cable Fridtjof Nansen. Perhaps he will know what this should mean.

SCOTT (TERMINATING) Thank you, Gran. Take the mails up, will you, give them to the Mate for distribution. And don't speak of this matter for the time being.

Gran takes the leather satchel, nods, confused; leaves. Scott stares blankly on at the cable.

KATHLEEN What will you do, Con?

SCOTT Nothing. (PAUSE) Nothing.

KATHLEEN I have a private address for Nansen, if you need it . . .

Scott looks hard and searching at her for a moment.

SCOTT (FINALLY, BLEAK CU) *Damn* him. How *dare* he.

Trail dog wails and pony snorts from scene 18.

18. *Quail Island, New Zealand. Oates, stooped, examining an aged*

pony's hind quarters, face grim, bleakening. Drizzly late spring November day. PO Evans holds the horse's head, talks to it ('Ain't no Norskie gonna beat *me* to the Pole, pony, I'm tellin' yew . . .' *and* 'In Wales yew'd be down a *pit*, boyo, so don't go feelin' sorry for yewself . . .') *In longer shot, they move on methodically through the small wire enclosure, watched from outside by Bowers, Meares, Anton and Dmitri (the Russian handlers). The dog compound beyond is a sporadic bedlam. The nineteen white ponies shiver in the dull rain.*

Oates approaches the wire entrance, wiping hands on a filthy cloth in his belt; leaves the enclosure through the gate Evans dutifully opens for him. Bowers approaches, clipboard to chest. Meares stays back a few paces, hair long and unkempt, a vast beard shrouding his features.

BOWERS I'll need them aboard by nightfall, Titus. The stalls'll be ready within the hour. All right?

OATES (TERSE) Thanks, Birdie.

Bowers marches off towards the wharf some fifty yards away and the ship he's busy restowing.

Oates looks at Meares, who stands his ground, defensively.

OATES (QUIET, NOT A WHISPER) Cut back to the ship, PO, will you, present my compliments to the Captain. (LOOKS DIRECTLY AT EVANS) Tell him I need to speak with him about the ponies before he leaves for his hotel.

PO EVANS Aye aye sir.

He's gone. Oates looks back at the ponies. Crosses to where Meares waits.

OATES (CAREFULLY) I congratulate you, Meares. Five thousand miles and not a beast lost.

117

MEARES   Thank you. (HE SAYS SOMETHING TO THE RUSSIANS, WHO STEP FORWARD AND GIVE A FORMAL HEAD-BOW) Anton Omolchenko, a jockey from Moscow; Dmitri Gerve, dog-handler; they shared the work.

Oates shakes hands with them, states his name very simply to each. Meares addresses them in Russian again; they move off to their chores. Oates wanders the few paces back to the compound, stares at the dank ponies through the wire. Meares joins him.

MEARES   (QUIETLY) Bad as that, eh? (OATES SNIFFS, SAYS NOTHING) I'll have to ask you to accept they're the best I could do.

OATES   I should have gone with you. I should have insisted. (PAUSE) These won't do.

MEARES   I know dogs. That's what I joined for. (THEY STARE ON IN SILENCE, IN THE RISING MIST) Scott's seen 'em, by the way. He's declared 'em first rate. (OATES LOOKS AT MEARES; A SHARP, BITTER LAUGH) I'll come with you when you see him, if you like.

OATES   Kind of you, but I'll do it.

PO EVANS   (OOS SOME DISTANCE AWAY, VOICE SLIGHTLY SLURRY) Captain Oates, sir, Captain's compliments, says 'e's occupied with the Governor-General all day but he might be able to spare you a few minutes after dinner at the hotel, sir. About nine, sir.

Oates deliberates, quite taut, then waves Evans back to the ship.

MEARES   (LEAVING) I have to feed my dogs. (RETURNING A PACE) Know what he said to me? Get a haircut, he said.

Meares smiles, prepares to melt off into the mist.

OATES   (SOFT) Whose idea was it to bring only white ones, Cecil?

MEARES   Wasn't mine. Shackleton claimed his whites lived longest. (BEAT) I hadn't heard you could tell a beast's qualities by its colour.

OATES   You can't.

19. The British Hotel. Lobby. A hung banner proudly announces that officers of the British Antarctic Expedition are in residence. Oates sits on a mock Louis-Quinze chaise longue, in work-clothes as before, like a hobo in from the rain. Hotel staff watch him with disdain, suspicion: passing guests mutter comments. Oates massages his thigh; glances at the great clock: 9.56; at the great chandeliers, like formations of ice. Clarety male laughter from the banquet-room lifts around a woman's clear voice.

20. Dining-room. Scott and guests at a round table: twenty seated, most of them dignitaries (Joseph Kinsey and wife; a Cabinet minister; magnates; a Governor-General and lady; Wilson and Ory; Teddy and Hilda Evans). Kathleen regales the menfolk with her views on the Women Question, through the slow crab about the table. The men are delighted, enthralled (save for Wilson and Evans). Her thesis is winningly simple: she's never thought of herself as a woman, has always considered herself totally free to do as she pleased. 'If women want to be merely *women*, they have only themselves to blame . . .' *and on into her familiar scathing attack on the contemptibility of her sex. Ory Wilson listens coolly, not part of it; Hilda Evans clearly hates the woman, simmers uneasily behind her fan. The crab reaches Scott, happy with her success; and the scribbled note, on his glass-mat, which reads:* 'Captain Scott, arrived as requested for discussion of ponies. Oates.' *Scott's glass down, to cover it.*

21. Lobby. Oates sits upright now, hands on thighs, watching the clock waver on 10.29. A tall old man and two younger aides stand watching and discussing him from the banquet-room doorway. Within, the party's breaking up. The clock strikes the half. Oates gets to his feet rather deliberately; one of the aides detaches and approaches him.

AIDE (EVENING DRESS) Oates, isn't it? (OATES NODS) Charlie Eyre, we met in Capetown during the war. (OATES SHOWS LITTLE INTEREST) You're going south with Scott, eh? (OATES NODS) I mentioned your name to the Duke of Connaught. (INDICATES THE OLD MAN, WHO'S WATCHING THE EXCHANGE) His Grace wondered if by any chance you knew his son at Eton?

Scott's party have begun leaking from the banquet-room in clots of three and four.

OATES (OBSERVING IT) No, I don't believe I did. A fellow can't be expected to know everybody at a school . . . Excuse me, will you?

He's seen Scott, makes to make sure he's seen. Scott is shaking hands: evening dress and decorations, cigar. Teddy Evans stands dutifully with and a dutiful half-step behind him. Wilson and Ory are already on the stair. Guests bonhomously drain off to their carriages. Scott spots Oates; flushes, a little angry. Approaches, Evans a pace behind.

SCOTT (COOL) Oates, you still here? Thought you'd have been abed long ago . . . All right, tell me the problem, I have five minutes . . . (CHECKS WATCH)

OATES (PLAIN) The ponies are no good. I thought you should know.

Scott looks at Evans, a sort of paranoid reflex: Evans stares dumbly at Oates.

SCOTT (SCORNFUL; A CHOICE) No good? What do you mean, no good? I saw them for myself, they're in remarkable condition, given the ordeal of travel they've undergone.

KATHLEEN (OOS, FROM UP LOBBY, NOT A SHOUT) Con, try not to be long, you need your sleep and we're taking cocoa with the Kinseys . . .

He waves acquiescence, she retires.

SCOTT   (TO EVANS) Thank you, Teddy, you get off to the ship, you have your watch. I'll give you final instructions in the morning before you sail.

Evans is dismissed like a schoolboy; stiffly thinks of saying something; leaves it; stiffly leaves. Oates misses none of it.

SCOTT   Captain Oates. Is there some grudge you bear me? You weren't allowed to pick the animals yourself, is that it? 'The ponies won't do'. Now what does that mean? Does it mean I shouldn't take them?

OATES   (IMPERVIOUS) *I* wouldn't.

SCOTT   (BLINKING) Are you *serious*?

OATES   There's not a one that isn't aged, windsucking, slit, scarred, lame or ringwormed. There's not a one I'd trust to carry me in a dog-cart down an English country lane.

SCOTT   (FAST) Oates, I'll read your *report* on the matter when I have the time, for the moment I have nothing more to say. If I were you, I should get some sleep, you look all in.

OATES   (TAKING SHEAF OF PAPERS FROM POCKET) The report is here, sir. I should be obliged if you would take it. (HE HOLDS IT OUT, PATRICIAN SUDDENLY; SCOTT DARKENS; TAKES IT, OUCLASSED) Thank you. I would not want their failure to be considered my responsibility. Good night.

He turns, limps away towards the main doors. Scott watches him out; slaps the rolled report like a baton against the palm of his hand.

22. Terra Nova. *Night. Slung lamps light irregular areas, thicken the mist. Two men — eventually Evans and Oates — walk the piled decks, past motorsledges and petrol drums, dogs, food, coal and a mass of gear. Evans talks in low tones, almost finished. Fragments*

121

float on the mist, flecks of his lukewarm 'loyal' defence of Scott's style and manner and of its sub-text, a guilt-based justification of his own supinity. ('You have to pick your moment with a man like the Owner.' 'Scott's a man of moods, everyone knows it.' 'Do you think I enjoyed being relieved of the ship in South Africa?' 'Grin and bear it . . .' *and so on.) Bowers appears suddenly from a pile of boxes stamped 'Gift of Government of New Zealand', clipboard active. Evans stops talking until they reach the rail by the high gangway. He leans forward, stares down through gluey light at the wharf below. Oates joins him, morose now. Evans casually checks that Bowers is out of earshot. Someone sings a hymn, high tenor, blurred and arhythmic* (The Message, *from scene 1) in the murk of the wharf.*

EVANS The Owner's under a great deal of pressure; a bit stretched, do you see. This Norwegian thing . . . Must be gnawing at him. Won't say a word, of course. Victor Campbell showed him a cutting he'd taken from an Auckland paper, clammed up. Wouldn't even acknowledge let alone discuss it. (BEAT) I'll see you get the extra fodder you ask for to fatten the little beggars up, that's a promise, but I can't ask the Owner to ditch them and hang around here for a month until you can arrange a shipment of Army mules from India, it's unrealistic, and we can't afford it. (THE SINGING BELOW HAS GOT LOUDER, PUNCTUATED WITH ADDLED SHOUTS ABOUT 'NORSKIES' AND 'THE BRITISH RACE'; BUT STILL BARELY IMPINGES.) Talk to me whenever you need to, old chap. But keep your counsel. You'll find it's rarely needed.

Oates stands upright, stares at the dead bowl of his pipe.

OATES Can I ask you a question, Teddy?

EVANS By all means.

OATES Is loyalty to the leader the *highest* virtue? Does plain *reason* not occasionally override it?

Silence, save for the broken hymn from below.

122

III   O PHILOSOPHY!

EVANS   (STIFFENING SLIGHTLY, AS HE STANDS UPRIGHT) I'm afraid
I consider that an improper question, Titus.

OATES   (THINKING IT OUT) Well, that's as maybe, Teddy. One
day you may not. I'm to bed.

*He heads for a hatch. Evans watches him recede; finds he's trembling,
complex angers — at Scott, at self — seething just below the skin.
He uses the rail to brace himself, the reflexive reach for control.
From below a loud shout, a splash, more shouting, then men from
the watch shouting 'Man overboard'. Evans glares over the side.*

EVANS   (SHARP, HARSH, SUDDEN) Who is that man?

MAN   (BELOW) It's PO Evans, sir.

EVANS   (VICIOUS, LARVAL) Pack his bags! Get him off this ship!
He's *fired!*

23. *Blood-red gong of sun over sea, two hours from setting.*

24. *Headland, high over bay. A man and a woman stare as if
tranced.*

25. *The Kinseys' peach-white residence and gardens, at some distance behind the two figures.*

26. *In closer shot, Scott and Kathleen, washed by the unreal,
salmony light, stare at the sun.*

SCOTT   (EVENTUALLY) Everything . . . passes.

KATHLEEN   Some things endure. (BEAT) Love endures. And the
deeds of great men. (HE SAYS NOTHING. THEY STARE ON AT
THE GIANT SUN) In London it will be dawn outside his
window. (SHE BLOWS A SOFT ISADORAN KISS ON HER HAND)
Good morning, my son.

SCOTT   (FARAWAY) Poor K. A babe at one end of the earth, a

123

husband at the other.

KATHLEEN   Poor? My men straddle the earth.

Silence again.

SCOTT   K.

KATHLEEN   Mmm.

SCOTT   Will you cope?

KATHLEEN   Yes.

SCOTT   If I don't return, I mean.

KATHLEEN   I know.

SCOTT   I've begun to feel recently I might not.

KATHLEEN   Heroes dream of failure. Which is South?

Scott checks, indicates. Kathleen reflects her body to face it. She locks her gaze on infinity for several moments, as if fierce in prayer.

KATHLEEN   (INTENSE) I entrust this my man to your care and charge you to return him whole and unscathed. (SHE TURNS TO HOLD HIS FACE IN HER HANDS, KISSES HIM WITH PASSION)

27. Rear of Kinsey house, in long shot. A maid shows a large navy man round the building and points down the garden towards the headland, where two tiny figures embrace. The man thanks her, proceeds down the garden, bulging roll-bag over shoulder.

28. Scott hugs Kathleen fiercely, as if scared to let go. She finally detaches.

KATHLEEN   I must go up to the house, if I'm to find anything at all to wear for this damned farewell dinner. I really want to spend the whole night with *you*.

29. The navy man stands by the perimeter gate. His POV, the woman has detached and is walking towards him.

30. Scott, touching bruised lips with finger pads; in back of shot, Kathleen meets the man, points on down the track towards Scott. Close on the face, losing the approaching man: fragments of Wilson's speech at the Farewell Dinner, pledging the loyalty and dedication of the scientists to the leader; and Scott's mini-press conference as the formal functions end and the odd mess rowdiness begins to appear.

MAN'S VOICE   (OOS) Captain Scott, sir.

Scott blinks, turns sharply. Sees PO Evans, roll on shoulder, cap in hand, a dozen paces away, abject.

In CU, we see his face is raw with tears.

31. Shot of Kathleen at upper window.

32. Her POV of the headland. The two men face each other, dramatic dots on a vast landscape.

33. The men from another angle, closer, still long, still mute. Evans has removed his tunic, unbuttons his shirt, rolls his sleeve up to show his bicep, his trouser leg to show his calf, dedicating all of it to Scott's leadership of the expedition.

34. Kathleen's POV again. The small dot consoles the large one. Very slow mix to 35. Over this, journalist's question at Farewell Dinner conference: 'Is it true that you've been forced to dispense with the services of a senior petty officer for indiscipline, Captain Scott, while you've been our guest here in New Zealand?'

35. Hotel. Large room for Farewell Dinner. Banter at large table where full officer complement and scientists and top wives drink and chatter. Scott has left the table, stands in corner of the room with four New Zealand reporters. Teddy Evans has approached unnoticed, listens from the shadows.

SCOTT (CU) No, sir, it is not true, though I cannot see it is any of your business. We leave for Antarctica tomorrow with a full complement as happy and determined to succeed as any I have had the honour to command. A final question? (HE CATCHES EVANS IN THE CORNER OF HIS EYE, LOOKS AWAY QUICKLY.)

JOURNALIST Perhaps you'd care to say something about the rival expedition from Norway and its prospects of success.

Scott has frozen. Looks again, almost involuntarily, in Evans's direction. Voices are rising at the large dinner table, Hilda Evans's rather tipsily prominent.

SCOTT I don't think I would care to say anything on that subject. (LONG PAUSE. HE KNOWS HE CAN'T LEAVE IT THERE) I do not regard myself as being in a race with anyone. My plans are meticulously laid, my men have been assiduously recruited, my animals are splendid and all in good condition. All will do their duty. Thank you.

Scott steps out of the group, leaves the room, crosses a lobby to the washrooms.

36. Washrooms. Scott enters, crosses to the raised stones, prepares to urinate. An old Maori attendant sits by the doorway in hotel uniform, a heap of clean towels on his table.

Teddy Evans in, crosses to wash hands in the ornate mirrored basins, eyes on Scott's reflection. Scott joins him eventually at the bowls. Catches sight of the tension in Evans's face in the glass. Splashes water on his own.

SCOTT Not now, Teddy, eh, there's a good fellow.

126

He collects a towel from the attendant's table, returns to the mirrors to pat himself dry.

EVANS   You've reinstated PO Evans, is that right?

SCOTT   (WEARY) That *is* right, Teddy. Strictly on grounds of his immense value to the work of this expedition. Evans is indispensible. Evans goes. I have his word there will be no repetition. There's no more to say.

EVANS   (TERSE) In that case, I believe I may have to ask you to accept my resignation.

Scott places the used towel on the table, returns to the mirrors to check his appearance. Evans dries his hands, returns the towel to the table.

SCOTT   And risk the taint of *funk*, Teddy? Come now.

EVANS   (QUIET) Oh, I think I have a case to put.

SCOTT   Case? PO Evans?

EVANS   (ONE BY ONE) A seriously defective ship, disastrously overladen, with inadequate pumping facilities and no engineering officer to replace the one you fired for purely personal reasons in Australia. I believe I might be able to make something out of that, Captain.

The men look at each other in the glass in silence. The attendant sits like a statue, unseen, unseeing.

SCOTT   Tell me what it is you *want*, Teddy.

EVANS   Simply. (PAUSE) Your assurance that you consider me as indispensible to this enterprise as PO Evans, for example.

Scott nods, seeing at last what's needed.

SCOTT   My dear Teddy, how can you possibly doubt it? Of course you're an *integral* part of my plans for the assault on the Pole. How remiss of me to have left you in doubt on the matter. Now I understand the source of your wild and largely unfounded grievances. Indeed.

Sounds of women's voices in lobby, raised, getting slightly angry.

SCOTT   Shall we go? (HE SMILES DISARMINGLY. EVANS NODS, BEADILY REASSURED.)

Scott leaves, Evans in his wake, the dutiful half-step behind. The Maori sits and stares. Clears his throat. Takes a small box from his pocket. Lips a clot of sputum into it. Returns box to pocket.

37. Scott, MCU, boat in motion, bunting, band, God Save the King, *naval salutes, cheering and the rest. He stares fixedly as if at something in the sky. On the reverse, we see it's the headland. A small figure stands on the brink, watching the ship.*

38. Kathleen, MCU, watching.

KATHLEEN   I didn't say goodbye to my man because I didn't want anyone to see him sad.

39. Scott, CU, still watching.

KATHLEEN   (VO) I felt his face radiating tenderness as the space between us widened, until I held only my memory of that upturned face, but held it for a lifetime . . .

40. Mix to Amundsen in his cabin, working meticulously at a notice in heavy swell. Three dogs lie or nose around the room, temporary squatters and pretty much at their ease. Amundsen talks to them under his breath from time to time, as he works.

41. Amundsen carries notice to the saloon, empty of crew. Lindstrom watches him from the galley as he pins the notice to the board, stands back to read it, leaves. Lindstrom sidles up to read it:

128

III   O PHILOSOPHY!

'Landing Party Planning Meeting, 8 p.m. Agenda: Dogs (Hassel), Ski (Bjaaland), Food (Lindstrom), Hut (Stubberud), Provisions (Johansen), Navigation (Prestrud), Clothing (Amundsen).' *And underneath:*

> Victory awaits those who have everything in order — people call that luck.
> Defeat awaits those who don't — this they call bad luck.

> Amundsen

42. Shot of dead pony floating in swollen wake of a ship. Develop shot to reveal debris, splintered spars, petrol drums, coal sacks, packing cases. Reveal finally the Terra Nova *in far distance, heading on south. Bring up journal voice, as we cut to*

43. Terra Nova, *in closer shot, main deck in massive disarray, swarms of seamen clearing up, in the aftermath of the storm. Two drowned dogs are jettisoned over the side.*

SCOTT'S JOURNAL   (VO) As far as one can gather, besides the damage to the ship, we have lost two ponies, two dogs, ten tons of coal, sixty-five gallons of petrol. All things considered we have come off lightly, but it was bad luck to strike a gale at such a time.

Images of Oates and Anton, under this, all in, stoically massaging ponies' hearts and feeding them brandy.

On deck, Scott offers prayer of thanksgiving before muster of available crew at unsteady attention.

SCOTT   O Lord, who has brought us to the beginning of this day, and who seest that we have no power of ourselves to help ourselves, grant that this day we run not into further danger and keep us always in thy safe ways. Through Jesus Christ our Lord.

ALL   Amen.

Scott studies his clipboard of announcements. The heroes of the storm emerge through a hatchway to wash on deck: Lashly, Crean, Keohane, Chief Officer Williams; and Teddy Evans. A cheer sets up from the mustered men, swells to spontaneous acclaim when Evans is finally sighted. Scott, CU, teeth clipping lip.

44. *Pack ice.* Terra Nova, *at distance, locked in. Slow track in, under*

SCOTT'S JOURNAL   (VO) Coal is now the great anxiety — we have come 240 miles since we first entered the pack streams and we have less than 300 tons of coal left in a ship that simply eats coal. It's alarming. And then there are the ponies going steadily downhill . . . No, it looks as though we've struck a streak of really bad luck, that fortune has determined to put every difficulty in our path . . .

Images of Bowers in crow's nest, scanning for leads and calling down his findings; Wilson, sketching penguin; Scott in cabin, writing his journal; Oates and Anton, black from their blubber stove; scientists dredging, measuring thickness of ice, wind-speed; and finally into shot, a group of ship's company on a floe some hundred yards away, plunging around on ski under Gran's instruction. During next piece from Journal, close on this group, to pick up ineptitude and cheery contempt of the sailors for 'these foreign planks' etc. (PO Evans). Gran's dismay and confusion are ignored by the Brits.

SCOTT'S JOURNAL   (VO) After breakfast we served out ski to the men of the landing party. They are all very keen to learn, and Gran has been out morning and afternoon giving instruction. Fortune would be in a hard mood indeed if it allowed such a combination of knowledge, experience, ability and enthusiasm to achieve nothing.

45. *Night.* Fram. *Full watch alert, watching and listening. Beck leans on the rim of the crow's nest, head forward, watching, listening, sniffing the bitter air.*

BECK   (SUDDEN, CALM) Berg starboard, four hundred metres!

130

The call is bounced from watch to wheel. Johansen swings to port decisively. The boat responds, cuts left before the wind. Amundsen and Prestrud, on bridge, watch something out to the right, wonder in their eyes. Their POV reveals a quarter-mile berg a bare hundred yards from the boat. Prestrud says something to Amundsen, who shrugs, sniffs.

PRESTRUD   (CALL TO CROW'S NEST) What's your secret, maestro?

Beck looks down briefly, taps his nostril, sniffs on into the night.

46. Day. Officers, scientists and crew line the Terra Nova's *rail. They stare in wonderment, faces intense, white.*

SCOTT'S JOURNAL   (VO) No other ship, not even Shackleton's *Nimrod*, would have come through so well. But I trust that the New Year will bring us better fortune than the old. The weeks wasted in the pack ice will not easily be made up.

On reverse, the Barrier, hundreds of feet high, many miles long, slips unendingly past the steaming boat. Ponting active, with camera and cinematograph. On the bridge, Wilson shakes Scott by the hand: he has brought them through. At the rail, Teddy Evans, Pennell, Atkinson, Cherry-Garrard, Bowers form one group, deeply awed by the weight of the experience. Oates, Meares and Campbell form another, absorbed but more sinewy in their regard. Lashly, Crean, Keohane and PO Evans form a third. Their stares are hard, unfriendly, unsentimental. Crean spits a stream of plug-juice over the side.

CREAN   Will ya look at the bastard!

47. Fram, *in midnight sun, emerging from pack. Prestrud climbs to crow's nest to relieve Beck.*

48. Saloon. Crowded. Amundsen with maps and charts spread on table, drawing a navigation line due south to Barrier then east, ending at a preset pot of ink, under which he writes Bay of Whales.

Beck pushes door open, scans for Amundsen across the smoky space. Amundsen looks up, sees him.

BECK She's through, Chief.

AMUNDSEN You said a week, it's taken three days.

BECK We had luck.

He leaves. No one in the meeting feels getting through the pack very remarkable. Several have been studying the maps.

STUBBERUD (HESITANTLY) But what if it isn't **there**, Chief? Ink-pot Bay there. Where do we land then? (GRUNTS AND MURMURS ASSERT THE QUESTION'S IMPORTANCE)

AMUNDSEN (TAPPING A PILE OF BOOKS) It's there. Ross saw it seventy years ago. Shackleton two years ago. A permanent feature. A land bay.

JOHANSEN (COLD) Which no one has actually *landed* in, though.

AMUNDSEN (NOT LOOKING AT HIM) That's right. Not yet. Questions?

49. Terra Nova *steaming down McMurdo Sound, by Cape Evans. Scott stares across the Sound at the far black cliffs and mountains, sun glinting behind them. The ship is very active, as they approach the ice-locked basin of the bay; but Scott is in a deep dream, scanning the high black cliffs. A peak. His face in CU. The peak again: a black cross stands out starkly against the skyline. (A prefiguring of the cross the expedition erects when they leave in 1913.) Scott's face again, overwhelmed by the image.*

Calls for the Captain. Teddy Evans appears.

EVANS What do you want to do, sir? We've reached the limit of the ice. We're still ten miles or so from the Hut.

SCOTT   (COMING TO) What? (HE LOOKS, SEES THE ICE FRINGE)
   Damn. Damn. Will nothing go right!

EVANS   Shall I look at the land around the Cape?

SCOTT   I suppose so. If we cannot go on.

*Evans gathers a body of men for the recce. Scott waits some
moments, then stares back at the peak. No cross, but the sun is now
directly behind it; a monstrance of white light.*

*50. Fram glides down whalesprayed waters. Crew and dogs line
rails, stare whitely about them. POV shots gradually establish
distant coastline of bay and ice barrier beyond. Wisting at wheel,
Shark on a box beside him, enjoying a fondle. Amundsen appears
casually on deck from below, makes for the rail. Men clap him
through their ranks. He smiles, easy, relaxed, unassuming. Dogs
begin barking, excitement building, Amundsen takes their applause
ironically.*

*Amundsen joins Hanssen, Hassel, Bjaaland and Stubberud towards
the prow of the boat. Stares with them at the advancing land.
Stubberud stares at him until Amundsen looks. Stubberud gives a
grave little salute, stiff fingers to shiny neb. Amundsen smiles, calls
something up to Beck in the crow's nest.*

AMUNDSEN'S JOURNAL   (VO) Before us, a great bay, so deep it
   was almost impossible to see the end of it from the crow's
   nest. Without striking a blow, we had entered our kingdom.

*51. Cape Evans. Around dawn. Campbell's voice booms and volleys
around the main deck of Terra Nova, pushing to complete the
unloading of the gear. Crew scuttle around in the tense air. Distant
bark of motorsledge at work ashore.*

*Scott appears from below, buttoning his naval windproof, joins
Campbell, taking his salute. Surveys his expedition from the rail,
spread across two miles of sea-ice and the sand-and-rock littoral of
Ross Island. Caravans of dog-sledge, pony-sledge and man-haulers*

*cross and re-cross the sea-ice from ship to shore, where one of the
two motorsledges gathers the loads behind it to haul down to the
base hut, all but erected, a mile or so down the rocky beach.*

*Scott pleased with the activity. Notes the remaining motorsledge
still not unstowed.*

SCOTT   I thought we'd agreed you'd put the sledge ashore first
thing, Victor.

CAMPBELL   Waiting for petrol, sir. Appears it was all taken off
the boat with the others.

Scott shakes his head, pained to hear of such carelessness.

SCOTT   Not very clever of somebody, was it? (LEAVING FOR THE
GANGWAY, COLLECTING SKI EN ROUTE) The sledge is a priority
item, Victor. I'll be at the hut should I be needed.

*Campbell watches him strap on his skis at the bottom of the
gangway.*

CAMPBELL   I've got Abbott keeping an eye on the ice.

SCOTT   Why not get a scientist to the job? Dr Simpson's the
meteorologist, see if he's free.

CAMPBELL   (SLOWLY) If you think so, sir. I wasn't sure how
much practical experience of sea-ice Sunny Jim has had.
And with Abbott having spent a season here with Shackleton . . .

SCOTT   (READY, NO LONGER LISTENING) Beautiful day.

He stifflegs off towards the shore.

52. *Telescope's image of figure on ski approaching on sea-ice.*

53. *PO Evans removes glass from eye. He straddles the hut's roof,*

tarpaulin-laying with Davies, the carpenter in charge of hut erection.
Throws glass down into Crean's waiting hands.

EVANS   Put it back in Mr Bowers' pouch, will you, Paddy, and
say the Owner's on 'is way.

CREAN   (LEAVING FRAME) Stand by yer bunks, is it.

Evans's eyes return to the smudge approaching across the glare.
Sniffs. Spits thick phlegm onto the ground below.

Between hut and approaching figure, in a wide arc of mounds of
gear, cases, drums etc, the huge inventory of base camp requirements
(see excellent pics of this scene in Scott's Last Expedition*).*

54. On the sea-ice, Scott approaches a stooped figure, sees finally
it's a seaman flensing a clutch of slaughtered seal. Blood splashes
everywhere. Scott averts his eyes, the pain of seeing clearly too
much for him.

55. Int. The completely empty hut (50 ft × 25 ft), four walls, a small
window towards the end of one of them. Bowers and Scott stand at
different ends of the hut, about 40 ft apart, thinking.

SCOTT   Ideas?

BOWERS   (JOINING SCOTT DOWN ROOM, HIS NOSE SUNBURNED
RAW) Well, I thought possibly cubicles. (HE SORT OF INDI-
CATES CUBICLES WITH HAND AND CLIPBOARD. SCOTT THINKS
ON DELIBERATELY FOR SOME TIME) What do *you* think, sir?

SCOTT   I think the seamen would appreciate having their own
mess deck, Birdie. It occurs to me you might be able to use
provision cases for a bulkhead (INDICATES ROUGHLY WHERE)
and as they empty they can be used as personal cupboards.
(CHECKS WATCH)

BOWERS   Very good, sir. I'll get the details worked out at
once.

Scott walks to the top of the hut, stares at the small window.

SCOTT   Put me here, will you, Birdie. If there is anything to see, I suppose I should be the one to see it.

Lashly in, hat in hand. Stands in a pool of water forming from his trouser legs.

LASHLY   (TO BOWERS) Beg pardon, sir. I've got the ward-room provisions outside, sir, where would you like them?

BOWERS   Bay F, PO.

LASHLY   Aye aye sir. (PUTS HAT ON, SALUTES SCOTT) Morning, sir.

SCOTT   Morning, PO. Got a soaking, eh?

LASHLY   Went through to the knees, sir, few hundred yards from the ship. Tiny hole, too.

He leaves. Scott ponders. Bowers waits.

SCOTT   Get a signal off to the ship, will you.

BOWERS   (PENCIL POISED) Ready, sir.

SCOTT   Unload motorsledge at once. Time of the essence. (SEES HE'S FINISHED) Right away, if you please.

BOWERS   I'll do it myself, sir.

SCOTT   Not a bad procedure, Birdie.

56. Sea-ice. Ship about 200 yards away. Sunny Jim Simpson probes with his rod, seeking break-up. His efforts are random, lack conviction. The work is unenjoyed. He looks back at the ship. Four seamen, in harness, manhaul an eight-hundred pound sledge of equipment towards him, en route for the shore.

57. Goetz-glass image (from ship) of the sea-ice. The shot takes in the four man-haulers, moves on to the watching Simpson, then further, to pick up a dog-sledge advancing from the shore, driver perched on two lashed fuel drums.

CAMPBELL   (VO, CALLING) Ah, they've sent Uncle Bill!

58. Terra Nova *deck. Campbell lowers glass, calls up to winch-operator.*

CAMPBELL   (CALLING) It's on the way. Take the strain.

The winch begins to inch the motorsledge from the deck. Seamen guide it carefully from each corner. A distant volley of cries from the sea-ice. Campbell raises the glass to his eye.

59. Goetz-glass. The sledge as before, doing quite well; down through the figure of Sunny Jim, who's striding out in the direction of the ship; and on to the man-haulers, or two of them, kneeling on the ice, trying to drag their companions out of a decent sized water-hole

PENNELL   (OOS FROM BRIDGE: CALLED) Message from the Owner being received, Mr Mate!

CAMPBELL   (SHOUTING) Four men on the ice *now*, come on, shake your stumps, there are men through out there!

On the ice, through the glass, it's touch and go still. Men's heads appear and disappear in the water. A loud barking commotion sets up. The glass cuts past the puffing Simpson towards the expected path of the dog-sledge, catches only a fragment of it as it disappears frame left in an uncontrolled careen. The glass searches, eventually finds the plunging team of frightened dogs, Wilson hanging on for his life, heading north now, in the direction of Cape Barne.

CAMPBELL   (SHOUTING) And there goes the bloody petrol! Damn and *blast*!

60. Pennell, in MCU, over rail of bridge.

PENNELL   (CALLING) Owner wants the motorsledge ashore by
    noon at the latest!

*61. Campbell, without the glass, watching the rescue party running
(on foot) towards the struggle of man haulers in the distance. In the
further distance to the left, the dog-sledge continues its crazed waltz
around the ice, and three seamen chase bolting ponies hither and
thither. It's a Breughel.*

Campbell CU, quite grim.

PENNELL   (VO, CALLING) What shall I tell him, Victor?

CAMPBELL   (EVENTUALLY) Tell him: Aye aye, sir.

*62. Seamen drag the motorsledge across the sea-ice, foot by foot, in
a low back-track, the machine ominous against the dead sky in the
back of the shot. The pace is slow; slows further; almost stops, the
strain growing in men's faces; stops; very slowly, the men are
dragged backwards; and (as if in slow frame), the motorsledge begins
first to up-end and then to sink from the shot.*

Over this:

SCOTT'S JOURNAL   (VO) It appears that getting frightened of the
    state of affairs, Campbell got out a line and attached it to
    the motor — then manning the line well he attempted to
    rush the machine across the weak place. Half a minute
    later nothing remained but a big hole. The actual spot
    where the motor disappeared was crossed by its fellow
    motor with a very heavy load only yesterday . . .

*63. Bright summer night. Exterior shots of Scott Base Hut, dwarfed
by sea, ice, volcanic mountains. Gramophone recording of Dame
Clara Butt drifts over Ross Island. The Dame tails away, chairs
scrape loudly.*

*64. Hut. Interior. Scott arriving at head of ward-room table, packed
with officers and scientists. Seamen move from mess deck to line the*

III O PHILOSOPHY!

ward-room walls or back chairs, on the fringes of the light.

SCOTT (SITTING, PAPERS IN HAND) Be seated, please. (CLATTER
OF PEOPLE RETURNING TO SEATS) I want to announce the
various expeditionary parties for this season and the
expected time-table of operations. The Western Party will
be led by Griff-Taylor, Messrs Debenham and Wright will
accompany, PO Evans will provide experience and back-
power . . . The Eastern Party to be led by Lt Campbell; Dr
Levick as surgeon; Dr Priestley will head the scientific
team. Petty Officers Abbott, Dickason and Browning to
accompany. When the Eastern Party have been safely
landed, Lt Pennell will assume command of the ship and
head her to New Zealand for the winter. You will have your
full written instructions before you leave, Parny. Depot-
laying Party. (LONG PAUSE. HE RUFFLES HIS PAPERS IN THE
ENSUING MURMUR OF ANTICIPATION. WILSON SITS CLOSE ON
ONE SIDE, PUFFING AT HIS PIPE. TEDDY EVANS SITS ON THE
OTHER, A TOUCH TENSE.) We'll be twelve in all. I shall lead.
(PICK THE FOLLOWING UP AS THEY POSE FOR HERBERT
PONTING FOR AN HOUR BEFORE DEPARTING ON THE DEPOT
RUN. AND ON, TO THE DEPARTURE ITSELF, SCOTT IN TIGHT
CONTROL, THE REST MORE OR LESS IN THE DARK . . . RETURNING
VISUALLY TO THE SCENE IN THE HUT ONLY FOR THE QUESTIONS
AT THE END) Dr Wilson, Lt Evans, Lt Atkinson as surgeon,
Lt Bowers, Captain Oates, Mr Meares, Gran, Mr Cherry-
Garrard, Petty Officers Crean, Keohane and Forde. Eight
ponies, twenty-two dogs in two teams. (PAUSE) Our goal,
gentlemen: to carry one ton of provisions to 80° South and
so secure our run for the Pole next season. A round trip of
some 300 miles. Birdie, I've written out your provisioning
instructions in full . . . (HANDS BOWERS A LARGE MANILLA
ENVELOPE) You'll need to liaise with the leaders of all the
parties . . . We leave on the 25th. You have six days. (A
COLLECTIVE BLINK AROUND THE TABLE, WHICH HE NOTES) In
addition, since it has become abundantly clear that the sea-
ice can no longer be trusted, at least this far north, I've
decided to use the ship to transport us down to Glacier
Tongue. (TO CAMPBELL) I'd like you to undertake the

restowing of the ship, Victor, along with Birdie, there. Pity, but there we are. Questions?

Long silence. Scott waits, in command.

CAMPBELL (EVENTUALLY) It's hardly important, sir, but I wonder if you have any information from home as to the whereabouts of the Norwegians. (THE WORD IS NOT WELCOME. THE ROOM STILLS A LITTLE) It's a question of the protocols, should my Eastern Party by chance encounter them.

SCOTT (CAREFULLY) The Eastern Party's instructions are to explore King Edward Land; that is, to remain wholly within the British sphere of operations. (PAUSE) If the Norwegian is here at all, he will undoubtedly base himself around the other side, almost certainly the Weddell Sea. (PAUSE) In any case, as my own work has shown, there is but one spot on this side of Antarctica from which the Pole can be reached; and we are in it, Lieutenant. Yes, Dr Priestley?

65. Framheim. Midnight sun. Shot follows a solitary sledge, six dogs in Greenland fan-harness, along the broad avenue of blue flags that marks the route to the base camp, four kilometres from the water's edge. Johansen drives, enigmatic, seasoned. He sits with his half-load, whipping the dogs into a sprint as they reach camp.

66. The whole party (minus Lindstrom, Gjertsen and Johansen) stand in silence, bareheaded, outside the finished hut. Around them, a tented village, perfectly articulated. Johansen joins them, removes head gear. The silence is ceremonial, not religious: grave, respectful, realistic.

AMUNDSEN First, we owe our thanks to Jorgen Stubberud and Olav Bjaaland for this fine work. (ALL CLAP. THE TWO MEN ACKNOWLEDGE BRIEFLY. THE RESPECT IS SERIOUS) Second, we need a name. What do we think?

NILSEN I asked around earlier, Chief. Most of us like Home of Fram. It's Prestrud's idea.

III   O PHILOSOPHY!

AMUNDSEN   It's good. (LINDSTROM OUT, WITH TRAY OF MUGS OF
SCHNAPPS — OR WHATEVER — AND HOT BISCUITS. MEN TAKE,
SETTLE, MUGS RAISED, LINDSTROM TOO) I name you: Framheim.

*The name is repeated, drink drunk. Sundbeck steps forward, hands
Amundsen a metal object.*

SUNDBECK   Made this for the roof, Chief.

Amundsen examines it. It's a beautifully worked iron weather-vane.

AMUNDSEN   We'll cherish it, Knut. Thank you.

LINDSTROM   Let's have your mugs and everyone inside,
speeches are all very well but they fill few stomachs . . .

*Lindstrom collects mugs, as men file into the bright-lit hut. Takes
Johansen's from him; notes the untouched drink.*

JOHANSEN   (LEAVING) Keep my dinner warm, will you, I have to
unload.

LINDSTROM   (CALLING AFTER HIM) You don't **have** to unload,
you could eat first and do it after . . . (AND TO SELF) but you
won't. Not you.

*67. Int. Hut. Dawn. Men sleep noisily. Lindstrom pads around the
galley preparing breakfast.*

68. Telescope's view of features of Framheim landscape.

*69. Amundsen, a few paces from doorway, routinely scanning
terrain, his first act of the day. He completes a half revolution, now
focusses on the bay.*

70. Telescope shot of Fram, *on ice-anchors. The shot pans left fairly
casually, gathers a little speed.*

71. Amundsen beginning to sweep the glass across the bay water.

141

Stops suddenly. Adjusts a few inches. Stares for a long time.

AMUNDSEN (LOUD, GLASS STILL UP) Adolf!

LINDSTROM (APPEARING) What?

AMUNDSEN (CALM, URGENT) Rouse the drivers. We're needed at the ship.

72. Fram. *Bridge. Gjertsen stands staring fixedly at something some distance away. He's tense, shocked, unprepared. His hands, out of sight, hold a pistol and a Handbook of Helpful Phrases in English.*

73. *In the reverse, we see two figures approaching the boat over sea-ice.*

74. *Gjertsen, watching, still anxious and resolute.*

VOICE (OOS) Ahoy there. We'd like to pay our respects to Captain Amundsen, is that possible?

75. *Gjertsen's hand releases the gun, raises the phrase book.*

76. *He studies it.*

GJERTSEN Good day. Captain Amundsen is not at home. Try again later.

77. *Sea-ice at foot of* Fram. *Campbell, Pennell and Levick stare up at the bridge.*

CAMPBELL (STILL IN SHOCK, AND SOURING; CALLING AS IF TO A CHILD) May we wait on board? We are members of the British Antarctic Expedition.

PENNELL (URGENT) Victor!

Campbell swings round. Five sledges, thirty dogs, five men, at full stretch, streak towards them down the slick avenue of blue flags. The

142

noise increases as they near the boat. The lead-sledge slows for a moment, at the top of the final sharp slope to the water, then plunges towards them, followed by the remainder. They stop on a farthing a few feet from the visitors in fizzy clouds of snowspray. Sledges are flicked casually onto sides. Quiet words to dogs, who lie at once.

Amundsen approaches, huge in full furs, to within a few paces of the visitors. Bjaaland, Hanssen, Hassel and Wisting back him, fierce in their gear.

CAMPBELL Captain Amundsen? (AMUNDSEN NODS) Campbell, sir, leading the British Expedition's Eastern Party. Lt Pennell, Levick . . .

AMUNDSEN (FORMAL, WATCHFUL; NO HANDSHAKE) How do you do.

Amundsen stares flintily at the Terra Nova, *anchored four hundred yards away in the bay. Campbell takes the look.*

CAMPBELL We do not seek to stay here, sir. (AMUNDSEN LOOKS AT HIM, THE QUESTION TOUCHED) We're on our way back from King Edward Land, quite impossible to find a landing there . . . The lookout spotted the bay and we slipped in to take a look. When we saw *Fram,* I thought it proper to call and pay our respects.

Amundsen nods again, the tension leaving him. Looks at the faces of his men a moment.

AMUNDSEN Perhaps you would do us the honour of joining us for breakfast, gentlemen.

Amundsen walks forward, shakes each man by the hand, begins to introduce his men. Sledges begin to be righted, the Brits are assigned to their drivers.

On the bridge, Gjertsen slides the pistol into a mahogany drawer.

Over this, hut acoustic, Campbell, Pennell and Levick completing a fairly random account of the journey out and the work of the first few weeks ashore, over breakfast, under Amundsen's casual and relaxed prompting.

78. Hut. Interior. A dozen or so men, the Brits among them, eat pancakes and honey, drink coffee from metal mugs, at the long table. The room is already homely, finely organized, linoleum on the floor, rugs, pianola, gramophone, books, magazines, a dart board . . .

CAMPBELL   Of course, we lost the best part of three weeks wasn't it, Penny, three weeks in the ice pack. Did you find it as tiresome, Captain?

AMUNDSEN   We found a good route. (GLANCES AT BECK) Three days.

Pennell whistles. Campbell can't believe it.

PENNELL   How long altogether, sir, from Madeira, I mean?

AMUNDSEN   Four months. Pretty well to the day. We didn't stop anywhere.

CAMPBELL   That's (HE RUNS IT AROUND HIS HEAD, TRIES TO COPE WITH IT) 16,000 miles!

AMUNDSEN   About.

The British look around the table at the Norwegians, beginning to sense their weight. Lindstrom in, like a penguin, spruced for the occasion, with a new pot of coffee.

LINDSTROM   (POURING ROUND TABLE) I bet no one's told them the one about how the Chief decided to drive the first sledge from the ship while we all watched in admiration. Only the dogs didn't realize they were a part of an exercise in leadership so when the Chief's finally ready and gives the signal to go and cracks his whip with a mighty flourish

144

they all sat down and started cleaning their paws and the Chief was there twenty minutes knocking seven kinds of demons out of his team before he even got them back on their feet . . . Anybody tell that one? Golden moment!

Cups have been filled. He's gone, to applause and laughter from the Norwegians, Amundsen included.

AMUNDSEN   (TO TABLE) And what did we learn? We learned that a Greenland dog can't work in an Arctic harness system. Just as well, eh?

Johansen enters rapidly.

JOHANSEN   I don't know if anyone's interested, but there's four of the Britishers headed for the ship. (HE SEES THE BRITS, STOPS, EYES THEM TENSELY)

AMUNDSEN   It's all right, Johansen. The British are our guests. Come and meet them.

Campbell has stood, gazes shyly at Johansen.

CAMPBELL   Forgive me, are you *the* Johansen, who went with Nansen?

JOHANSEN   I am.

CAMPBELL   (IN AWE, LIKE A SCHOOLBOY WITH A HERO) It's a very great honour indeed to meet you, sir. (THEY SHAKE HANDS) Victor Campbell.

Campbell explains his holidays in Norway, his boyhood worship of Nansen and Johansen and their exploits. Amundsen watches closely, over the rim of his mug; sees Johansen relax, bask a little, swell slightly; checks the attraction of eyes in Johansen's direction. Only in the last frames of the shot do we locate dislike below the neutral scrutiny.

79. *Shot of* Terra Nova *at anchor.*

80. Ward-room, Terra Nova. Campbell, at table head, raises the loyal toast. The toast is drunk, seats resumed. The long meal is ending: its debris litter the room's surfaces; carcase of roast lamb; bowls of junket, three wine glasses per setting, silver, champagne bottles, now cigars and brandy. Two seamen pour and carry. The Brits — Campbell, Pennell, Levick, Rennick, Priestley — are dressed formally; Amundsen, Nilsen and Prestrud have come from, and will return to, work. The lull is cigars and brandy-warming. Beneath the brittle bonhomie, some tension at work.

AMUNDSEN (FACING CAMPBELL, FROM BOTTOM OF TABLE) Do you have wireless, by the way?

CAMPBELL Wireless? (BEAT) No. (WAITS. AMUNDSEN DOES NOT ELABORATE)

PENNELL If it's a question of messages, Captain, I'd be happy to telegraph them on from New Zealand.

Amundsen smiles, nods his appreciation of the offer. Lull. Puffing. Campbell flicks a look at Priestley, who takes the baton.

PRIESTLEY I imagine you'll have little time here for purely scientific work, Captain Amundsen.

AMUNDSEN Our real work begins in the North, Dr Priestley. This is just a diversion for us.

LEVICK Do you have a doctor with you?

AMUNDSEN No.

CAMPBELL You don't say.

AMUNDSEN Without doctors, men learn how to be well. But I don't expect a Navy surgeon to agree. (HE SMILES, RATHER CHARMINGLY. LEVICK GRINS) Do you find the ponies can work out here, Lt Campbell? (CAMPBELL BLINKS, OFF-GUARD, FROWNS) I noticed your two on deck, and it has always been

Captain Scott's declared intention to use Siberian ponies . . .

CAMPBELL   (EASING AGAIN) Yes, of course. (PAUSE) I believe
they're doing as well as was expected. Of course, they're
not what you'd call 'untested' exactly, Shackleton reached
88°23' using 'em.

AMUNDSEN   But ponies *and* dogs, different speeds, different
food, different care, different handling.

RENNICK   (STIFFLY, FROM NOWHERE) I believe the Navy can
handle it, Mr Amundsen.

AMUNDSEN   (NODDING, STUBBING CIGAR) I'm sure the Navy can,
Lieutenant. (CHECKS HIS WATCH) That was a fine luncheon,
gentlemen, we're most thankful.

CAMPBELL   (TO WAITING SEAMAN) More brandy, if you please.
(AMUNDSEN BEGINS TO PROTEST) Sir, I will not hear of you
leaving until you have at least given back the toast.

*Brandy's poured. Amundsen thinks a moment, stands, glass in hand, is
joined by the rest.*

AMUNDSEN   I give you (PAUSE): Skol! Og lykke til. (THE BRITS
WAIT. NILSEN AND PRESTRUD BOTH FLICK LOOKS AT THE CHIEF)
To success, gentlemen!

*The toast is picked up in English. Nilsen and Prestrud repeat 'Skol Og
lykke til'.*

*Campbell studying Amundsen's face. Amundsen returning the scrutiny
down the length of the table.*

*81. Deck. Terra Nova. Norwegians about to leave. A courtesy of
handshakes. Amundsen stares about the decks. Sees Campbell watching him.*

AMUNDSEN   I was noting the absence of motorsledges. I imagine

Scott has use of them for his principal work.

CAMPBELL That's right. (PAUSE. AMUNDSEN WAITS FOR MORE. CAMPBELL KNOWS IT) As a matter of fact, we have already put one of them on terra firma.

Amundsen looks away, towards the Barrier and the distant sky-line. (Terra Firma? Ross Island? The Beardmore Glacier?) Campbell watches closely.

AMUNDSEN Terra firma, eh?

82. Shot of the Norwegians being rowed ashore in a whaleboat. The British party watch from the deck. Their casual exchanges cover the shot.

PENNELL (VO) Extraordinary crowd, wouldn't you say?

RENNICK (VO) Rather wild, I thought.

PRIESTLEY (VO) They'll give a good account of themselves, I shouldn't wonder.

LEVICK (VO) Good of them to offer to let us stay. I must say, I found them very nice, very modest and very well-meaning.

A sour barking laugh from Campbell.

83. Campbell, close up, real anger in his eyes.

CAMPBELL *Modest,* Tofferino? Well-meaning? He! I've lived among Norwegians, I know 'em. You know what the toast he gave us *meant?*

LEVICK Success, he said.

CAMPBELL Correct. And when you say 'Og lykke til' in Norwegian, you're also saying 'Break a leg', or something pretty damned nasty.

Pause, as this is examined.

LEVICK   (EVENTUALLY) Wouldn't that be true of English too?

Campbell's exasperated. Returns his gaze to the receding whaleboat en route for the Fram.

84. In the boat. Amundsen and Prestrud sit opposite Nilsen. Amundsen is inturned, brooding; Prestrud watches Nilsen's furtive efforts to remove something from his trousers without being seen by the British seamen who row them. Over this, the Terra Nova *discussion continues.*

PENNELL   (VO) You're absolutely sure protocol forbids us to accept his invitation to land you here? It's a perfect spot. Just imagine if Captain Scott had come here in the first place. Straight up onto the Barrier, sheltered, all of sixty miles nearer to the Pole.

CAMPBELL   (VO) (BITTER) Really, Penny, you don't have to rub it in. They're seasoned professionals engaged in a race and they know what they're doing. That's why they're in this place and we're not. But just remember, every step he takes south is unknown territory, a thousand miles of it. Mmm?

Nilsen has finally managed to extract it unobtrusively from his trousers. Covertly shows it to Prestrud, whose eyes light up. It's a huge iron spanner. Nilsen demonstrates its precautionary utility in apologetic deadpan. Prestrud has a bit of a coughing fit. Nilsen slips the spanner into his jacket pocket. CU Amundsen, watching. Bring up boat acoustic.

AMUNDSEN   (VERY QUIET) What did you suspect? They meant to carry us off, wreck our chances?

NILSEN   (SIMPLY) It crossed my mind.

Amundsen leans back a little, stares at the sky, very slowly places his right hand in his coat pocket.

AMUNDSEN   Mmm. Mine too.

85. Terra Nova *Deck. Officers and Priestley still watching.*

CAMPBELL   You're going to have to take us back, Penelope, land us at Cape Adair or thereabouts. And I'm afraid to say you're going to have to take news of all this to the Owner before you head for New Zealand. (PENNELL TAKES IT ALL STOICALLY) I'm sure you'll enjoy giving him our thrilling news. (GLANCING BACK AGAIN AT THE WHALEBOAT, TYING UP TO THE FRAM IN THE DISTANCE, HE HEAVES A SUDDEN SHOUT OF FURY ACROSS THE WATER, AT THE DISTANCE SAFELY UNHEARABLE) Og lykke til! (THEN TO PENNELL AND THE OTHERS) Let's *go!*

86. Amundsen and Nilsen, on bridge of Fram, *watch the* Terra Nova *steam off north.*

NILSEN   (QUIETLY) Og lykke til. (SMILES AT AMUNDSEN) I suppose you trawled a fair bit from that, Chief?

AMUNDSEN   Enough.

NILSEN   Are they still ahead?

Amundsen drops the Terra Nova, *turns to look south.*

AMUNDSEN   Perhaps. It's close. Scott's already on the Barrier, laying his depot for next year, we leave on Thursday. Plenty of time to overhaul them before we lose the sun.

NILSEN   (CAREFUL) So what's worrying you, Chief?

AMUNDSEN   Worrying me? Nothing. (RUBS HIS CHEST) Too much fine food.

He heads for the gangway, collects ski on the way.

NILSEN   Prestrud brought the shore party's mail up today, I shall need yours by tomorrow, we'll be gone by the time you're back from depoting.

AMUNDSEN   (NOT TURNING) I have no mail. But be here next
   spring, Thorvald, I might have something for you then.

*87. High wide shot of sea-ice from bay. A dot, on ski, moves
smoothly across glassy terrain. Wind howls. In the distance, Framheim and the sixteen 14-man bell tents of the village. Fade figure and
hut into blank white, fade up simple caption: Laying Depots,
25 Jan–21 April 1911.*

*88. In the whiteness, an animated graphic — a mapping device —
emerges, on which we can follow and evaluate the progress made by
each party on the Barrier and the glacier beyond. The map
contains lines of longitude and latitude, but topographical detail
exists — from Cape Evans to the Plateau via the Beardmore Glacier
— on Scott's half of the terrain only. On Amundsen's, across the
blankness, the words 'Terra Incognita'. Dated lines of march push
south from base camps; Scott's will eventually reach 79°28½' (One
Ton Depot), then return to Corner Camp and Safety Camp, return to
Corner Camp, then back to Safety Camp, Hut Point and Cape
Evans; Amundsen's to 80°South and back; to 81°South and 82°South
and back; to 80°South and back. Amundsen's line will generally
travel at about twice the speed of Scott's; in addition it will generally
be straight, free of the whirls and curls of Scott's movement. Scott's
party has already been named in the text (see page 139); Amundsen's
three runs employ (i) Amundsen, Prestrud, Johansen and Hanssen,
three sledges, eighteen dogs; (ii) all except Lindstrom (8 men,
7 sledges, 42 dogs); (iii) all except Amundsen and Lindstrom (7 men,
6 sledges, 36 dogs).*

*Within this frame, the essential imagery of the depot runs can be
laid down: a montage of characteristic moments, brief scenes and
occasional words, bound one to another by journal voices.*

*89. Montage, to be mixed from both narratives, and melded via the
mapping device.*

(Amundsen's first run. Great Ice Barrier, 12 Feb.) Hazy day.

Prestrud as forerunner. Hanssen first sledge, with compass; Johansen, with compass; Amundsen last, with bicycle-wheel sledgemeter. They become tiny stationary figures on an immense plain of ice. In closer shot, they share a thermos of hot chocolate for their midday meal.

Over this:

AMUNDSEN'S JOURNAL   (VO) Our fight for the Pole was entirely dependent on this autumn work, in laying down large supplies of provisions as far to the south as possible in such a way that we could be certain of finding them again . . . I cannot understand what the English mean when they say that dogs cannot be used here.

(80°South) The depot they're building is 12 ft high. Johansen plants a bamboo pole in it bearing a black flag. From his POV we see the other men stretched out along several miles of identical marker poles on each side of the cairn. Along the route they came, Johansen's POV, a line of stockfish marks the route at 100 yard intervals.

(80° 32'South) Second run. Blizzard. Warm. Eight men, seven sledges, forty-two dogs making deliberate progress into its face. Prestrud forerunner, Amundsen again in rear.

(81°South) Fine, bright. A second cairn. Beyond it, five men go on to 82°South. Bjaaland, Hassel and Stubberud return towards camera, heading for Framheim.

(Night) Cold. Three green tents, sledges, dogs. The dogs howl, pitiful. Inside, sleep. Amundsen dreams. A mute, imagic, haunting recall of the farewell dinner for the Frampeople at Framheim. Beck and Ronne dance a breathless polka. Nilsen receives his letter of instruction from Amundsen, a handshake. Nilsen weeps quietly. Campbell's face appears. Out of synch, he says: 'One of the motor sledges is already on terra firma . . . '

(82°South) The third cairn, at long distance, the flag and markers still clearly visible. Pan half-circle, reveal five men receding north.

152

III   O PHILOSOPHY!

(79°South) Extreme cold. In a tent, Prestrud's frostbitten foot is heated on Wisting's chest. Outside, Amundsen watches ten dogs devour a dog-carcase.

AMUNDSEN'S JOURNAL   (VO) Associations of ideas are curious things: sauce hollandaise suddenly came into my mind.

Framheim. Smoke from chimney. Interior. All nine sit at table, working at tackle, clothing, footwear, goggles, tents, ski-bindings, dog-whips, whatever. Amundsen gets up quietly, takes a towel, goes out into the snow, walks some distance from the hut. He appears to put the towel down the back of his trousers. Close up, he's sweating, face drawn. He draws the towel out, examines it for a long time, face impassive. We see the towel, bright with blood.

(Via map) Third run. Seven men, six sledges, thirty-six dogs. Prestrud again forerunner. Johansen in rear.

Framheim. Interior. Amundsen sweeps out the empty hut. Lindstrom sits stuffing a penguin at the table. Amundsen checks the calendar on the wall. It's April. The 8th has been heavily ringed; it's now the 11th.

LINDSTROM   Coffee? (AMUNDSEN SHAKES HIS HEAD, EYES ON CALENDAR) You'll make yourself ill again.

Amundsen sits in his customary chair at the bottom end of the table, takes up a pencil, resumes some calculations.

Crevasse, apparently bottomless. Hanssen and two dogs hang in the air in silence, black against the sky. Very slowly, barely perceptibly, they are inched upwards. Wisting's head appears in the hole of sky; Johansen's.

Framheim in distance. Amundsen, on ski, on ice-knoll, scanning the plain, through glasses. His shoulders suddenly tauten. Faint whisp of dog's barking on the air. Glass image of tiny smudges in the snow.

AMUNDSEN'S JOURNAL   (VO) The foundation was solidly laid: the

153

complete erection of the station, with accommodation for nine men for several years and the distribution of three tons of supplies in depots at latitudes 80, 81 and 82 degrees south. And when the sun left us for good, all the work requiring daylight had been completed. We are all in the best of health.

Shot of Amundsen still staring through glasses. Widen and lift, to reveal the approaching party. Amundsen skis forward to greet the forerunner. Greeting, shouts across the snow.

Interspersed with key images of Scott's journey, mediated through mapping device:

Blizzard. Corner Camp. 10 February. Tents. Inside. Oates, Meares, Teddy Evans, sitting in sleeping bags, reading or writing journals. Meares crawls to the furthest corner of the tent, pisses.

OATES (VO; WRITING) Things are not as rosy as they might be, mother. We are handicapped by lack of experience. Scott having spent too much of his time in an office, he would fifty times sooner stay in the hut seeing how a pair of puttees suited him than come out and look at a pony's legs or a dog's feet.

Scott's tent. Scott writing journal. The tent is schoolboy neat: everything is laid out at right-angles, like a naval rating's kit. Gran sits doing nothing, to Scott's irritation and displeasure.

GRAN (VO) One thing I am certain of. We will need luck if we are to reach the Pole next year. Especially since nobody understands ski . . .

SCOTT'S JOURNAL (VO) I withhold my opinion of the dogs, in much doubt as to whether they're going to be a real success — but the ponies are going to be real good. The dreadful weather meanwhile puts all thought of pressing on out of the question.

Cherry-Garrard stares around the tent's corners for a moment, then picks his way out of the tent. Outside, he pisses downblizzard.

Ponies flounder belly-deep in snow, buck wildly as men seek to drag them on. CU Oates.

OATES   (vo) Scott and Evans boss the show, pretty well, and their ignorance about marching with animals is colossal. Nobody understands severe marching with ponies . . . I can't run the lot . . . It is trying to work three kinds of transport that knocks me. They can't do it in the Army, so I'm jolly sure Scott's not going to . . .

A pony being gouged by Eskimo dogs. Scott howls orders for them to be pulled away, hysterical.

SCOTT   (vo) It is pathetic to see the ponies foundering . . . horrid to see them half-engulfed in the snow, panting and heaving from the strain.

One Ton Depot. Cairn not yet built. Only six ponies left. Oates and Meares crossing to Scott's tent.

Scott's tent. Wilson, Bowers, Evans, drinking hoosh around stove. Scott withdrawn, alone with his tin mug. Oates and Meares in.

SCOTT   Ah, Soldier. Sit down, won't you. It's no reflection on you, of course, but I believe that *all* the ponies will be lost if we continue. In consequence, I've decided to depot our supplies here and return to base. We're eleven or so miles short of our target, but that can't be helped. I shall want the animals ready for departure around evening.

Oates looks at the three diners, who indicate nothing.

OATES   I don't believe turning back will save the ponies, sir. It would be a great mistake, in my view, not to continue. If you would let me put Weary Willie down, he'd feed dogs and men for three whole days.

SCOTT   I have had more than enough of this cruelty to animals and I'm not going to defy my feelings for the sake of a few days' march.

OATES   (AFTER THOUGHT) I'm afraid you may regret it, sir.

SCOTT   Regret it or not, my dear Oates, I've made up my mind like a Christian.

Oates nods. Nods to Meares to lead on. They crawl out of the tent.

One Ton Depot, a flag on it, six feet off the ice. Tracks return from it, towards and past the camera.

The returning party, making slow desperate progress back. Behind them, less than a mile away, the cairn is already almost invisible, and wind obliterates their tracks.

Cape Armitage. The sea-ice has broken up. They stare at the sea. Scott's face black with impotence, as he glares north towards Cape Evans. Wilson stands by him.

WILSON   Bad luck, sir?

SCOTT   Damnable. Damnable. We could be here months.

Int. Discovery Hut. Sounds of door being forced. Scott pushes his way in, with Wilson and Bowers. They scan the room, a filthy wilderness of boxes and domestic disorder. Snow has pushed deep into the room through a smashed window and set hard. Scott skirts it to approach the blubber stove and the beam-head display: Discovery Expedition 1901–3; Leader : Capt. R. F. Scott; *and above it,* Shackleton & Co., 1907–9. *Photographs adorn an upright beam. One of Scott in full naval uniform. Someone has pencilled in a kiss-curl at the front of the forehead. Scott rips it down, crumples it.*

SCOTT   (GRIM) It is difficult to account for the manners of some who call themselves gentlemen, is it not, Bill . . . Sir. Ernest. Shackleton. All available hands, Lieut Bowers. The pig-sty must be cleaned.

III O PHILOSOPHY!

Bowers approaches, a leather satchel in one hand, its contents, envelopes, in the other.

Hut. Interior. Full of dark smoke and little light from blubber stove. Men asleep, cramped, restless. Scott sits at the table, reading a letter by the light of a small paraffin lamp. Close in on the face, paralyzed by panic, reading. Campbell's letter voice over gives a fragment of the encounter with Amundsen.

A shadow across Scott's face. Bill Wilson has joined him at the table.

WILSON   What is it, Con? (SCOTT HANDS HIM THE LETTER MUTELY. WILSON READS FOR SOME TIME) So. The race is on in earnest. No matter, Con, we're ready. And I pray God I may be found good enough for the final party, when next year comes round.

SCOTT   (SUDDEN) What a chance we have missed. We might have taken him and sent him back in the Terra Nova. There *is* no law down here, and we know Amundsen is acting against the wishes of his King.

Wilson has recoiled slightly, sensing mania. Scott's eyes gleam, passionate. Wilson watches him.

WILSON   Get some rest, Con. You push yourself *along* so.

SCOTT   (METALLIC) That the action is outside one's own code of honour is not necessarily to condemn it. One thing only fixes itself definitely in my mind. The proper as well as the wiser course for us is to proceed exactly as though this had not happened To go forward and do our best for the honour of our country.

Wilson sits in shadow. He's worried. Glances at Scott, whose eyes have grown glassy.

WILSON   It's ill to sit still and contemplate the ruin of things.

SCOTT   We leave tomorrow (GLANCES AT WILSON'S ASTONISHED FACE) Over the sea-ice. We'll be at base within two days.

WILSON   Isn't the sea-ice too young yet?

SCOTT   It's a chance we must take.

The line of march across the ice begins on the map. Inserts of men, dogs and sledges in swell of ice and water, ponies drowning, men on floes trying to save them. A dead pony is washed back on to a floe. Oates is everywhere; and Anton. Another pony drowns. Two dogs float by, still in harness. The line retreats in confusion to the hut.

Cape Evans. The hut and encampment, from a good distance. Distant shouts. Men run from the hut to stare across the sea-ice towards Glacier Tongue. In CU they're excited.

Scott and co. man haul their painful way across the sea-ice. Two remaining ponies are led. Faces are dreadfully blackened by blubber-smoke. Surgeon Atkinson is wrapped in a sledge, face and feet badly frost-bitten. They're well within range of men's shouts and ragged cheering, but see nothing in their slow impulsion forward, like the blind on traction. Shot of Wilson.

SCOTT   (vo) Well, we have done our best. And bought our experience at a heavy cost.

In long shot, the welcomers reach the returning party. PO Evans raises three cheers for the Owner. They ring out precisely. The heroes are home.

Scott, in CU, a mad, sullen stare, as he plods on.

SCOTT   (vo) No one will say we have not done our best.

IV

AS TO WAR

Pretitle: Shot of Framheim. Slow track towards the hut, which is pretty well snowed under. Title: THE LAST PLACE ON EARTH. Sounds of shovels and picks at work on snow and ice. Cut to

An ice-tunnel, about six feet high, ten feet wide, deep beneath the surface. Amundsen and Bjaaland, lightly clad in fur underwear, sweating, drive their shovels into the wall of snow ahead of them. Some way behind the two, Stubberud is tapping supporting props into the tunnel walls. All have thick beards, long hair; in fur, they seem like natural beings, perfectly adapted.

Cape Evans. On the sea-ice, in the strange gloom of early winter (4 May) sun low and lurid on the horizon, twenty men play football, gentlemen versus players; in long shot, voices pure but transilient on the air, a sort of dance of the dead. Cut to

Ice tunnel. Amundsen is relieved by Johansen, who has brought Bjaaland a mug of cocoa. No words. Amundsen stoops off down the tunnel, passes Stubberud with a nod. The passage widens, turns into a large, brilliant ice-workshop. Wisting and Hassel are hanging outfits from the ceiling; Wisting carries a modern treadle sewing machine through an alcove into a second workshop. Amundsen watches awhile, smiles, when they catch his eye, moves on. Hanssen and Prestrud are glimpsed at work in their separate spaces, as the whole underground system of workshops, dog-shelters, latrines,

159

American vapour baths and the lean-to is revealed, en route to the hut.

Lindstrom sees Amundsen enter; carries a tin mug of chocolate to the bunk, where Amundsen has removed his soaking vest to towel himself down; hands Amundsen a vest he's been airing in the galley. Returns to his work. Amundsen sits, sips his chocolate, stares sombrely into space. Lindstrom watches him carefully from the galley.

LINDSTROM Game of cards?

Amundsen starts uneasily, frowns.

AMUNDSEN No. I have work.

He stands to put on the aired vest, drains his chocolate; Lindstrom reads the tension in him.

LINDSTROM Relax. It's winter for them too.

Amundsen nods tersely; smiles. Continues dressing. Cut to

Scott on bicycle, two dogs in his wake. He rides determinedly towards the distant hut. On the rim of the shot, ghostly men drain from the ice-pitch towards base, steam rising in clouds above their shoulders.

SCOTT'S JOURNAL (VO) Of hopeful signs for the future none are more remarkable than the health and spirit of our people. It would be impossible to imagine a more vigorous community, and there does not seem to be a single weak spot in the twelve good men and true I've chosen for the southern advance. All are now experienced sledge-travellers, knit together with a bond of friendship that has never been equalled under such circumstances.

Shots of gentlemen — Wilson, Bowers, Teddy Evans, Atkinson, Cherry-Garrard — frolicking their way off the ice. PO Evans shares a fag with Lashly and Crean, some paces behind.

SCOTT'S JOURNAL   (VO CONT.) I find it exceedingly difficult to settle down to solid work just at present . . . and keep putting off the tasks which I have set myself . . .

Shot of red rim horizon: the sun has gone.

IV. As to War.

(Scenes and images of wintering distilling characteristic processes of the two parties.)

1. Int. Hut, Cape Evans. Galley. Clissold prepares a tray for the Owner. Sounds of pianola, mid-evening chatter, dominoes clacking on mess-deck table. Over this, in short spasms, a stiff exchange between Scott and Evans in Scott's den at the other end of the hut. Clissold flicks glances up the room, a touch nervous; re-positions the cakes he's made, as he waits for the tea to brew.

2. Clissold carries the tray up the room, past the messdeck table (Evans, Crean, Keohane, Hooper at dominoes), through the packing-case doorway to the ward-room. Lt Evans appears from Scott's den at the far end of the long table, face taut and white; passes Clissold, who gives him berth, and leaves the hut by the Cook's table at the bottom of the room. Clissold glances in the direction of the 'Tenements' where Bowers, Cherry-Garrard, Debenham and Day discuss the fracas in looks and gestures; then enters the Owner's space by the window. Places tray on desk. Pours tea.

Scott sits facing the window, his ancient naval overcoat over his shoulders. He smokes his pipe; stares in silence at the glass. Clissold follows the gaze. The glass gives back Scott's image, as if in the form of a portrait. His journal, pen and ink stand ready before him on the desk.

CLISSOLD   (FINISHED) Hope you enjoy it, sir.

SCOTT   Thank you, Clissold. Ask Dr Wilson to step in when he has a moment, will you?

CLISSOLD   Very good, sir.

SCOTT   And I think it's about time you got busy with scissors and comb again . . .

CLISSOLD   Very good, sir.

Clissold out. Scott reaches for his tea, stretching across the open journal, returns to his self-scrutiny.

SCOTT'S JOURNAL   (VO) (IMAGE OF BLANK JOURNAL PAGE) Hooper sweeps the hut after breakfast, washes the mess traps, and generally tidies things. I think it is a good thing that in these matters the officers need not wait on themselves; it gives long unbroken days of scientific work and must, therefore, be an economy of brain in the long run . . .

Clissold scans the Biology cubicle, then Geology, discovers Wilson sitting on a box in Gran's bedspace, deep in confessional murmur with Gran, who sits on his bunk, face troubled.

CLISSOLD   Beg pardon, doctor, Captain Scott would like a word when you've a minute . . .

WILSON   Thanks, Thomas.

Clissold goes. Wilson faces Gran again. Gran's miserable.

WILSON   (BARELY AUDIBLE) . . . Command puts men under terrible stress, my boy. Mmm? My advice to you, Trigger, is very simple. Don't let him catch you sitting around doing nothing, nothing will inflame him more. If you see him coming, untie your shoelaces and be doing them up — anything — when he passes. (HE STANDS, MOVES A PACE TOWARDS THE CUBICLE ENTRANCE) We'll talk again . . . (TURNS, SMILES HIS SAINT'S SMILE)

GRAN   (UNCONSOLED) I came to teach ski, I'm treated like a
    drumstick, making cocoa, running errands . . .

WILSON   Domestic. (BEAT) The trouble is, you remind him of
    things he would sooner forget.

*Wilson goes. Gran sits on. On the wall behind his head, photographs
of Haakon and Maud, Nansen, St Olav. A pony neighs close by;
once, twice. Cut to*

3. Pony stalls. Oates soothes a sick pony. It neighs again.

OATES   All right, calm down, come on, buggerlugs, it's not as
    bad as all that . . .

*Beyond Oates, in the eerie light of the blubberstove, Meares, Atkinson
and Evans sit drinking cocoa in silence. Oates returns to the group,
resumes his place. Waves to Anton to join them from his detached
seat in the shadows. Anton edges nearer. Meares says something to
him; he smiles, nods. Their attention returns to Evans who stares
whitely into the fire.*

MEARES   (EVENTUALLY) So come on, Teddy, what did he say?

EVANS   (BARELY AUDIBLE) He told me to mind my own bloody
    business.

*Light from the fire plays on Oates's grim smile, as the group absorb
the not unpredictable information.*

EVANS   Like some bloody middy.

*Silence again, at the familiar humiliated bitterness. Fat spits,
hisses.*

ANTON   (FROM NOWHERE) Captain Oates, good to horses, good
    to Anton.

He smiles, pleased, subsides. Oates sucks his corncob.

EVANS   I made a perfectly rational suggestion: abandon the Western Party expedition and use men and equipment to augment the Polar party. Can anyone seriously doubt, after Campbell's account of their men and equipment, the Norwegian threat? And did anyone enlist for this expedition believing that being *second* to the Pole was our goal? Our claim to this Pole is historic. We should ensure that we stake it.

ATKINSON   (MILDLY) I agree with the Owner, as a matter of fact, Teddy. If it is ours, we shouldn't have to race for it. We're a scientific expedition, we should behave like one.

EVANS   (TERSE) I don't say we should race, Atch, I say we should ensure we get there before the Norwegians. For that it requires but the smallest alteration to the season's plan . . .

MEARES   (QUIET, BITTER) Plan? Is there a *plan*? I hadn't heard that.

It's enough said. Bleakness descends. Oates suddenly chuckles. They look at him.

OATES   I was just remembering a lady who arrived late at a ball. She said the reason she was late was because the cab-horse had played up terribly on the way. 'Ah', said the host, 'must've been a jibber.' 'No,' said the lady, 'I think he was a bugger, the cabby called him so several times . . . '

Laughter, slow to build but steady and persisting. Oates is pleased with himself, in a shy way. Clissold appears in the doorway, speaks over the noise.

CLISSOLD   (TO OATES) Wondered if I might have your trousers, Captain Oates, I've got a wash on and I could have 'em dry for you in no time. Would you mind slippin' 'em off, sir?

Oates smells for the rat.

OATES   That's very kind of you, Tom, but why mine?

They all look at Oates's incredibly blubber-soaked corduroys, ponder the answer solemnly, laughter slowly building again.

CLISSOLD   Just thought you might fancy a clean pair o' trousers, sir, that's all.

OATES   Well, I think I would, Tom, I rather think I'd enjoy that, thank you kindly.

He lays his pipe down, begins to remove his trousers, still seated. His long johns are ancient, tattered things: through a tear in the thigh we see the long raw divot of his wound. Atkinson stares at it, frowning.

OATES   I think I shall adore clean trousers, yes, o yes.

He throws his pants to Clissold across the cramped space.

OATES   Excellent. Well held.

Clissold grins, leaves. People settle again, pipes active.

MEARES   (EVENTUALLY) What do *you* think, Titus?

OATES   (SIMPLE, SLOW) I don't know anything about who has rights to what down here, not being a Navy man, but I agree with Atch about putting all thoughts of racing out of our heads, *racing* is quite beyond the capability of these ancient duffers. (INDICATES THE EQUINE SORRINESS, STUFFED IN THEIR STALLS) Getting there at all will probably prove quite enough, all in all. (PIPE AGAIN) As for the Norskies, I believe they're a tough old lot who know what they're doing and I wish 'em luck. That's what I think.

EVANS   (SLIGHT EDGE IN THE DISTINCTIVENESS) No one wishes the bounders *harm*, Titus, though God knows they've behaved abominably in the matter.

A horse coughs. Oates listens, alert for it, stretching a little. Atkinson gazes at his thigh wound agleam through the rent underwear.

ATKINSON How'd you come by that, soldier?

Oates looks at it briefly, covers it over.

OATES Bullet. South Africa.

ATKINSON Get the bone, did it?

OATES Yes.

Oates looks at Atkinson, spits into the stove. They listen to the hiss in silence. Evans gets up suddenly, at the end of a long thought.

EVANS Ah well, I did what I could, I'm washing my hands . . .

He picks a careful way out, through the soft, unforced goodnights. No one speaks when he's gone. Oates spits on the stove again.

SCOTT (VO, SOTTO) I'm really feeling quite low, Bill, as a matter of fact. There are times (LONG PAUSE) I can't remember how I came to let myself in for this thing.

4. Scott's den. Scott sits on his bed, the greatcoat across his legs. Wilson sits forward in his chair. It's tête-à-tête. Wilson's a touch concerned: Scott's more than usually fragile, shivery, on the edge of something.

SCOTT Advancement? Rear-Admiral by 1913 if I pull it off, was that it? Or Kathleen, living for her heroes? I'm forty-three next month, Bill, this is a young man's sport.

WILSON You're as fit as a flea. (SCOTT PULLS DEEPER INTO HIMSELF. WILSON WATCHES THE FAMILIAR CONTOUR OF STRESS AND PANIC IN THE MAN'S FACE AND FRAME) How's the plan coming?

166

SCOTT   Plan? Oh yes. It's coming along. I keep putting it off, actually. I'm secretly convinced we won't get much help from the motors, the dogs won't go far. (THE GLOOM SEEMS TERMINAL; WILSON'S CONCERN INCREASES) I wish we could leave tomorrow, get it done, there's nothing worse than sitting tight and waiting for the next disaster.

WILSON   (CAREFULLY) I've been talking with young Gran . . .

SCOTT   Idle. Malingerer. I watched him through the window, limping away, until he thought himself out of sight, then off comes the limp like a false moustache, the leg's as right as rain. Well, he must learn the hard way, if he will not play the game.

Wilson sees he cannot penetrate the carapace of Scott's fearful despair.

WILSON   (PUSHING CHAIR BACK A LITTLE) I'll organize the lecture programme as you suggest, then . . .

SCOTT   Evans is useless, thank God I have Bowers, I can trust my number one with absolutely nothing . . .

WILSON   (STANDING) Well, I think I'll do a spot of reading . . .

SCOTT   Don't go, Bill.

Scott's eyes are red, rather inflamed. They plead.

SCOTT   Please.

Wilson sits down again, drawn by the pain, the dependence.

SCOTT   I'm a bit in the dumps, that's all. (BEAT) We'll get there, Bill. Shoulder to shoulder. Past Shackleton's mark and faster too. Two old chaps together, eh?

He laughs, a short crack of sound on the hard palate. Wilson chews his pipe.

5. *Moonlight on Cape Evans. White on white, the hut toylike in the waste. The pianola music flickers, unreal.*

6. *Int. Hut. They sleep, coughing and snuffling. Gleam of lamp and moon liquescing the air. Low pianola persists. In the Tenements, Oates is slowly readying himself for bed. Cherry-Garrard, Bowers, Meares and Atkinson sleep in their bunks. Oates drags the shirt from his head, stills the movement as he sees his trousers, cleaned and creased, on the high bunk, the hung pony-tackle beneath. He touches the corduroys lovingly, hugs them to his cheek.*

In long shot, a soft wheel, the naked soldier waltzes the trousers into the dim room and around the ward-room table. Men sleep on, steeped in dreams of flower, grass and petticoat.

7. *Lindstrom's hand clashes fierce notes from the ship's bell in the galley.*

8. *Fast images of men in the ice workshops, as the bell summons them:*
Bjaaland lightening sledges;
Stubberud lightening provision cases;
Wisting enisled in tent material at his Singer;
Hassel and Hanssen testing whipstocks, as if duelling;
Johansen stacking sledge cases with thousands of biscuits, sausages of milk powder etc.

Final image, as the bell subsides, of Amundsen in vapour bath. Only the shaggy head is visible, swathed in steam, eyes closed. Slow inch in to close up: Campbell's voice reports that one of Scott's motorsledges is already on terra firma. Amundsen's voice repeats 'terra firma' several times, examining meanings. In CU, he opens his eyes: they're a little tense; fearful.

9. *Int. Framheim. Flash. Freeze. Eight men at table, festive food over, drink and tobacco on. They sit in comically sombre silence, self-patented snow-goggles on their faces.*

LINDSTROM   (vo) Smile, you devils, smile. You'd smile if you were standing here, I can tell you.

Flash. Laughter, hoots. Sledging flags, pics of royalty, a banner proclaiming Midwinter Eve etc. The hut clock begins to strike midnight.

On cue, Lindstrom in from galley, to cheers from the table. He carries a large flat round object in his hands, over which he has spread a concealing red-white check cloth. Speculative chat as he lays the object at the bottom of the table, by Amundsen's left hand.

Amundsen stands slowly. Calls of 'Speech, speech.' *He quiets them with wide palms. Regards the watching men for a moment, as they settle. Hanssen tries to peek under the cloth; Lindstrom, at table, bats his knuckles with a spoon.*

AMUNDSEN   (FINALLY) Gentlemen, friends, I wish you, one and all, a happy midwinter's . . . (TABLE SLAPPING, GLASS CLINKING, GENERAL JOSSING) To make this particular midwinter memorable, I asked Lindstrom there to create something special. And this is what he came up with.

He flicks the cloth away. Cheers, laughter, loud bravos as the huge iced cake is revealed; then gradual absorption, as they deal with the representational detail of the chef's work. It's a contoured and perfectly lined replica of known Antarctica, with a hut and a flag at Framheim and at Cape Evans, depot cairns on the Norwegian route at 80°, 81° and 82° South.

AMUNDSEN   With a little help, I might add. (GRINS AT THEIR GRINS) Well, I see you're thinking the thing to do with a cake is eat it.

HANSSEN   (KNIFE IN MITT) That's what I'm thinking . . .

AMUNDSEN   Before we do, however, I want to say a few words about the trip. There it is, nineteen hundred miles of it. (HE TRACES A STRAIGHT LINE FROM THE BAY TO THE POLE, ACROSS THE BLANK ICING, WITH THE KNIFE) Looks easy enough on a cake, mm? But from 82 south we must be prepared for anything . . . Shackleton met these, remember . . . (KNIFE-TIP HOVERS OVER THE HUGE TRANSANTARCTIC MOUNTAINS AND THE BEARDMORE GLACIER) and found a glorious way through, in case anyone imagines the British can be entirely discounted from our reckoning. (HE SCANS THE STILL FACES, THE ENTRY THEY'VE MADE INTO THIS REHEARSAL) Scott has motors, three of them: one . . . possibly already here, (HE POINTS TO THE FOOT OF THE BEARDMORE) four hundred miles south . . . on terra firma. He has ponies, dogs, four times the men we have. (BEAT) We have ourselves and the mutts outside.

JOHANSEN They'll be enough.

Growls of agreement. Amundsen nods.

AMUNDSEN (MILD, DELIBERATE) They'll be enough if we do this winter's work on equipment properly and if we do it in time to make the earliest possible start in September.

Silence. Frowns. Hassel flicks a look at Hanssen; Hanssen at Lindstrom, then Johansen, then back at Hassel.

HASSEL You think that early?

AMUNDSEN I do. We can't take chances, Sverre. Sixty days there, sixty back, all right? *Fram* returns in January, with perhaps no more than two or three weeks before the sea freezes her in. There's no point winning the Pole if we can't get out with the news, friends. In any case, we have business at the other end of the earth, remember. Well (HE REMOVES THE NORWEGIAN PIN-FLAG FROM THE ROOF OF THE MODEL FRAMHEIM, CASUALLY PLACES IT IN THE CENTRE OF THE CAKE PLATEAU) It means we have to be here by Christmas. (PICKS UP THE KNIFE, HOLDS IT POISED ABOVE CAKE) Who'd like a piece?

HANSSEN Thought you'd forgotten the damn thing; me.

*Amundsen cuts the cake in large deft slices. Lindstrom shuffles it into
hands. The cake is tasted ceremonially. Amundsen pours wine into
tin mugs around the table from a large white jug. The cake is liked.
Wisting revives the gramophone. Amundsen sits down unfussily in
his chair, finished. The table is quiet, not silent; a sort of tension
persists, under the habituated ease, a matter unresolved.*

JOHANSEN   (EVENTUALLY) As you say, looks easy on a cake, and
being second interests no one. (BEAT) But then, neither
does being dead.

*The room stills momentarily, then lifts a fraction, to close the hole.
Johansen, hard, knotted, contained, picks at his cake. Men glance
down the table, where Amundsen peers shortsightedly at the sock
he's begun to darn.*

AMUNDSEN   (QUIETLY) I would say (LONG PAUSE, AS HE
BITES THROUGH THE GRAY WOOL) that goes without saying,
Hjalmar.

BJAALAND   (SUDDENLY) Who cares, so long as we get some fun
out of it. I'll lay five cigars to one it's the Chief sees the
mountains first, if there are any. Anyone?

LINDSTROM   I'll take that, skiman. The Chief can barely see the
hole he's darning.

BJAALAND   Maybe. But he's bloody tall.

*Tickles of laughter round the table. Amundsen grins at Bjaaland.
Johansen picks at his cake.*

*10. Cape Evans. Int. Hut. Night. Clissold and Hooper dealing with
the debris of the officers' dinner in the galley area, working around
PO Evans (blanket round shoulders), who is gathering their claret
leavings in his tin mug. In the ward-room, relatively distinct, Bill
Wilson is finishing his University of Antarctica lecture on Antarctic
Flying Birds. PO Evans flicks glances through the packing-case
passageway at the illumined huddle of officers and men about the*

ward-room table. Scott's at the head of the table, sucking on his pipe; Wilson next to him, standing, a sheaf of notes in his hand. Evans gestures facial responses, sardonic, alienated, to the gentlemen's exchanges, as the wine bites; remains nevertheless in touch with their progress.

Evans carries the tin mug to his bed. Crean lies on the next bunk reading a copy of Girl's Own *for 1902. Evans lies on his bunk, places his wine on the floor. We hear Scott ask for more questions by name, the ward-room voices more distinct at this closer range. Bowers dutifully invents a question about pigmentation: why are white gulls white, when they inhabit a terrain completely devoid of predators. Wilson doesn't know. Griffith-Taylor thinks it might have something to do with heat-preservation. Scott doubts it authoritatively.*

EVANS   (SOTTO) What you got there, Thomas? (CREAN SHOWS HIM, ANGLING THE MAGAZINE. EVANS TUTS) Dirty bugger. After you with it. (TAKES A SWIG OF WINE) You should be in there, improving your brain, boy. (CREAN IGNORES HIM) Bloody University of Antarctica, did you ever hear of such. I reckon I'll stay stupid.

Out of the ruck of contributions to the whiteness of skuas, we hear Meares wonder why Shackleton's ponies were all greys. A silence. Wilson says he doesn't feel competent to answer the question.

SCOTT   (OOS) Of course, the fact of the matter is, Shackleton's ponies weren't all greys. But the ones that did best and survived longest were. I'm not concerned whether Science can explain that, it appears to be a fact, and that's good enough for me.

Some comments around the table. PO Evans primps his face at Scott's voice, mimicking the Owner's characteristic mode of senior-prefect delivery.

EVANS   (SOTTO) Horseshit.

CREAN   How are you feeling, Taff?

EVANS   I'll live.

MEARES   (OOS) You any ideas, soldier?

OATES   (OOS, SLOWLY) None at all. Perhaps it has something to do with intelligence.

WILSON   (OOS) What do you mean, Titus?

OATES   I don't know, maybe greys are more stupid than blacks and chestnuts. I mean, if you were a horse in snow lugging a damn great load behind you, wouldn't the clever thing be to kick the bucket early and get it over with?

OOS the young officers and scientists chuckle intemperately at the puncture. Scott taps his pipe on a tin plate for order.

PO EVANS   (CU) Too bloody true, boyo.

WILSON   (OOS, SCOTT'S LONGSTOP) Incidentally, since we're raising the questions Science cannot presently answer, perhaps the meteorologists among us would care to say something about the meteor old Atch there saw falling yesterday. Come on, Sunny Jim, any ideas?

PO Evans's eyes look heavenward, the boredom massing.

SIMPSON   (OOS, A YOUNG ANCIENT) The problem there, Uncle Bill, is quite simply: was it, indeed, falling?

Silence, as it's pondered. Evans's face contorts further.

OATES   (EVENTUALLY) What, you mean it might have been pushed, Jim?

Hilarities, schoolboys corpsing in Scripture Knowledge. Evans mimes his own contemptuous version of the laughter. Scott's pipe raps the tin plate again with some vigour. Evans begins to get into his sleeping bag; turns on his side, eyes closed, to sleep.

SCOTT (OOS; PATERNAL, AS THEY QUIETEN) Before the evening degenerates into levity, there are one or two announcements that may be of interest to those who see themselves as potential members of next season's polar party. (EVANS'S EYES OPEN SHARPLY. HE HISSES CREAN TO LISTEN. EVANS LEAVES HIS BUNK, FINDS A SHADOWED POSITION WITHIN THE MESS DECK AREA FROM WHICH HE CAN SEE A TELLING FRAG-MENT — CRUCIALLY SCOTT — OF THE WARD-ROOM PROCEED-INGS) The final plan is currently being laid and will be ready for presentation within a week or so. When it is ready, it will be revealed much as Uncle Bill revealed his work on Antarctic Flying Birds this evening; that is to say, in the context of the scientific lecture series I have construc-ted for the winter months. Because in my view, the British Antarctic Expedition is pre-eminently a *scientific* enterprise concerned with increasing the store of *knowledge*, not an unseemly scramble to be first past the post. Despite advice received, it is my intention to achieve the full programme as discussed with senior men in England: the Northern Expedition, already under way; the Eastern Expedition, which Griffith Taylor will lead to Granite Harbour, a Winter Expedition to Cape Crozier under Dr Wilson; a Spring Journey to the Ferrar Glacier, which I intend to lead myself; and, of course, the advance to the Pole. On this last, I propose to say for the moment only this: our desperate misfortunes with the ponies last season, and the known limitations of both dogs and motorsledges, make it all the more imperative that those who are chosen should be in the peak of physical condition, since from the foot of the Beardmore Glacier to the Pole, and all the way home, it will be on *back*-power that our success or failure will largely depend. And quite frankly, gentlemen, in these days of the supposed decadence of the British race, I would have it no other way. Of the so-called 'Norwegian threat' I say only this: no journey ever made with dogs can approach the height of that fine conception which is realized when a party with their own unaided efforts go forth to face hardships.

BOWERS Hear, hear.

Hear, hears pick up, the table suddenly enlarged, lifted by the scent of heroism on the horizon. Scott begins to thank Wilson for the lecture etc. PO Evans returns to his bunk, as chairs begin to scrape and clatter, and general chatter builds on the other side of the divide. Crean has heard everything. Evans sits on his bed, facing him.

CREAN   What is it you're thinking, Edgar? Will we be in or what?

PO EVANS   Oh yes, Thomas. We'll be in all right. Man needs donkeys, you see.

He flexes his arm: the bicep bulges.

11. *Ext. Framheim. Dark waste of the depot. Johansen feeds his dogs; on his own. A tenor — Herold — sings a romantic song in thin relay from the hut gramophone.*

12. *Int. Hut, lit by spirit lamps; the 200-candle Lux lamp has been switched off. A honed sledge being weighed. Bjaaland steadies it; Amundsen adjusts the scale. Hanssen and Hassel look on, absorbed in the work. Around the table, Stubberud, Prestrud and Wisting work quietly on details of personal gear: boots, socks, sleeping bags, fur underwear, snow-goggles. Lindstrom in from galley carrying knives and spoons for polishing.*

LINDSTROM   (STOPPING BRIEFLY, EN ROUTE FOR THE TABLE) What's it weigh, then?

AMUNDSEN   Unbelievable. 48 lbs.

LINDSTROM   Hundred and sixty five pound sledge down to forty-eight? You're crazy.

He takes his place at the table. Amundsen winks at Bjaaland.

AMUNDSEN   Am I?

He checks with Hassel; Hanssen.

175

HASSEL It's damned light.

BJAALAND That's the point. (TO AMUNDSEN) Do I do the rest?

Amundsen runs strong testing hands around the racer, stressing and flexing. Nods. Bjaaland grins. Removes sledge from the room, as Johansen enters, discards furs in his bedspace without speaking.

13. *Later. They sit, the nine, round the table, working on personal gear. Lindstrom's finishing his knife-polishing. The room is quiet, creaky. Stubberud writes a letter in large, awkward hand. Johansen pushes and pulls a needle through leather with deft power, remodelling boots. Amundsen calculates provision requirements on a large sheet of paper, column after column of weight and mass. Lindstrom returns the utensils to their tray, sits idly watching the others, eventually gathers something from his bunk and returns to his seat at the head of the table. Begins winding a key. Hassel frowns at the disturbance; Johansen sniffs. Lindstrom releases the object: it's a doll; blouse, skirts, petticoats, ankle boots. Slowly the long-haired woman performs perfect somersaults on the table. Lindstrom chuckles to himself, engaged, childlike. The movement gradually breaks the men's resistance: face after face succumbs, absorbed by the bounce of lace and the dance of hair, into private remembering. Even Johansen is touched, in a hard, curious way.*

We reach Amundsen. He stares at the doll, eyes thin, unyielding. He remembers nothing.

14. *Snowscape. Dark, desperate blizzard. Three men — Bowers, Cherry-Garrard, Wilson leading — lean into the gale, lugging 280 lbs a man. Wilson stops, calls back to the others, a rasping croak. The three stare at the dim outline of the half-buried hut.*

15. *Ext. Hut. The men are lovingly helped in. Wilson clutches a small box to his chest. Inside, Atkinson, the POs and the young scientists are stunned by their appearance. Facial flesh has been withered, frost has bitten deep into feet and hands. Wilson's right eye has been seared by blubber fat.*

176

Scott appears from his den to greet them. Wilson hands him the box. Scott opens it. Inside, three Emperor Penguin eggs.

SCOTT   I'm proud of you, Bill. Proud of you all.

He bites his lip, moved. Cherry-Garrard slumps to the floor.

LINDSTROM   (VO) Crazy, crazy, this is crazy, this is crazy . . .

16. Framheim. Through the horizontal door of the snowcover, a packed sledge is being slowly extruded.

17. Int. Hut. The men shave in silence. Mirrors glint in the Lux light. Remnants of beards and hair litter floor and surfaces. Lindstrom stands in the galley doorway, mittened and balaclava'd, a ladle in his hand.

LINDSTROM   (BAWLING AT AMUNDSEN UP THE ROOM) Apart from anything else, it's a Friday, dark things happen on Fridays, you're a grown man, you should know that.

AMUNDSEN   (FINISHED, HOOD UP) Three days running the thermometer's told the same story. We go. Will you say goodbye?

LINDSTROM   Go to hell.

He sulks back into the galley. Amundsen pushes on through the door, followed by Bjaaland, Prestrud and Wisting. Johansen is left, tying a finnesko.

18. Ext. Framheim. They pour out onto the dark snow. Hassel, Hanssen and Stubberud are harnessing dogs and aligning sledges. The new men join them.

19. Int. Lindstrom comes out of his galley. Sees Johansen.

LINDSTROM   I told him: Scott won't be out there, too cold. Crazy. Will he listen? Ba.

JOHANSEN   (BITTER) They never do. He's like Nansen. He wants
the prize.

LINDSTROM   (LIVERISH) That's as may be, he's a great man and
don't you forget it out there. (BEAT) *We're* as bad anyway,
what the hell are *we* doing here, we should be out to grass
with all the other old folk. Grass, eh? (CHUCKLES, MIRTH-
LESS) Grass.

Johansen cowls his head in fur.

JOHANSEN   *I* know why I'm here.

*20. Ext. Framheim. Dawn sun just above horizon. Eight men on ski,
seven sledges, eighty-four dogs. Amundsen skis the line, checking
details, brief words. Returns to the head.*

AMUNDSEN   (LOW KEY; ANTI-DRAMATIC) Let's give it a try, shall
we?

BJAALAND   (DOWN THE LINE, CALLING) Piece of cake.

*Amundsen waves to Hanssen, lead driver. The whip cracks. The
dogs strain and gather.*

*In high long shot, the teams head south, dark stains across the cloth.
Over, a fairly tuneless rendering of* Onward Christian Soldiers.

*21. Cape Evans. Int. Hut. Brief images of a service: gentlemen and
sailors sing with little gusto. Scott watches, tight-lipped, a bible in
his hand. Cut to*

*22. Int. Pony stalls. Perspectived sound of hymn continues over
long shot of Oates, squatting by blubberstove, trousers filthy again,
writing a letter. Slow track in.*

OATES   (VO) Dearest mother, I am afraid this letter is very
disjointed and badly written and I feel the occasion is one
for a special effort but our life here is so monotonous and I

find it difficult to write a decent letter. (THE HYMN FINISHES WITHIN. SCOTT'S METAL VOICE INDICATES HE REQUIRES IT TO BE SUNG PROPERLY. 'Once more, Mr Cherry-Garrard, if you please.' THE PIANOLA RESUMES) They have service but I do not attend as Scott reads the prayers and I dislike Scott intensely. I would chuck the thing if it was not that we are the British Expedition and must beat the Norwegians. (LISTENS TO THE SINGING A MOMENT: IT'S LITTLE CHANGED) The fact of the matter is he is not straight, it is himself first, the rest nowhere, and when he has got what he can out of you, it is shift for yourself. (SCOTT INTERRUPTS THE SINGING, CALLS FOR A FRESH BEGINNING. INTRODUCTORY CHORDS) I learnt last week I'm to be in Scott's tent for the start of the polar journey. Whether this means I am to be in the final party or not I don't know but I think I have a fairish chance, that is, if Scott and I don't fall out — it will be pretty tough having four months of him. If Scott was a decent chap I would ask him bang out what he means to do. (THE SLOW TRACK STOPS, FRAMING THE PLAIN FACE ABOVE THE PLAIN PROSE) From what I see it would not be difficult to get to the Pole provided you have proper transport but with the rubbish we have . . .

He looks down the stalls at the wormy survivors. Clicks his tongue at them. Mad Christopher neighs and snickers in vehement response. Next door, Scott halts the hymn yet again. Oates grins. Introductory chords. 'Onward Christian soldiers, marching as to war . . .' *Oates clicks. Christopher responds. Scott calls a halt. Oates's grin widens.*

23. *Mapping device. Amundsen's line of march pushes slowly forward towards 80°South and the first depot cairn. Inset images of the terrible journey, dank bitter wind, fog, blizzard, ice waves, falling thermometer −45°, −53°, −67°), inching progress, bicycle-wheel sledgemeter; frozen sleeping bags, tight swollen faces, dogs' feet minced by ice, blood printing snow beneath them. The line stops at 79°40'.*

24. *Barrier, 79°40'. Fog. The shot tracks through swirls of nothing. Clink of picks and shovels on ice, grunts of exertion, some distance*

away. Two men loom — Hanssen and Johansen, feeding dogs; then sledges; finally the main group, constructing a large ice-hut. Beyond them, a pitched tent, flaps open; Wisting prepares the evening meal.

25. *Int. Ice-hut, lit by paraffin lamps. The eight eat pemmican stew around the primus. Faces are lined, split; eyes raw; fingers cracked, and blackened. They eat in silence. Amundsen scans for meanings; makes no contact.*

PRESTRUD (FINALLY) I have to take a reading . . .

AMUNDSEN Here. (HANDS HIM A LAMP) There's a leather satchel in Helmer's middle case, could you bring it?

Prestrud furs up, crawls out with the lamp. Wisting hands out oatmeal biscuits; three each. Mugs of boiled snow passed round.

26. *Ext. The sledge thermometer. Lit by Prestrud's lamp. It reads −69.3°C. Prestrud stares at it in wooden disbelief.*

27. *Ext. The light finds the aluminium side-lid on the middle packing case. It's prised off, the satchel fished out. A sudden hideous whining cry from a dog. Prestrud turns, listens.*

28. *Ext. The lamp lights the snow ahead of the advancing Prestrud. A prone dog comes into view; a second. They've frozen to death.*

29. *Int. Ice-hut. Eating gear has gone: sleeping bags have appeared. Prestrud returns, satchel and lamp in hands.*

HASSEL What do you make it, Krystian?

PRESTRUD (HANDING AMUNDSEN THE SATCHEL) 69.3 below. (SQUATTING AGAINST ICE WALL) Two dogs gone, Chief. (AMUNDSEN FROWNS, HOW GONE?) Froze to death.

Silence. Looks. Amundsen's slow fingers unfastening the leather clasps.

PRESTRUD (TO WISTING) Adam and Lazarus.

They look at Wisting, who blinks, frowns.

WISTING   (QUIET) Damn.

AMUNDSEN   (HANDS GROPING IN THE SATCHEL) Hold your mugs
up, I've been saving this, we need something to cheer us . . .

*He draws out a bottle of geneva. It's frozen solid, a huge crack down
the length of the glass.*

BJAALAND   Or a chew.

HANSSEN   (FOOD IN HAND) Hunh. The devil.

He shows the heel he's just discovered. It's dead; a lump of tallow.

HANSSEN   (TO STUBBERUD) How're yours, boy?

Stubberud holds both feet out, both badly bitten.

AMUNDSEN   (AS IF TO HIMSELF) We'll hole up here a day or two,
see how it looks . . .

JOHANSEN   (FROM NOWHERE) We've made a mistake, I think we
should face it. If we go on, we risk everything.

AMUNDSEN   (SOFTLY) Will Scott turn back?

JOHANSEN   (AFTER THOUGHT) Beating the English isn't all there
is. There are wives, children, the years left to us . . .

*Amundsen slowly checks for support on the faces of the remainder.
Gets a taut headshake from Hassel, another from Hanssen, silence
from Wisting.*

PRESTRUD   I think he's right, Chief.

*Amundsen nods. On through Stubberud, who's deeply miserable, to
Bjaaland.*

BJAALAND   I'll go on, if you think so, Chief. (BEAT) But it won't be fun.

It's decisive. Amundsen lies down in his sleeping bag. Others follow suit.

AMUNDSEN   (EVENTUALLY) We'll move everything up to Eighty Degree Depot tomorrow. (BEAT) Then we'll head home.

30. Ext. Shots of Amundsen, anxious, morose, frosty, as they depot supplies at 80°South and turn; as they struggle over sastrugi, crevasses, drifting fog, deep cold; as they press to get out of the cold. The features tighten, as the journey continues with empty sledges, drivers up. Mapping device traces them back towards Framheim: stops about forty miles out. Shots of the men, worn, hurting. Stubberud in bad shape, finding it hard to move his feet. Amundsen, no longer forerunner, sits with Wisting in the second sledge, dealing tensely with the crisis in his leadership.

31. Ext. Morning. The weather lifts uncertainly: they glimpse a thin sun. Amundsen calls a halt down the line. Hanssen, leading, doubles back to join the others. Amundsen stands up on the back of Wisting's sledge.

AMUNDSEN   How far, Helmer?

Hanssen checks the bicycle-wheel sledgemeter behind his sledge.

HANSSEN   Forty miles, a little less.

Amundsen scans the drained men, the rat-like dogs, bellies stuck to the hard snow. Looks up at the smear of sun and the hard waste ahead.

AMUNDSEN   (VOICE LIFTED TO BE HEARD) This break may not last and there's another forty miles. I want it doing at a stretch. You have your biscuits. Tonight we dine at Framheim and sleep in our bunks. Let's go!

He grabs a whip, cracks it viciously across the heads of Wisting's team, who lunge forward instantly. Hanssen and Hassel exchange dark, uncomprehending glances.

HANSSEN   Better do as the man says.

He cracks his team forward. Hassel drives forward more conservatively. Stubberud's team flounders, quite weak, Prestrud, weak himself, stops to help him forward. Johansen climbs a small hump on ski, to watch the shrinking figures of the leading teams. There's a sudden wildness in him now.

JOHANSEN   (A HUGE SUDDEN VOICE) Look to your men, you bastard! Look to your men!

The scream rolls across the barrier, dies in their icy wake.

32. Ext. Barrier. Amundsen, on a packing case behind Wisting, watches Hanssen brilliantly overhaul them.

AMUNDSEN   (RELEASED, HALF MAD) Come on Oscar, come on, come on, come on . . .

Hanssen draws level, grinning grimly. They battle for the lead like kids on push-bikes. Whips slap the air.

33. Ext. Framheim. Late afternoon (4 p.m.). Lindstrom feeds the Base dogs inside the giant sixteen-man dog-tent. Is distracted by distant barking. Comes out to see a sledge and team top the rise a mile or so away; then a second, two men up. They careen towards the base. The base dogs pour excitedly out of the tent, rush off to greet the returning teams. Lindstrom watches for more sledges to appear; they don't.

34. Ext. Approaches to the hut, Lindstrom waits. Hanssen skews to a halt before him, dismounts, hobbles stiffly towards the roof door and Lindstrom.

LINDSTROM   Too cold, eh?

HANSSEN   (CURT, ALL IN) Mmm.

He lifts the door, lowers himself gingerly down the steps.

LINDSTROM   Don't say I didn't tell you.

Amundsen and Wisting arrive.

LINDSTROM   (CALLING) Don't say I didn't tell you!

Wisting passes Lindstrom without a glance, lowers himself exhaustedly into the hut. Amundsen approaches Lindstrom. He's gaunt, icy, his mood at freezing point.

LINDSTROM   Where are the rest?

AMUNDSEN   (NOT CHECKING STRIDE) Coming. (LIFTS ROOF DOOR)

LINDSTROM   Don't go on a Friday, I said. Do you remember?

AMUNDSEN   (DISAPPEARING) See to the dogs.

35. Int. Framheim. Lux lamp-light. The clock's at 9.31. Bjaaland wolfs food at table, furs still on but loosened. Stubberud lies on his bunk, moaning and weeping with pain. Wisting tends him: boracic compresses to the grotesquely blistered feet etc. and a mug of seal broth, which he feeds the sick man. The atmosphere is bad. Lindstrom skulks moodily in his galley, preparing more stew.

Amundsen in from vapour bath. He stands naked in his bedspace, towelling himself dry. Glances at Bjaaland, who eats on, head down.

AMUNDSEN   You're back then, eh.

BJAALAND   Ahunh.

AMUNDSEN   See anything of the others?

Bjaaland shakes his head. Amundsen gets into his sleeping gear, crosses to Stubberud's bunk.

AMUNDSEN   (TO WISTING) Go and get your bath, I'll look after
   this.

Wisting nods, surrenders the mug, leaves.

AMUNDSEN   How are you, son?

STUBBERUD   Sore, Chief.

*Amundsen   removes   the   compresses   delicately,   studies   the
feet.*

AMUNDSEN   It'll pass.

*Bark of dogs, quite close. The dog tent responds. Lindstrom brings
buckwheat cakes for Bjaaland. Catches Amundsen's eye.*

AMUNDSEN   (RELIEF NOT ENTIRELY MASKED) Here they come.

*Hassel in. Picks a slow, painful route down the room to his chair at
table. Lindstrom has a bowl of seal stew waiting, cakes, coffee.
He takes them in silence, looks at no one.*

AMUNDSEN   (EVENTUALLY) You on your own, Sverre?

HASSEL   (EATING) Yes. (AMUNDSEN WAITS. HASSEL EATS, SLOW,
   DELIBERATE) Passed Prestrud in a bad way sixteen miles
   out. Dogs played out, he had to cut 'em free. Johansen's
   bringing him in.

AMUNDSEN   (EVENTUALLY) Good.

*36. (MUTE DREAM) A thirteen-dog team, driver's POV, toils
through festering fog over snow. Amundsen drives them on, looking
behind him fearfully. Ahead something briefly looms, disappears.
Amundsen cracks the whip, desperate to catch up, but still conscious
of his pursuers closing him down. Nansen is one, in Viking garb;
Betty; his brother Leon, a sheaf of notes in his hand; Frederick Cook,
long hair streaming behind him; King Haakon and Queen Maud. He*

whips the dogs on, draws away from his demons.

With a supreme effort he overhauls the thing ahead. It's a motor-sledge, with a Union Jack engine pennant. He sees it's driverless. For a moment he looks set to pull past it. A sudden cough and clatter out of the muteness; the motorsledge accelerates, begins to leave him behind, is rapidly swallowed by the fog. A voice behind him, Lindstrom's: 'Crazy. Crazy. This is crazy.'

37. Int. Framheim. Amundsen's eyes are open, alert. He listens to the shuffling in the room beyond the curtained bunk. Low voices, Lindstrom's, Johansen's; a man whimpers with pain.

With his fingers he parts the curtain a fraction, watches Johansen and Lindstrom shoulder the ruined Prestrud to his bunk at the other side of the darkened room. There are grim mutters, as they help get Prestrud to bed. Amundsen lies back on his pillow. Stares at the roof. The clock strikes two.

38. Int. Framheim. Morning. Amundsen at Prestrud's bedside, changing the compresses and tending the badly swollen face. Stubberud lies on the next bunk, feet bandaged, eating breakfast. At the table, Wisting, Hassel, Bjaaland and Hanssen. Hanssen and Hassel rest swathed feet (one each) on stools, while they eat. Wisting and Bjaaland smoke in silence, finished. Lindstrom, in galley, prepares more food. Amundsen enters the galley, to wash his hands. Lindstrom gives him a brief look, goes on with his work.

AMUNDSEN (QUIETLY) All right. It was a mistake.

LINDSTROM Mistake. It was a fiasco. When the old dog barks, we would do well to look out of the window.

He leaves the galley, carries a fresh pot of coffee to the breakfast table. Amundsen dries his hands, follows him down to his seat at the foot of the table, a plate of buckwheat cakes in his hands. Eats in silence for a while.

AMUNDSEN (FINALLY) It's fairly obvious the boots won't do.

They'll have to be redesigned. It's an ill wind, I suppose.

WISTING   (SUDDENLY) It's true. And we've doubled the depot at 80°. That must count for something.

HANSSEN   (CAREFULLY) Yes. (GLANCING AROUND HUT) But I reckon we paid for it.

Johansen in, from his ablutions. He restores his gear to his bunkside, takes a place at the top of the table. Lindstrom in with jam and cakes. Johansen begins to eat. Tension in looks, glances, as the silence mounts.

AMUNDSEN   I hear you came in at two . . . (JOHANSEN STOPS CHEWING MOMENTARILY, CONTINUES WITHOUT SPEAKING OR LOOKING. AMUNDSEN CALCULATES. PRESSES ON) It's hard to imagine how it could take so long.

Johansen stands up, gathers his mug and plate, and begins to walk towards the galley, snaps suddenly, hurls plate and mug at the galley wall with tremendous force and swivels round to face the foe.

JOHANSEN   Hard to imagine? Hard to imagine? Why in Jesus Christ's name should a leader have to imagine? He should be there, with his men, in contact. Men could've died out there, but where were you, tucked up in your bunk. We should never have started out and everybody knows it including you. The truth of the matter is, you're not fit to lead, Amundsen, all you care about is polar glory and clearing your debts. Men's lives come nowhere with you. I don't call this an expedition, I call this panic. Panic. Look at us! (HE SWEEPS HIS ARM AT THE ROOMFUL OF WALKING WOUNDED) Look at us!

He stops, rubs his hand down the seams of his trousers, reaching for control. The men watch him in silence, appalled, fascinated. Amundsen stares on at his coffee.

Lindstrom crosses to collect the mess by the galley wall.

187

LINDSTROM   (HARD, AS HE PASSES) If you don't like the food, say
    so, don't throw it around.

*Hanssen looks at Hassel. Both look at Amundsen. Amundsen looks
carefully at the men round the table, ignores Johansen.*

AMUNDSEN   (CALM) Another twenty-four hours on that ice and
    limbs would have been lost. We had to get in fast. That's
    why I ordered the distance to be done at a stretch. That was
    my judgement anyway. It was hard — but it was right. And
    we survive.

He stands, collects his furs at the bunk, leaves the hut.

JOHANSEN   (FISTS BUNCHED, IN LOW RAGE) Bastard.

HASSEL   (FAST) You've had your say, now shut your mouth.

*39. Ext. Amundsen crouches by sledges, checking wear and tear, in
line some distance from the hut. Lindstrom, in wolf furs, approaches
him slowly. Amundsen hears him, does not turn.*

LINDSTROM   It's bad, Chief.

AMUNDSEN   Yes.

LINDSTROM   What'll you do?

Amundsen stands slowly, stares south.

AMUNDSEN   I don't know.

*40. Int. Framheim. Evening. Shot of bandaged feet etc. below
full table. Sounds of eating, polite mumbled requests for salt, bread
etc.*

*41. Shot of table and the men at dinner, nearly over. Pipes are being
lit; a certain unease, glances down the table at the withdrawn
Amundsen.*

AMUNDSEN   (AT LAST, ALMOST CASUAL) The events of this morning have caused me to reconsider our plans. (BEAT) I've decided to reduce the polar party to five. (BEAT) Prestrud and Stubberud, when their feet are healed, will undertake a journey into the unexplored territory of King Edward Land. Johansen will join them. Prestrud will lead. I'm sorry, but I think it's for the best.

Prestrud and Stubberud exchange miserable glances. Hanssen, Hassel, Bjaaland and Wisting chew on their pipes, holding off. Amundsen looks at Johansen.

JOHANSEN   (QUIET) Go to hell, Amundsen. (STARES DOWN TABLE) I've given my life to the ice, and you're going to put me under the command of a novice? I want that in writing.

Amundsen opens a notebook, takes out a script, folds it, passes it along the table. It reaches Johansen. He studies it. We read: 'To Hjalmar Johansen from Roald Amundsen: I find it most correct, with the good of the expedition in view, to dismiss you from the journey to the South Pole.' Johansen folds the paper, carries it to his bedspace, draws his curtains.

AMUNDSEN   (STANDING) I'll be in the galley. I'd like to speak to you all in turn. Helmer, you first.

42. Int. Framheim. Shot of galley from living quarters. Hassel and Hanssen watch Amundsen talking quietly and intensely with Wisting. Wisting emerges, nods to Bjaaland, goes to his bunk, draws his curtains after him. Bjaaland stands, we follow him to the galley.

AMUNDSEN   Sit down, Olav. (HE POURS HIM A GENEVA. BJAALAND SWALLOWS IT) I'm asking everyone to reaffirm his loyalty to me as leader. Will you do that? Just say yes or no.

BJAALAND   Yes.

AMUNDSEN   Thank you. Ask Sverre to step in, will you.

Bjaaland stands, as if to go; then turns.

BJAALAND   Chief. I say yes, because I know there has to be someone who leads if there's a crisis. It doesn't mean I think you're God — or even always right.

Amundsen nods; a grave smile. Bjaaland returns to his bunk. Lindstrom into his galley.

LINDSTROM   What about me? Want me to swear?

AMUNDSEN   Do you need to?

LINDSTROM   (ANGRY) No.

43. *Montage of shots of the sun over the Barrier, a rising arc of warming weather. At length the shot completes the parabola onto the ice. Four sledges, five men, fifty-two dogs stand ready for the off. Prestrud takes cinepics of the departure.*

44. *In closer shot, the men say their casual goodbyes. Stubberud weeps openly. Johansen stands, detached from the main body, hard and pathetic. Lindstrom hurries from the hut, a large package in his hands, gives it to Bjaaland.*

LINDSTROM   Something for Christmas. (TO AMUNDSEN) It's *another* Friday, you know that, don't you?

AMUNDSEN   I can't help that.

Lindstrom says his personal goodbyes. Johansen detaches, crosses to Amundsen, removes his glove, extends his hand.

JOHANSEN   Good luck.

Amundsen nods, turns away without taking his hand. Johansen watches them set off. Takes a flask from a wolfskin pocket. Takes a long, deep draw.

*45. Ext. Film. Cape Evans. Late October. Slow track into Ponting,
behind his camera and tripod, taking cinepics of the departure of the
polar party. Close on shot of Ponting's camera lens. Cut to*

*46. White caption on black screen, in the florid mode of early
silents:* 'First to leave are the mighty motorsledges, in the
capable hands of Lt Evans and Mr Day.'

*47. Jerky monochrome mute film of the motorsledges inching off
towards Glacier Tongue and Hut Point beyond. Teddy Evans and
Day wave to the camera: Lashly and Hooper pay it no heed.*

48. Caption: 'Next the turn of the slower ponies.'

*49. Film (as in 47) of Silas Wright and PO Keohane dragging
Jimmy Pigg and Jehu and their sledges towards the sea-ice.*

50. Caption: 'Meanwhile, as the expectancy outside grows . . .'

*51. Film (as in 45) of Scott at his desk, dressed for off, writing a
letter for the camera.*

52. Caption: 'The intrepid leader calmly pens a last loving
line to his beloved spouse back home in England.'

53. Int. Hut. Film (colour), shot as in 51. Scott writes away.

SCOTT'S LETTER   (VO) Evans is not at all fitted to be second-in-
        command, as I was foolish enough to name him. So I take
        him with me, so as not to risk leaving him in charge here in
        case I am late returning . . . I am quite on my feet now, and
        I realize that the others know it, and have full confidence in
        me . . .

54. Caption (as in 46): 'Some of the men who will go with
Captain Scott: Captain Oates, a very gallant cavalry officer, and
Mr. Cecil Meares, gentleman-adventurer and dog-expert.'

55. Film (as in 47): Oates and Meares flapping arms across chests as they wait on the ice for Scott to appear. Neither looks at the camera. Mix through to

56. *Ext. Film (colour). Oates and Meares, cold, alienated.*

OATES (BLOWING ON GLOVES) This is one hell of a circus, Cecil. Damn the bloody motors. A thousand quid apiece, the ponies cost a fiver and the dogs thirty bob, and he leaves the design engineer in England.

MEARES (SEEING SCOTT BEYOND THE CAMERA) He dropped Skelton for Teddy Evans, they say. (BEAT) Somebody should buy the man a shilling book on transport, soldier.

Anton arrives, with a present of tobacco for Oates. Oates shakes his hand, moved.

57. *Caption (as in 46):* 'The Captain arrives to place himself at the head of the main party.'

58. *Film (as in 47): Scott says his farewells to the base party (Simpson in charge) for the camera. Cut to*

59. *Film (as above): Scott, hand on Snippet's bridle, waves his arm forward and the caravan of eight ponies sets uncertainly off towards the sea-ice. Wilson, Oates, Bowers, Cherry-Garrard, Crean, PO Evans and Atkinson pass jumpily through the shot.*

60. *Caption (as in 46):* 'We wish them Godspeed and safe home. They are boys of the British breed. They will do their duty. May Fortune smile on them.'

61. *Ext. Film (colour). Long shot from the Hut of the long wavy ribbon of men, ponies and sledges trudging away from camera towards Hut Point. The shot holds: a pony goes out of control, a long way from camera — its handler chases and catches it; a moment later, another.*

62. *Int. Hut, Cape Evans. Close-ish shot of a field telephone. It*

buzzes, loud and long. Simpson picks up the receiver. Listens to the rather emotional voice at the other end for some time.

SIMPSON Right away, sir.

He puts the receiver down, screws up his nose, thinks. Griffith-Taylor has come out of his cubicle.

GRIFFITH-TAYLOR What is it?

SIMPSON They forgot to take the flag. He's at Hut Point. Wants it sending on.

GRIFFITH-TAYLOR Well, how the hell are we supposed to catch 'em?

SIMPSON (THINKING) Gran? He could ski.

Griffith-Taylor thinks, uncertain.

GRIFFITH-TAYLOR (EVENTUALLY) A bit bizarre, don't you think? He *is* a Norwegian.

63. Ext. Close fast track of Gran on ski, racing. Fastened around his chest, the Union Jack. Cut to

64. Mapping device (with relevant dates) charts simultaneously: Scott's four layers of transport (motorsledges, slow ponies, remaining ponies and dogs) from Cape Evans to Hut Point to Corner Camp; and Amundsen's single straight line, much faster, through 80°, 81° to 82°South and the last depot cairn. Mix through to

65. Ext. Cold deep drift on the Barrier. Night. Dark blue tent, sledges, dogs protected by constructed ice walls.

66. Int. Tent. The men lie propped or sit in their sleeping bags, smoking or reading or doing nothing. Amundsen has a chart on his lap, a notebook and a pencil; works in absorbed silence. Bjaaland reads a detective thriller, The Rome Express, *but there's little light to read by.*

BJAALAND   Helmer, you've read this, who did it? I'll never get it finished.

HANSSEN   (BINDING A WHIPSTOCK) Don't remember. Wasn't it the guard?

BJAALAND   It's the guard who was murdered. (POINTS TO HIS PAGE)

HANSSEN   (NOT INTERESTED) Oh.

HASSEL   (QUIETLY) Suicide.

Bjaaland looks at him, takes it in; begins to nod his head.

BJAALAND   Suicide. Yes. I had a feeling it was, you know.

Hassel nods, confirming the hunch. Bjaaland puts the book away, prepares for sleep. Hassel looks at Hanssen and Wisting. Winks once, quite dry. They bed down. Amundsen puts his chart and notebook away, turns down the light, lies down with the others.

BJAALAND   Think there'll be mountains, Chief?

AMUNDSEN   We're at the end of our rope. There could be anything from now on. Tomorrow our work begins in earnest.

Silence, save for breathing.

BJAALAND   I wouldn't mind mountains. Mountains could be a lot of fun, don't you think?

Silence from the others. He props himself on his elbows, finds they're already asleep.

67. Mapping device takes them on through 83° and 84° South. Intermix shots of the five in low-visibility weather — fog, mist, swirl, blizzard, low cloud; shot from below of a snow-ledge over a bottomless crevasse — Hanssen inches the lead-sledge over the divide with extraordinary skill and control, the others follow; the five of them building beacons every fifteen kilometres, depots every degree; a dead dog stiff on top of a depot cairn; etc. Final image of making camp at 84°South in a blizzard.

68. *Ext. Dawn. A brilliant sun. The blue tent in the vast ice-plain.*

69. *Int. Tent. Amundsen, dressed, preparing snow for chocolate on the primus. The others sleep. He puts his boots on, crawls outside.*

70. *Ext. Tent entrance. Amundsen comes out, elevates from the crouch, eyes narrowing in the strong sun. He sees something in the far distance. Stares for a long time, then stoops his head back into the tent to rouse the others.*

Amundsen takes a few paces forward. Raises his glasses, studies the thing ahead. Hanssen, Wisting and Hassel straggle out. Amundsen points. They see. Are smitten; awed. Bjaaland joins the line of men.

BJAALAND   Lindstrom owes me a cigar.

On the reverse, we see the Transantarctic Mountains, a sweep from the Beardmore right across their route south, about 200 miles ahead.

AMUNDSEN   (OVER THIS) Now we know the worst . . .

Slow pan of their separate faces facing south. Hanssen, Wisting and Hassel are versions of Amundsen: resolute but concerned.

BJAALAND   (ALMOST HAPPY) My God but they are beautiful, aren't they?

Amundsen puts his glasses up again. We follow the long scan along the unbroken chain from the Beardmore in the south-west to the peaks directly ahead of them.

AMUNDSEN   (SARDONIC; VO) Oh yes. They're beautiful all right, Olav.

Mix via mapping device charting Scott from Corner Camp out onto the Barrier to

71 *Ext. Barrier, 79°20'. Scott leads the main pony-sledge party through deep soft snow in brilliant sunshine. The ponies are belly-deep and desperate. Forward progress is minimal. In close shot, Scott's gaze is fixed on something ahead and to the left. His slow-track POV reveals the abandoned motorsledges.*

72. *Ext. His POV almost abreast of the motorsledge, slow tracking to a halt.*

SCOTT'S JOURNAL (VO) The dream of great help from the machines is at an end . . .

A shout. Bowers hurries towards Scott with his pony, a can in his hand.

BOWERS Message from Day, sir. Big ends have gone. Couldn't repair them, so they've pressed on as instructed.

SCOTT (STILL STARING AT THE MOTOR SLEDGES) Thank you, Birdie.

BOWERS Would this be a good place to camp, sir? The men seem pretty well done.

Shouts behind. Ponies and men scatter as Meares and Dmitri come through, very fast, whips flailing. Meares waves cheerily in Scott's direction and is gone, the dogs flying over the soft snow. Scott's nostrils flare with anger.

SCOTT We stop when *I* say so and not before, Lt Bowers, is that clear?

BOWERS Yes, sir.

Scott calls forward. The murderous trudge continues. Mix to

73. *Ext. High shot of the dogs and the sledges. The five men lie on*

their backs in their Netsilik fur underwear, hands clasped behind heads, staring upwards.

74. Ext. We take their view: they're off the Barrier, at the very foot of the first mountain (Mt Fridtjof Nansen). It rises 12,000 feet into a clean blue sky.

HANSSEN   (VO) What shall we call it?

HASSEL   (VO) Mount Bastard.

AMUNDSEN   (VO) Mount Fridtjof Nansen.

75. Ext. Amundsen closes his hook-and-eye ski fastening.

AMUNDSEN   Let's go.

76. Ext. Amundsen, Bjaaland and Wisting ski off south-east along the foot of the mountain. Hanssen and Hassel are pitching the tent and making camp.

77. Ext. The three skiers in long shot, dwarfed by Mt Nansen. Suddenly the mountain opens up to their right. The leading skier signals the gap. They begin the climb.

78. Ext. The three dots edge up the first glacier.

79. Ext. Amundsen reading for way ahead through the glasses. Lets the glasses hang, turns to Wisting, some yards away.

AMUNDSEN   What do you make it, Oscar?

WISTING   (READING HYPSOMETER) We've climbed about 2,000 feet. See anything?

AMUNDSEN   Mountains. (PICKS UP A ROCK, HOLDS IT LIKE A STRANGE OBJECT) Maybe we should take some of this back for Hassel and Hanssen.

BJAALAND   Shall we go on?

AMUNDSEN   This'll do well enough. We still don't know whether Greenland dogs know anything about climbing.

He walks past Bjaaland, lifts the glasses to study the Barrier to their rear. The Goetz-glass image picks out their endless chain of guide-cairns across the ice.

AMUNDSEN   (VO) At least we know the way back.

80. Int. Tent. They eat their pemmican stew. Amundsen has his chart out, and the notebook. He makes quick calculations, then thinks a long time.

AMUNDSEN   All right. We take sixty days provisions on, depot everything else here. All the dogs to the top, the best eighteen go on to the plateau, back to here, if we're lucky, with twelve. (BEAT) Helmer, can these dogs do it?

HANSSEN   Is the king an aristocrat, of course they can do it. These fellers'll fly if you ask 'em to. Might have to double 'em up, but they'll get there.

Amundsen checks with Hassel, who's as confident, but more quietly.

AMUNDSEN   I've allowed ten days for the climb. Seem enough?

HANSSEN   Ten days, eh. (THINKS ABOUT IT. GRINS) Bit like snakes and ladders really. Depends how many times we fall down.

WISTING   How many dogs d'you say go on, Chief?

AMUNDSEN   Eighteen.

Wisting nods. Sniffs. Lays down his bowl and spoon. Begins to put on his boots.

BJAALAND   I was conceived on a mountain. According to my mother.

Wisting, half-unseen, quietly leaves the tent.

81. Ext. Night. Strange light, in the lee of the mountain. Wisting walks to his dogs. Begins to talk with them. The Shark paws his chest, licks his face hungrily. Wisting speaks dog with them. They answer.

82. Int. Tent. The four men listen. Mix to

83. Ext. Extended montage of the four-day climb: a mainly wordless narrative of co-operative and highly dangerous action, punctuated by occasional scenes of dialogue. Day One covers 11½ miles and 2,000 feet; two ski reccess follow that day, one by Bjaaland ('climbing the steepest part of the mountainside like a fly'), one by Wisting and Hannsen. Hassel and Amundsen make camp and prepare a meal. Hassel asks Amundsen what Scott is like as a man. Amundsen: 'Very English'. *Day Two covers 17 miles and brings them to an altitude of 4,000 feet by mid-day. It's the lowest part of the Axel Heiberg Glacier, between Mounts Nansen and Christopherson, riven by giant crevasses, buckled between the two land-masses. By evening they reach a very small flat terrace, which ahead of them drops steeply to a long valley. Images from Day Two include hard, single-team dog-work, Hanssen and Hassel prominent, Amundsen either forerunning or helping to push; about them, on all sides, summit after summit; beacon laying; Hanssen and Hassel indicating they've reached the limit of their Day One recce; the five staring at the further monstrous course of the glacier; applying rope-brakes to sledge-runners; travelling gingerly and dangerously down ice-slope from terrace; up again, Bjaaland on ski as forerunner, in his element; hypsometer reading of 4,550 feet; framing glimpse of mapping device, charting line through glacier to 85°South and beyond; heat:* '. . . we sweated as though we were racing through the tropics'; *final recce ahead in evening; camp in deep soft snow; Wisting tends a slit paw.*

84. Ext. Glacier. They relay, dogs doubled up, towards a high terrace, Hanssen on ski urges his dogs on, leading. The work is telling in the thinning air.

85. Ext. They drive the dogs down again. Begin the ascent with the next sledge.

86. Ext. Evening. Moon and sun. The terrain straightens to flat. Hanssen leads, seen from Amundsen's POV on the second sledge. Ahead of Hanssen by a good twenty yards is Bjaaland, forerunning on ski. Amundsen turns head to check the following teams. When he looks forward again, Hanssen has disappeared. Amundsen calls Bjaaland, stops his dogs, skis forward carefully.

87. Ext. Hanssen hangs by his traces over a mile-deep crevasse. The sledge lies across it, slightly skewed.

88. Ext. Above, some yards from the edge of the crevasse, Hanssen's dogs brace and dig in against the weight of the dangling master.

89. Ext. Hassel and Wisting bring Alpine ropes. Amundsen and Bjaaland take the trace-weight, ease the strain on the dogs. The sledge shifts a little further askew, threatening to plunge down onto the man below. There are no orders or panic. Wisting, roped, begins a slow methodical descent down the side of the crevasse, passes the rope he carries round Hanssen's body and reefs it. Hanssen grins. Wisting smiles.

90. Ext. They pull him gently out. Hanssen lies on his stomach getting his wind, his feet within feet of the crevasse edge.

HANSSEN Never saw the damn thing. (CLIMBS SLOWLY TO FEET. TURNS TO STARE DOWN THE CREVASSE. CALLS DOWN IT) Hard luck, shitface! Not your day, I'm afraid.

The voice smashes into the chasm.

BJAALAND (CHUCKLING) It'll have you yet if you hang around long enough.

A sudden huge crash and roar from the far side of the glacier valley. They turn, startled, to see a million or so tons of snow puff from the side of the mountain to the glacier below. Clouds of snow begin to rise in the air all along the Heiberg. Crash after crash, roar after roar, a shot from Mt Nansen, a fusillade from Christopherson, on and on.

BJAALAND (AS IT SEEMS TO END) Now see what you've done.

They laugh, tension expelled. The laughter lifts, builds. The mountains respond with more landslides in the eerie moonlit far distance.

91. *Int. Tent. Wisting, Hassel and Hanssen sleep. Amundsen works at his chart and log. The hullaballoo of dogs outside distracts him. He listens. Bjaaland in. Amundsen pours him chocolate, as he unwraps, unboots. He puts both hands round it, sips it slowly, staring into the lamp.*

BJAALAND You really missed something, Chief. They're good mountains. They're very fine.

AMUNDSEN (QUIET) You found a way?

BJAALAND (SIMPLE) Oh yes. All the way up. We'll be there tomorrow evening.

Amundsen blinks, looks down at his notes. Bjaaland gets into his sleeping bag.

AMUNDSEN Are you sure?

BJAALAND Ahunh.

A dog howls. Another. Amundsen listens. An excitement builds behind the eyes.

92. *Ext. (Day Four) Overcast, dismal. They continue their breathless dizzying toil. Wisting calls out a hypsometer reading of 10,325 ft. Amundsen is tense, driving the group forward, keen to make ground.*

93. *Ext. Long shot from bottom of glacier valley of the men and sledges, on a narrow outcrop near the top of Mt Don Pedro Christopherson.*

94. Ext. Night. Dark under the cloud. Amundsen and Hassel are pitching tent; Wisting and Hanssen are unloading supplies and equipment. They're all in, men and dogs alike.

Bjaaland skis in along a narrow ledge.

BJAALAND   I've checked, fifty yards and you can see the plateau . . .

AMUNDSEN   Here's fine, Olav. We're there. (HE LOOKS AROUND THE GROUP) Good work. Dogs too. Feed 'em well. (BEAT) All of 'em.

He crawls inside the tent, lights the primus. Outside, the men contemplate the work ahead.

95. Int. Tent. Amundsen preparing stew stock on primus, face impassive. Outside, a calm, rare night.

A shot rings out, another, another, a volley, another single shot. Amundsen's face never changes. The shots pour out now, a ragged but methodical firing squad. Amundsen works on, as methodically. At length it's silent. Amundsen closes his eyes; they move a little behind the lids; opens them again, as the men return. Hanssen, Hassel and Bjaaland crowd round the pot in silence. Amundsen stirs the stock, drops more snow in.

Wisting appears in the entrance. His hands are full of prime cuts of Eskimo dog. He crawls forward, drops them into the pot. Amundsen watches; stops his hand suddenly with his ladle. Wisting looks at him, half angry suddenly.

AMUNDSEN   (GENTLY) Not the liver, Oscar. The eskimos say, never eat what a dog won't eat.

Wisting goes to his sleeping space, climbs into his bag, turns onto his side, away from the group.

BJAALAND   (MOROSE) Who's hungry anyway?

No one answers. Amundsen studies them quite carefully.

AMUNDSEN   I am. Those dogs served us well. (TAPS THE POT WITH HIS LADLE) And continue to serve us. You've seen scurvy, Helmer, Sverre. I've had it. Fresh meat's your best protection. You think it benefits the dogs to refuse the flesh you've just stilled forever? This is what we planned, God help us. This is what we do.

He takes each man's gaze in turn, in control. Each gives his signal of assent. Wisting's face remains averted.

96. Via mapping device, we trace back from the Transantarctic Mountains across the Barrier to Scott's miserable journey, several hundred miles in the rear. Mix to

97. Ext. The Barrier, One Ton Depot. Blizzard blowing itself out. Tents are pitched. Ponies and dogs huddle and dig for survival. The ponies are ragged, helpless. Men move about between the tents on pointless errands. Oates tends a sick pony. Lashly arrives with a message. Oates leaves the pony and enters Scott's tent.

98. Int. Scott's tent. Scott, in sleeping bag, in conference with Wilson.

SCOTT   Ah, Soldier, just the man. I've been checking the log, and I have to tell you we're falling further and further behind and it really won't do.

OATES   Further behind who?

SCOTT   Shackleton, who do you think? Look, the fact is, these ponies are a bloody shambles, is there nothing you can do to speed 'em up a bit? (SEES MEARES IN ENTRANCE) Meares, come in, I'm getting pretty sick and tired of you waltzing past us every day. You will kindly follow your orders in future and leave four hours after us, not three or two or whenever you feel like it.

MEARES That's what I've been doing, Captain Scott.

SCOTT Thank you, Meares, that's all.

Bowers replaces Meares in the entrance.

SCOTT (SEEING HIM) I want to talk to you. I want you to weigh my sledge-load, I suspect you've contrived me fifty or sixty pounds more than anyone else, I can't think why.

BOWERS Now, sir?

SCOTT Now, please. (TO OATES) The ponies must do better, Captain.

Oates leaves the tent. Catches Meares's eye. The look says most things. Inside, Scott sinks into moroseness.

WILSON You all right, Con?

SCOTT Fine, Bill. (BEAT) Never better. Just showing 'em who's in charge.

99. Ext. Barrier. Scott trudges his pony under strange, streaky sky. The rest strung out behind. A light glints remorselessly at him from a source up ahead.

100. Ext. Scott closes on the light source. There's a monster cairn, fifteen feet high, on the path ahead, two sledges drawn up beside it, three men watching the main party's approach. On top of the cairn, a mirror in his hand, is Teddy Evans. He salutes Scott in to Mt Hooper, calls out they've been waiting a week for them.

SCOTT (CONTEMPTUOUSLY) Get down from there, you bloody fool.

101. Ext. Early morning. Amundsen crawls from the tent, begins to put on ski. Gradually becomes aware of Wisting, down on one knee in the midst of the carnage. Amundsen crosses to the bloody pile. The snow is splashed with red in all directions. Wisting kneels by the Shark and others of his team.

AMUNDSEN   They'll need flensing.

Wisting nods, stands on his skis.

AMUNDSEN   You ready?

Wisting nods. They ski off along the narrow ledge.

100. Ext. Fifty metres on, or less, they see the plateau ahead, bathed in pink sunlight. They stare at it in wonder.

AMUNDSEN   Four days and here we are.

WISTING   We win.

AMUNDSEN   Not quite. But we have a chance now.

WISTING   What shall we call it, this place? Plateau View?

Amundsen looks down the slope towards the carnage on the snow below.

AMUNDSEN   (SUDDENLY SICK, HARSH WITH DISGUST) Call it what it is. The Butcher's Shop.

V

THE GLORY OF THE RACE

Pretitle: Ext. Mountain camp-site. Blizzard. Tent, sledges, dogs under drift. Snow. Wind snarls. Caption: Butcher's Shop, 85°30', 20–25 November 1911.

Slow pan across the site and on up to the corner ledge established in the final scene of Part IV. A tall figure, ski and skin, back to camera, stares into the thick white rage to the south. Title: THE LAST PLACE ON EARTH.

CU Amundsen, head on, eyes slit against the wind. He stands for some moments longer, turns.

Begins a careful line down from the ledge corner to the camp. Approaches the tent, removes ski, unclips bindings, enters.

Int. Amundsen crawls through the others to his sleeping bag. Sits. They're barely disturbed by his return, a glance and back to their separate processes. Hanssen writes in a small black book: long thought-pauses; slow, difficult and brief entries. Wisting's in the entrance section, a can of snow simmering, preparing delicate cutlets of dog. Hassel and Bjaaland play cards in self-absorbed silence. Amundsen unhoods, scans the comrades. He looks old, tense.

HANSSEN   No change, eh, Chief?

AMUNDSEN   No change.

HANSSEN   What's the day?

AMUNDSEN   Friday.

Hanssen goes back to his book. Amundsen sits on; does nothing.

AMUNDSEN   (QUIET) I think it's time we went. (THERE'S A MINI-
MAL ARRESTATION OF PROCESS WITHIN THE PHLEGMATIC
MINIMAL RESPONSE. AMUNDSEN CHECKS FACES. THE TENT
WHINNIES IN THE WIND.) I don't insist. If there's a voice
against, we stay put. But this is our fifth day holed up here,
and it could be another week before it's clear enough to go
on with safety.

*He waits now; looks at no one. Hassel checks with Hanssen,
Bjaaland.*

HASSEL   It makes no difference to me, my sledge is depoted. (HE
LOOKS AT HANSSEN) It'll be the drivers who take the risks,
sledging blind at ten thousand feet.

Hanssen thinks, unhurried. Amundsen watches.

BJAALAND   (CLAPS HIS HANDS ONCE) This place is the devil's
arsehole. Anything's better than sitting here waiting for
your hair to grow.

*Amundsen receives this with a nod and a wan smile. Hanssen thinks
on. Wisting, out of it, has begun singing* Solveig's Song *(as played
on the gramophone at Framheim, Midwinter's Eve, Part IV) in a
breathtakingly inadequate voice in the outer section.*

BJAALAND   Piece of cake.

AMUNDSEN   Helmer?

HANSSEN   Is it up or down, do we have any idea?

AMUNDSEN   Bit of both.

HANSSEN   We'll need forerunners, probably two together, plenty of rope, and depot what we can where we can, while we travel blind . . . (AMUNDSEN NODS, WAITS. HANSSEN GRINS SUDDENLY) Otherwise I agree with Olav, piece of cake.

Something is released. The air eases. Bjaaland chuckles, flicks a card at Hanssen's head.

WISTING   (APPEARING IN GAP BETWEEN TENT SEGMENTS) Stew's on.

He withdraws again.

AMUNDSEN   (THROUGH CANVAS WALL; DISTINCT) We were talking about pushing ahead, Oscar.

They wait. Wisting appears in the gap again, fastening his hood for out.

WISTING   (PREOCCUPIED) Fine, count me in, somebody keep an eye on the pot there, I'm off to feed the mutts.

He's gone. Dogs greet Wisting outside, as grins are exchanged.

AMUNDSEN   (EVENTUALLY) Good.

Ext. Blizzard. Sledges packed, dogs harnessed, depot cairn being marked. Wisting carries a broken ski, scales the six-foot cairn, drives it securely into the snow-blocks.

Whips crack. They begin their almost blind climb to the corner.

Mix to

Mountainous terrain in heavy blizzard. Amundsen and Hassel, roped together, forerunning like yoked snails. One by one the sledges appear: Hanssen, Wisting, Bjaaland.

V. The Glory of the Race.

1. Ext. Deep silence. Fog, almost black. Amundsen forerunning, ten dim paces ahead of Hanssen's lead dog. Hanssen's POV shows the spectre of Amundsen ahead. Wisting, invisible in the rear, asks if they're climbing or dropping. Bjaaland, last, says both. The voices are remote, unreal, disembodied. Amundsen calls hold, sharply. Sledges hold.

HANSSEN (CALLING) You there, Chief?

Amundsen's cowled face, through the V of his ski, from below the lip of the crevasse. Fog boils about the image. Hassel joins him in the shot.

AMUNDSEN (CALLING BACK) How far, Helmer?

HANSSEN (OOS, CALLING) Wait.

Amundsen looks at Hassel.

HASSEL Want me to unpack the wings?

Amundsen grins, estimates the gap with his ski-stick. Hassel peels off, to look for a bridge.

HANSSEN (OOS, CALLING) Nine miles, a bit more, dead reckoning.

2. Ext. Snow bridge, from below. Ghostly images of Amundsen testing it, crossing. The lead sledge looms: Hanssen coaxes, taut, purposive. Hassel pushes from behind. Snow and ice flake from the bridge, drop into the silence below. Hanssen's clear; Wisting appears, jockeying forward, clucking, dog-voiced. Hassel helps again. Bjaaland now. Heavier crumbling. Bjaaland stops mid-bridge.

BJAALAND (TO THE HOLE BELOW) Shut your mouth, you devil.

This is Olav Bjaaland and he's spoken for.

The dogs scramble forward. The sledge clears, vanishes.

AMUNDSEN   (SHARP; OOS) Hold!

3. Ext. A tent peg being driven into ice with an axe-head back.

HANSSEN   (OOS) More damned holes than ice in these parts . . .

4. Int. Tent. They sleep. Amundsen's watch by his head says three o'clock. A slow smear of light through the blue canvas greases his face. The eyes open abruptly. He studies the canvas, sensing; quietly wakens Hanssen.

5. Ext. Tent, dogs, sledges. The two emerge, in close-ish shot, stand upright to survey the sky.

6. Ext. Shot of sun through thickish mist: 'a pat of butter'.

7. Ext. Slow, upward widening shot of them, in which their blind terrain takes shape: a huge distorted glacier, fractured and riven, linking mountains and plateau. They stand in wonder for a while, as the shot is extended, then begin a gestural anaylsis of the route ahead.

8. Ext. The overhead shot rests. They stand marooned in a surreal and terrifying ice-scape.

AMUNDSEN'S JOURNAL   (VO) We called it the Devil's Glacier, and
   his Majesty graced us with his presence every step of the
   way across his icy kingdom.

Mix to

9. Ext. Montage of low-visibility images of tortuous progress: roped traverses of polished ice; giant sastrugi; warm blizzard; cold fog. Men's voices call hollowly, left, right, hold, back; dogs talk.

Amundsen's voice calls 'Hold!'

10. Ext. Amundsen in CU, shrouded in thick dark grey fog, Hassel a pace behind him in the back of the shot. Amundsen studies something just ahead of them, scans left, right, then back to the object of scrutiny.

HASSEL   What are they?

Amundsen shakes his head; squints on.

11. Ext. Ahead in the murk, their POV, clusters of pressure hummocks in the shape of haycocks, higher than men, look like alien beings. The two men move forward with great circumspection. The first sledge looms.

12. Ext. They study the ice-formation gingerly. Hassel pokes the side with a broad flat knife; makes no impression. Hanssen leaves his sledge, burls up through the darkness with an axe.

HANSSEN   The devil, I *said*, we'd been climbing, we're on the moon . . . What do you make of 'em, Chief?

AMUNDSEN   Must be pressure.

HASSEL   Question is, what's underneath.

HANSSEN   One way to find out. (HE SWINGS THE AXE IN A FULL ARC AT THE HAYCOCK; HALF OVER-BALANCES, AS IT SINKS IN ALMOST TO THE GRIP, THE ICE CAVING LIKE A CHOCOLATE EGG) Jesus . . . (HE PEERS INTO THE HOLE) All the way down to the basement . . . Black as a sack . . .

His voice squirts and bubbles beneath them. Dogs bark, back in the murk, frightened. Wisting skis up. Sees the haycock, the hole; scans ahead.

WISTING   Dogs're getting spooked. (HE SHIVERS)

AMUNDSEN   We'll sleep. Wait for the sun.

V THE GLORY OF THE RACE

13. Ext. Pale, ghostly light. Deep cold. In wide long shot, mute, they toe a discreet path across the lunar landscape, mile upon mile of pressure hummock.

14. Ext. Indoor echoey acoustic. Montage of images, close to, of this crossing of the Devil's Ballroom: dogs' legs crunching through ice-crust; men's, Bjaaland to the hips. Always the impulsion is implacably forward. In CU, we see and hear the signs of cost, in bleeding paws, frost-sores on lips, frozen flesh, raw eyes, the rasp of thin air on lung.

AMUNDSEN'S JOURNAL   (VO) In spite of all hindrances, and of being able to see next to nothing, we put in almost twenty-five miles today and camped at 11,070 feet above the sea, a good thousand feet higher than the Butcher's. Perhaps, after all, we have come through . . .

15. Ext. Wet clinging blizzard. Tent up. Bjaaland and Hassel build snow walls for the dogs; Amundsen and Hanssen feed them.

16. Int. Tent, outer section. Wisting at work on the hypsometer and primus. The others crawl past him, exhausted, climb into their bags. Wisting works on, makes the odd calculation on a pad. Eventually he's done; crawls to the gap.

WISTING   11,780 feet two days running. I'd say we were on the plateau . . .

He peers into the dimness of the tent. The four lie in their bags in silence, barely conscious.

Over this:

SCOTT'S JOURNAL   (VO) One cannot see the next tent, let alone the land to the west. I doubt if any party could travel in such weather.

17. Mapping device, superimposed over blizzard, connects the Norwegians' positions around 87° with the British at 83°30'.

213

SCOTT'S JOURNAL (VO) There is food for thought in picturing our small party struggling against adversity in one place whilst others go smilingly forward in the sunshine.

18. *Ext. Through this, on the track, glimpses of Blizzard Camp: snow walls, desperate ponies, tents, sledges, dug-in dogs in the warm whining blizzard.*

19. *Caption over this: Blizzard Camp, 83°30', 5–8 December.*

20. *Ext. A lone figure — Bowers — humped against the storm, struggles between tents. He passes Oates, who crouches in the lee of a snow wall over a prone pony. Bowers calls, indicates the tent ahead. Oates stands, waves Bowers on, indicates he'll follow, watches Bowers enter the tent, produces a pistol from an inner pocket and shoots the pony through the head. He waits until the pony rests before heading off after Bowers. En route, he stoops to peer inside a two-man tent amid the three larger ones.*

21. *Int. Tent. Dmitri bathes Meares's heavily inflamed eye with a piece of lint.*

OATES How is it?

MEARES Sore. More dog food? (OATES NODS) Want to come in?

OATES Can't. Called to a meeting.

Meares grimaces. Oates leaves.

22. *Int. Scott's tent, alive with the drip and trickle of melting snow: poles, canvas, groundsheet, clothing, bedding, personal gear. Bowers, snow-pasted, just arrived, sits in an oozy puddle, waiting. Scott, opposite, works on his journal, sucking a dead pipe. Wilson reads. Bowers works a small black book from his clothing. Scott checks his watch deliberately. Bowers might speak; doesn't. Wind rips at canvas: flap and tug.*

SCOTT'S JOURNAL (VO WHILE WRITING) Resignation to

misfortune is the only attitude, but not an easy one to adopt. It seems undeserved where plans were well laid and so nearly crowned with a first success.

Oates crawls into the tent during this, gets a grave smile from Wilson, nothing from the scribbling Scott, as he squelches down beside Bowers. Scott closes his book, places it methodically away, pockets the pencil. Checks watch again.

SCOTT Was that a shot I heard just now?

OATES Michael. Done for.

Scott nods, looks at Wilson.

SCOTT Makes one feel just a little bitter, does it not, Bill, to contrast such weather with that experienced by our predecessors?

WILSON We've had no luck, it's true. But we plug on . . .

Scott nods, smiles grimly.

SCOTT Well, gentlemen, our appalling luck with the weather on this leg of the journey and the delay it has caused mean that we have somewhat over-run our provisions — food and fuel — by some three or four days, right, Birdie?

Wilson loses some of his langour; shuffles to sit up a little.

BOWERS That's right, sir, we'll be forced to break into our Summit rations this evening, I'm afraid.

SCOTT So. The question I must resolve is whether it makes any sense at all to keep feeding the ponies during this infernal and unending blizzard or kill them here and now and use them as an additional source of food for men and dogs. The paramount consideration, to my mind, of course, is the welfare of the ponies themselves. Four, five, have already succumbed. Is it right to demand more of the remainder? Should we not simply put an end to their unspeakable misery?

Oates has covered his eyes with his hand. Bowers dutifully appears to be considering the problem.

SCOTT Any thoughts, Bill?

WILSON It's a cleft stick, I can see that. If the weather were kind tomorrow, the problem solves itself, of course . . . What does Titus think?

Oates uncovers his eyes slowly; sniffs.

OATES I see no point in killing the ponies here. The food they'd provide would barely cover the extra ration we'd need to manhaul their loads. (BEAT) Leaving none to depot for returning parties.

SCOTT And the suffering?

OATES (SLOWLY) I don't see how that can be helped, Captain.

Scott absorbs this. Wind whines. Water splashes down from disturbed canvas.

SCOTT Well, whatever I decide about the ponies, it's becoming clear that I may need to take the dogs on beyond the foot of the glacier. I'd like you to take a fairly detailed look at what that's likely to cost us, Birdie, in food and fuel, say two days on the glacier itself.

BOWERS Very good, sir. (BEAT) I know things aren't so rosy, sir, just now, but I believe we have the spirit to make it up somehow, later on.

SCOTT So do I, Birdie. (TAPS HIM ON THE SHOULDER WITH HIS FIST) Well said. Thank you, gentlemen. I'll let you have my decision when I've given the matter fuller consideration.

BOWERS   Thank you, sir.

Oates and Bowers leave the tent. Scott strikes a match, begins to warm his pipe bowl.

SCOTT   That's the spirit, eh, Bill?

WILSON   Mmm. (PAUSE) Whatever happens, we're going to have to make good the stuff we've borrowed already on this leg, aren't we?

SCOTT   It's in hand, Bill. Simpson has orders to get the dogs back as far as One Ton Depot with what we'll need.

Pause.

WILSON   (CAREFULLY) So . . . you won't want to take the dogs on *too* far, will you, in case they don't get back in time to replenish the depots? By rights they should have turned back a week ago.

SCOTT   (PATIENT) The weather is not *my* doing, Bill. (BEAT) We'll manage. (GRINS) We've done it before, eh?

Wilson smiles, less than happy. Scott pulls on his pipe.

WILSON   Have you spoken to Meares? (SCOTT SHAKES HIS HEAD) I said I'd take a look at that eye of his. (SCOTT LOOKS AT WILSON, BRIEF, DEEP, NODS ONCE, LOOKS AWAY) Two days, you say?

SCOTT   Mmm.

WILSON   It might be the time to raise again with him the whole business of next season, Con. (BEAT) It wouldn't do to find ourselves at the mercy of inexperienced drivers, come the spring.

SCOTT   (DISTANT) I'm not prepared to beg, Bill. I can't pretend I

217

find his decision to catch the ship other than deeply selfish, but there we are. (BEAT) We'll have Dmitri, of course.

Wilson takes a small pack from his personal gear, removes two small phials and an eye-dropper. Begins gearing up for out. Scott picks up the book Wilson has been reading.

SCOTT   Tennyson still.

WILSON   All I have with me. But fine stuff. (POCKETS HIS GEAR, CRAWLS TO THE ENTRANCE) I'll go and take a look at Cecil's eye.

Wilson leaves. Scott opens the volume at the book-mark. Holds the page under a lamp to study it. We read a title: Crossing the Bar.

23. *Ext. Wilson flops across the driven snow towards Meares's tent.*

WILSON   (VO) Twilight and evening bell
                    And after that the dark!
                    And may there be no sadness of farewell,
                    When I embark;
                    For tho' from out our bourne of Time and Place
                    The flood may bear me far,
                    I hope to see my Pilot face to face
                    When I have crossed the bar.

A burly figure crawls from a tent, passes Wilson en route for another.

PO EVANS   (CALLING) No chance of movin' on, is there, sir?

WILSON   (CALLING) Impossible to steer in this stuff, PO. Don't want to get lost . . .

PO Evans enters his tent. A hoot of greeting goes up.

24. *Int. Tent. PO Evans kneels in the entrance, a small bottle in his mitt. Keohane, Crean and Lashly watch him from the fug of pipe smoke.*

PO EVANS Spot of Napoleon, gentlemen? Give up your mugs, my boys.

CREAN (AS EVANS POURS) I'll be buggered, so I will, auld Taffie's knapped the swag.

KEOHANE Makes a change from playing with his knob. 'Ow'd yer come by it? Been dancing to someone's whistle, is it? Bit of knee-drill, eh?

Lashly watches from his sopping bag, the archetypal non-smoking teetotaller.

PO EVANS As a matter of fact I got it from Surgeon Atkinson, all fair and above board. (SWIGS FROM THE BOTTLE, THE POURING OVER) It's for old Bill's chest, there.

Chuckles, as they sink into the spirit. Lashly returns to his journal.

LASHLY So what've you found out, Taff?

PO EVANS. Well, it's still four for the Big One, the Owner and three others. Wilson probably — for Science, you see, never mind if the bugger can pull. Another officer, Evans, Bowers, Atkinson, someone like that . . . (BEST TILL LAST) And like as not someone from the lower deck. (HE SMILES, SERAPHIC. SWIGS AGAIN, FOLLOWS IT ALL THE WAY DOWN) An' if that's true, my boys, you could be perusing that very body right now.

LASHLY Think you'll get the nod, do you, Edgar?

PO EVANS (INTENSE SUDDENLY) I better, I tell you. Means a lot to me. Gonna call my little hostelry The South Pole, see . . . a picture of me there behind the bar in the best room. That's my future we're talkin' about, let me tell you . . . And no second place either. First or nothing s'far as I'm concerned, if I have to pull the other bloody three there myself . . .

Silence, as the wind gathers for another shriek. Evans drains the brandy, throws the bottle out into the snow. His passion has stilled the company a little.

PO EVANS   Listen to it, will yer.

KEOHANE   (SUDDENLY) Will I be readin' yee the wee rhyme I penned only this mornin' on that very subject, my gallants? (FISHES PAGE FROM POCKET, AS THEY CHUCKLE HIM ON. TENNYSONIAN POETRY VOICE)

> The snow is all melting and everything's afloat
> If this goes on much longer
> We shall have to turn the tent upside down
> And use it like a boat.

CREAN   Ach but that's a powerful verse you have there, Patrick, it is so.

Laughter, dizzied by the dram.

25. *Int. Scott, lying in his bag, hears the laughter, as he contemplates possible disasters.*

26. *Int. POs tent. Laughter rests. PO Evans wipes the spit from his lips.*

PO EVANS   Bowers says we go on Summit ration from this evening.

Lashly looks up, frowning. Evans sniffs.

27. *Int. Bowers' tent. Bowers, Oates, Teddy Evans, Atkinson, Wright and Cherry-Garrard sit crammed in moody silence in the gloomy wetness, smoking.*

BOWERS   (FINALLY) Well, it's not the end of the world. (THE OTHERS SAY NOTHING) The Owner's in a real paddy with the weather. I feel glad he has Dr Bill in his tent, Bill's best in adversity . . .

V THE GLORY OF THE RACE

28. Int. Meares's tent. Meares, in loose close shot over Wilson's left shoulder, bears a fresh pad of lint secured by a head bandage over the right eye. He sits for some moments, chewing his pipe-stem, mulling the question. Begins calm, hard; develops considerable acid ferocity by the time he's done.

MEARES   Let me be plain, Dr Wilson. Gentlemen do not make public their grievances and disagreements, and I am bound by that code as much as any man; but I would not want my reasons to be wilfully misconstrued, particularly by my fellows on the trip. (BEAT) I came to this . . . expedition with decent credentials: years of experience in the world's wilds — Siberia, Manchuria, India, Africa; some skill in Russian, Chinese, Hindustani; and a working knowledge of dogs and their habits. All these I offered for nothing, for a pittance, because I believed in the show . . . And while I believed in that show, I've been prepared to swallow my professional pride and follow the order of the day, however confused, stupid, inept or incompetent those orders may have been. (PAUSE) Well, the events of last season, and everything that's happened since, persuade me that any belief in this particular enterprise is sadly misplaced. My record shows I am no coward, no weakling: but when my *life* is put at risk by leadership as crass, as arrogant and as . . . irresponsible as that which Captain Scott displays every day we are here, I know what I must do. (PAUSE) Ten years ago, when I was twenty, I drove a team of dogs across Siberia, a journey of two thousand miles. It taught me many things, but chiefly I learned the narrowness of the line Man walks in Nature between farce and tragedy. It's a lesson those Norwegians have learned on sea and ice and mountain time and time again; it's a lesson Scott and his kind will never learn. (LONG PAUSE) Tell him, if you will, I would as soon agree to swim my way back to New Zealand as consent to another season under his command. I shall take the ship in February and wash my hands of it. Tell him: a man who sits in his tent in the Antarctic and whines about the weather is unfit to lead. (HE PRESSES HIS PALM AGAINST HIS BANDAGED EYE) Damn this thing. (PAUSE. THEN

221

WITHERING) Where does he think he is, the Isle of Man?

Cut to Wilson, in CU, over Meares's shoulder. He says nothing. Mix to

29. *Ext. Odd half-light, low sun and moon. The camp sleeps. The blizzard's ended. The snow buries most things.*

30. *Int. Scott's tent. Scott sleeps, his face in a deep pout. Oates and Keohane sleep. Wilson lies propped on elbow, writing a letter.*

WILSON (SOFT, POETIC VO, FLECKED WITH THE SAINT'S MORBIDITY)
O my dearest, ... I have been reading Tennyson's 'In Memoriam' during this blizzard and have been realizing what a perfect piece of faith and hope and religion it is ... It makes me feel that if the end comes to me here or hereabouts there will be no great time for you to sorrow ...

31. *Ext. Plateau. Still weather, larval-gray cloud over endless white plain. The five Norwegians stand, separate, silent, scanning the sky. Hanssen carries one sextant and artifical horizon; Wisting the other. Bjaaland carries a camera.*

WILSON (VO) All is as it is meant to be ...

They wait, scan, in tense silence.

HANSSEN (SUDDEN) There!

They follow the finger. The sky has lightened for a moment; closes down again.

They resume their waiting mode. The dogs lie still, glad to rest. They're worn; quite thin, losing condition. The men's facial skin is cracked and raw; Hanssen, Wisting and Amundsen have vast frost-sores from eye to chin.

BJAALAND (URGENT, SCANNING TERRAIN NOW) Come on, Chief,

let's make tracks, we've lost an hour already, there isn't time for this . . .

AMUNDSEN (QUIET, TENSE) If we're to claim the Pole we have to make it stick. Remember Cook up North. It's ninety miles since we were able to make a meridian. We need the sun.

Shots of upturned faces as they wait on, ending on Amundsen's. Very slowly the light values on it alter, uncovering a slow excitement in the eyes. Some cheers from the others. Dogs bark, disturbed.

AMUNDSEN (TO THE SUN, QUIETLY) Thank you, your Grace. (TO THE MEN) Let's do it!

32. Ext. Pared-down montage of sextant work (Hassel and Wisting; Hanssen and Amundsen; Bjaaland snapping their efforts); the growing tension of five separate calculations.

33. Ext. Amundsen finishes his. Checks with the figure for the dead reckoning. Waits for Hanssen to finish his computations, then calls each in turn to give his results. All four give 88°16' South.

AMUNDSEN It's what I make it too. (PLAYING IT A LITTLE) Which, strangely enough, is precisely our figure from dead reckoning.

HASSEL (STUNNED) I don't believe it.

AMUNDSEN See for yourself.

BJAALAND My God, we're going to do it! Helmer, we're going to *do* it man!

HASSEL (HANDING THE BOOK BACK; LOW VOICE, MARVELLING) Like an arrow.

Hassel holds his hand out. Amundsen takes it.

BJAALAND (OOS, CHILL) Jesus Christ, what's that?!

223

They turn quickly to look, squint at the broad waste behind them, following Bjaaland's extended arm.

34. Ext. In their POV of the horizonless white globe of plateau, a black speck is clearly visible. Tension reasserts among the group.

BJAALAND   I'm taking a look . . .

Amundsen nods tersely, watches Bjaaland ski off, takes in the speck again, encounters Hassel's white glance. A dog barks, unexpectedly; startles them all.

HANSSEN   He's stopped.

35. Ext. Their POV again. Bjaaland has drawn up fifty or so yards away. They wait. He begins his return. Their taut faces bring him back.

36. Ext. Bjaaland arriving.

BJAALAND   Mirage. It's a dog turd.

AMUNDSEN   (CALM) Fine. Let's go.

WISTING   No depot?

AMUNDSEN   One thing at a time, eh?

37. Ext. Amundsen forerunning, Hanssen lead-sledge, Bjaaland, Wisting, then Hassel skiing loose behind; a clean, silken movement under dust-grey sky.

38. Ext. CU of Norwegian flag tied to two ski-sticks laid flat across Hanssen's sledge.

AMUNDSEN'S JOURNAL   (VO) We had a great piece of work before
    us that day: nothing less than carrying our flag farther
    south than the foot of man had trod . . .

39. Ext. Head-on close shot of Amundsen forerunning, deep in abstracted reverie. (Possible images recovered from previous texts here: with Nansen, Leon, the German newspaper headline about Shackleton's Furthest South.) A sudden huge shout from Hanssen: 'Yeeees!' and a volley of cheers pull him back to now. He turns to look.

40. Ext. His POV Hanssen holds the flag aloft, points to the sledgemeter, laughing and calling.

41. Ext. Amundsen's face slowly absorbs the news.

AMUNDSEN'S JOURNAL   (VO) 88°23' was passed; so far as could judge, we were farther south than any human being had been before.

42. Ext. A grave handshaking ceremony around the lead-sledge.

AMUNDSEN   (VO) No other moment of the whole trip affected me like this. We had won our way by holding together, and we would go farther yet, to the end.

43. Ext. CU·Amundsen, bareheaded, by the flag on the depot cairn. Tears seep down his face as he speaks.

AMUNDSEN   On this day, 8 December 1911, at latitude 88°23' South, we salute the brave men who showed the way: Shackleton; Adams; Marshall; Wild. First to cross the Barrier, first to climb the mountains, first to set foot on the Plateau. Wherever stories are told of these parts, may their names be remembered.

Murmurs of assent from the others, who stand with bared heads in a small arc round the cairn. The silence holds for some moments. Amundsen reaches for his hood.

BJAALAND   I would like to say something. (PAUSE) I salute Shackleton not only for daring to come this far, but for daring to turn back within sight of the prize rather than risk the lives of his companions. For in this he showed true

courage. (HE NODS TO AMUNDSEN TO INDICATE HE'S FINISHED.
AMUNDSEN SEARCHES FOR MEANINGS; FINDS NONE)

*The others applaud with their mitts, Amundsen too; an odd, formal,
very civilized group in the middle of nowhere. Slowly they slip back
into their hoods and goggles and drift to their stations.*

Mix to

44. *Ext. Shambles Camp, foot of Beardmore Glacier. Fine, sharp
weather. Meares's dogs fight over a pony's head. Some yards away,
PO Evans, Lashly, Keohane and Crean bury sections of pony
carcasses in the depot cairn. Beyond, Scott, Wilson and Oates are
fastening themselves into their hauling gear.*

45. *Ext. Lower Beardmore Glacier. The two dog-teams tackle the
sharp slope briskly, eventually revealing the three man-hauling
teams as they pass them. The snow is deep, soft drifts: the man-
hauling, in close shots of backs, legs, and faces, is murderous.*

SCOTT'S JOURNAL   (VO; IN SHOT) Hereabouts Shackleton found
hard blue ice. It seems an extraordinary difference in fortune,
and at every step Shackleton's luck becomes more evident.
Things are not so rosy as they might be, but we keep our
spirits up and say the luck must turn.

*Teddy Evans's team (Atkinson, Wright, Lashly) are in difficulties.
Scott calls a halt; turns to look down the slope at the stragglers.*

SCOTT   (CALLING) Your sledge is badly loaded, that's why you
can't keep up. Put it right and follow on.

46. *Ext. Teddy Evans calls a fairly superfluous halt, his face grey
with effort, eyes heavy with loathing for his leader. Wright and
Atkinson flop down to their knees in the snow. Lashly leans over his
ski-stick, sucking air.*

47. *Ext. Camp on the lower glacier, a broad winding highway
between huge mountain ranges. Morning. Three sledges in file point*

up the hill. The two dog-teams point down. Meares and Dmitri are harnessing the dogs. The POs are active about the camp-site, reloading sledges and cleaning sledge-runners. Bowers moves amongst the tents, collecting mail for home. Caption: Lower Beardmore Glacier, 83°40', 11 December.

48. Ext. Scott leaves his tent, followed by Wilson. They walk a stiff distance from the site, fanning as they do, to urinate.

49. Ext. Bowers approaches Meares, now working on his sledge-lashings.

BOWERS   (LEATHER SATCHEL IN HAND) Mails, Cecil. (MEARES TAKES THE SATCHEL) Give my regards, won't you. It must be sad for you to leave the show so soon, but I suppose the Owner's right, we can't risk not having the dogs next season. Seems a pity though. They have out-pulled everything.

MEARES   (AMUSED AT THE INNOCENCE) Aye, but they're *dogs*, Birdie, aren't they, and that's not quite the thing.

Scott calls Bowers to him. Bowers shakes hands with Meares, then cuts off to the approaching Scott. Meares watches, dry and hard.

OATES   (HAND OUT) Safe home, Cecil.

MEARES   (TAKING IT) Good luck, Soldier.

Oates smiles gravely. Meares's eyes sadden. Oates moves off, waving without looking. Meares watches him a moment. Oates shakes hands with Dmitri, moves off again towards the tents.

SCOTT   (OOS, CLOSE) You're ready for off, then.

MEARES   That's right.

SCOTT   (HANDING HIM AN ENVELOPE) Please see that Dr. Simpson receives this on your return. (BEAT) They're my revised plans concerning the dogs and their work next season, so I shouldn't need to stress their importance to the enterprise.

MEARES I'll see he has them.

Scott looks away a moment, finding the line.

SCOTT At the end of this season you will have placed yourself outside my command, knowing full well that such a decision could undermine our chance of success. I trust it will not be a decision you have cause to regret in the years to come, Mr Meares.

Dmitri calls something in Russian, Meares answers, picks up his dog-whip.

MEARES I think that most unlikely, Captain Scott. I will stand ready to be judged by my actions. (PAUSE. HE CALLS THE DOGS TO READINESS) I hope you can say the same, sir.

He cracks the whip over the dogs, begins to push the sledge to free the runners. Dmitri follows suit. Men run to wave them off and call farewells. Scott watches for a moment, then calls Bowers to strike camp.

The dogs dwindle at a decent pace down the glacier, as Scott approaches the POs. They stand upright respectfully. He waves them on.

PO EVANS (INDICATING DOGS) Good riddance, I say, sir. Now we can get our backs into it with a will.

SCOTT Just like the old *Discovery* days, eh, PO?

PO EVANS Exactly. (WIPES BROW) Think we're winning, do you, sir?

SCOTT We're not engaged in a race, PO. But I must confess myself heartened by the absence of tracks on the glacier.

PO EVANS   You think the Norskie'd come this way, sir?

SCOTT   It's what I'd do, PO. He may be lucky, of course, and find an easy route through the mountains to the east. Then again he may not.

The meaning hangs, clear but unuttered. Scott peels away, chivvying for off. Long shot of decamping, bleaching slowly into long shot of white globe of plateau. Over this, the mapping device nudges Amundsen's route forward beyond 89°South and fades, leaving the plateau again. Wind gusts, falls, gathers, from the south, along the line of route-marker beacons.

50. Ext. The five — Hassel forerunning; Hanssen lead-sledge and compass; Wisting; Amundsen on ski with Bjaaland — head into the bitter southern wind and snow crystals.

Caption: 15 December 1911. 89°50' South.

AMUNDSEN'S JOURNAL   (VO) Last night in the tent it was like the eve of some great festival. Hair was lopped, beards clipped, as if in readiness for the great event we felt to be at hand.

51. Ext. Hanssen calls something to Hassel, points to the sledge-meter; Hassel skis back to join him. Hanssen indicates a halt with his whip.

52. Ext. Bjaaland reins in his dogs. Calls to Wisting, 'What's going on?' Wisting shrugs.

BJAALAND   (SCANNING THE PLATEAU; TENSE) Is this it? I don't believe it.

AMUNDSEN   (CHECKING BJAALAND'S SLEDGE-METER) Not according to this it isn't. (HE SCANS AHEAD. HASSEL AND HANSSEN ARE IN CONFERENCE THIRTY YARDS AHEAD OF THEM) Another hour at least, on the reckoning.

BJAALAND   (STANDING ON SLEDGE, CALLING) Come on, you two, if you're tired, drop back, I'll lead the way.

Hanssen waves his whip, ignoring him, continues the conference. Bjaaland rejoins Amundsen in the snow.

AMUNDSEN (STUDYING HIM) Still seeing the English flag?

BJAALAND Every hundred yards, damn it. What about you?

AMUNDSEN We're all on edge a little. It'll pass.

BJAALAND (TAUT) Will it?

They look at each other for a moment. Bjaaland looks back up the tracks.

AMUNDSEN You have some complaint, Olav?

BJAALAND How do you mean?

AMUNDSEN (SHAKING HEAD; SLOW) I suppose I mean about me, the way I lead. Something you said at Shackleton's mark made me think perhaps you were dissatisfied . . .

Hassel has doubled back down the sledges, reaches Bjaaland's. He seems soured by the discussion.

HASSEL (TERSE) Hanssen wants you to lead, Chief.

AMUNDSEN Why?

HASSEL You'd better ask him.

He skis off to Wisting's sledge. Amundsen waits for Bjaaland's answer.

BJAALAND (EVENTUALLY) I wouldn't be anywhere else in the world just now, Chief. And there's no one in the world I'd sooner follow. When I gave you my hand on that railway station two years ago I already sensed you were a man to trust. (BEAT) Now I know it. I'm sorry if I make difficulties.

I'm a Telemarker, you know what that means . . .

AMUNDSEN (WITH DIFFICULTY; MOVED) Nobody deserves today more than you do, Olav.

He skies off up the track, calls something to Wisting en route, reaches the lead-sledge.

AMUNDSEN What's the problem, Helmer?

HANSSEN Hassel's all over the place, Chief, I need someone who can ski straight, my mutts are worn out trying to follow his weavings . . .

AMUNDSEN (INDICATING SLEDGE-METER) What do you make it?

HANSSEN Couple of miles.

Amundsen studies his face for some moments for clues, finds none. Hassel calls something sharply from the second sledge, Hanssen waves at him in disgust.

AMUNDSEN All right, let's go.

Ahead, the plateau unfolds, white, unrelenting.

AMUNDSEN'S JOURNAL (VO) In most respects it was a day like any other. The wind bit our faces and the dogs complained at the going, but we did our work in the same methodical way as before. Not much was said, but eyes were used all the more . . . .

Hanssen calls, 'Chief.' Amundsen turns. The three sledges stand abreast some forty yards back. Above them the silk flag flaps and putters.

Amundsen nods, smiles; skis slowly back to the waiting men. Nobody speaks. Hanssen moves forward, to hand him the flag on the bamboo pole.

231

HANSSEN   Feel proud, Chief. You tweaked the lion's tail today. First man to the Pole. As luck would have it.

Amundsen smiles, acknowledging the subterfuge, exchanges brief looks with the others, then withdraws a few ski-lengths to plant the pole. Turns, flag in hand, to speak.

AMUNDSEN   Come, comrades. This must be done by all of us.

53. Ext. Five bared fists press the rod into the snow.

AMUNDSEN   (OOS) We plant this flag at the South Pole, and give to the plain on which it stands the name of King Haakon the Seventh Plateau.

54. Ext. Long shot of the five, the flag flapping. Solemn handshakes at first then a gradual release into excitement. The dogs have been freed and mill around the men.

55. Ext. The group again, closer in, watching Amundsen expectantly, the flag cracking in the wind at his back.

HANSSEN   Anything you want to say, Chief?

Amundsen scans their faces.

AMUNDSEN   Yes. (PAUSE) A lot. A lot. (THINKS) Comrades, this is a cold place. And we have work to do before we sleep.

Groans from the men.

WISTING   (QUITE SERIOUS) No, we have to have a speech, Chief. Things have to be marked.

Others laugh, as Amundsen grows grave.

AMUNDSEN   All right. (THEY QUIETEN, TO LISTEN) I thank you. From my heart. For your work. Your commitment. Your craft and your comradeship. (PAUSE) I have . . . no grand emotions, no profound thoughts to share with you, I have to confess it. I experience the excitement, of course, but I feel the irony. My dream since childhood has been the North, the North Pole itself, if I'm to be honest. And here I am at exactly the opposite end of the earth. (HE WATCHES THEIR SMILES, FEELS THEIR WARMTH) But above all what I feel is . . . not large or deep at all, it's just: how good it is. To be alive.

He looks around them again. Something is touched in each of them.

AMUNDSEN We'll make camp.

56. Ext. In long shot again, they begin their work of unloading and feeding and tent-pitching. The flag flaps in the wind, already forgotten.

57. Ext. Polheim. Hassel, Hanssen, Bjaaland and Wisting stand outside tent, watching the entrance.

58. Int. The tent, a single; clean, still, tomb-like. Amundsen, on one knee, unhooded, crouches as if in prayer. Gradually we see he's entering his name in a leather-bound notebook. Over his shoulder, we read the brief sentence proclaiming their visit and the appended signatures: Roald Amundsen, Olav Olavson Bjaaland, Helmer Hanssen, Sverre H. Hassel, Oscar Wisting, 17 December 1911.

Amundsen closes the book, lays it on the stack of implements and clothing they've left, smiles at the sewn-in messages of congratulations from Ronne and Beck, and leaves.

59. Ext. Amundsen emerges from the tent, hooding up; scans the northern horizon for a moment.

WISTING (AT HIS SLEDGE, INDICATING) What do you want to do about the surplus fuel, Chief?

AMUNDSEN (THINKING IT THROUGH) I think we should take it with us, Oscar. We might have need of it. (SCANNING

HORIZON) It's unlikely they'll lack anything material. (HE TURNS, SURVEYS THE GROUP: SLEDGES, HANSSEN AND WISTING DRIVERS, TWO TEAMS OF TEN, HASSEL AND BJAALAND ON SKI) For those who believe we have already won, let me say this: the British *will* be here, and perhaps soon; they do not give up easily. If we were to make the mistake of allowing them to reach the telegraph first, the issue of priority could get . . . quite muddied. We're a long way from home. Are we ready?

BJAALAND   (REMEMBERING SOMETHING) Wait, Chief. (TAKES A WOODEN BOX FROM HIS FURS) Let's go back in style, what do you say?

He hands cigars round the group. They're taken gratefully, as a gift; lit; puffed. Bjaaland lights Amundsen's last.

AMUNDSEN   Lead us on, Herr Bjaaland.

BJAALAND   (CIGAR IN TEETH) A pleasure, Herr Amundsen.

60. Ext. Long shot of the tiny group, against a low dark sun.

61. Ext. The wind cracks an unfurling sail, another. Cigar butts gripped in teeth still, as they begin their plain sailing.

62. Ext. Long shot again. Sails bellying forward, the sledges float against the sun like junks in an eastern sea. Bring up desperate scrape of air on lungs. Slow mix to

63. Ext. Long shot down Upper Beardmore Glacier. Through thin mist the first sledge materializes: Scott, Wilson, Oates, PO Evans. They suck at the thin air as they inch for the summit. Behind them at some distance, the second sledge looms: Teddy Evans, Atkinson, Wright, Lashly; and close behind, the third: Bowers, Cherry-Garrard, Crean and Keohane.

In the long lens, at a mile an hour, the work is Sisyphean.

64. Ext. Upper Glacier Depot, at about 10,000 feet. Wilson sits on a boulder sketching the Cloudmaker north down the track. He glances from time to time at the entrance to the Owner's tent. The camp is quiet; as if dead. Eventually Atkinson emerges on all fours, stands grimly.

WILSON   (CALLING) Atch. Could I have a word, old chap?

Atkinson approaches, lips tight.

WILSON   Tough luck, Atch. (ATKINSON SAYS NOTHING) If it's any consolation, the Owner hates it as much as you do. But we can't all go on.

ATKINSON   I don't mind for myself, Bill. I simply don't grasp the principle . . . Silas Wright's as strong as an ox, still . . . So's PO Keohane for that matter.

WILSON   Leading is deciding, Atch. It's always hard. (BEAT) What's your opinion of the men left? As a doctor, I mean. (ATKINSON FROWNS A QUESTION) I'm a touch concerned too, as a matter of fact. I believe it's Scott's intention to have the lower deck represented in the final party.

ATKINSON   Then it should be Lashly. Hard as nails. Without question.

WILSON   That's my feeling. And Crean?

ATKINSON   Pretty tireless. He'd make it.

WILSON   PO Evans?

Pause. Atkinson screws up his nose. There's a call from the entrance of one of the tents and Wright appears, striding towards them.

WRIGHT   (ARRIVING) Is it right we've been told off, Atch?

ATKINSON   Afraid it is, Silas.

Wright's eyes are bitter, face grim.

235

WRIGHT I'm going to see about this . . .

He strides off towards Scott's tent.

ATKINSON Silas, wait. Silas. (WRIGHT STOPS. DWELLS. TO WILSON) PO Evans is a bag of wind. Taking him on makes a mockery of sending chaps like Silas and Lashly back. But I don't imagine anyone's about to listen to me.

Wilson watches him clap an arm round Wright's shoulder and talk him gently back to his tent. Wilson returns to his sketch; relights his pipe. A shadow falls across the paper. Teddy Evans stands above him, rather menacing in the shadow of the rocks.

WILSON Evening, Teddy.

EVANS Evening, Bill. (LOOKING AT SKETCH) I believe you've really caught that, it's quite remarkable.

WILSON Just a sketch. I'll paint it when we're home.

EVANS (QUIET, CASUAL) Any idea who's going to the Pole, Bill?

WILSON (CAREFULLY) Still in the balance, I believe, Teddy. (PAUSE) Why not ask the Owner? (EVANS SMILES THE IMPOSSIBILITY) I think he's still watching performance and weighing condition. (BEAT) Atch, Cherry, Silas and Keohane return tomorrow, did you hear?

EVANS (HARD-EYED) No. But then I wouldn't expect to. So he'll take the fittest, will he? Good.

He leaves down the slope to the tents. Wilson watches. Scott emerges from his tent, pipe aglow, takes a magisterial promenade around the entrance. Teddy Evans walks past him. No word or look is exchanged.

65. *Mapping device and images of punitive hauling from Upper Glacier Depot to approx. 86°South and the Plateau.*

66. Ext. The leading sledge. The four strain in their separate vacancies. A distant cry from their rear shakes Scott from his dream and causes him to call a halt.

SCOTT   (DRAINED, LOOKING BACK) Damn that man, can he do nothing right.

67. Ext. Their POV of the second sledge, about three hundred yards to the rear, stopped.

PO EVANS   Someone's gone in, I think, sir. Shall I give a hand?

SCOTT   (VIEWING IT THROUGH HIS GLASS) Save your strength, PO. We'll rest. Looks like Lashly's found a blasted hole. (BITTER) And here was I looking for fifteen miles for Christmas Day. Ha.

Scott tuts and fumes as he watches. Wilson and Oates lean against the sledge, wet and ashen. Oates massages his thigh very slowly. PO Evans slides to his haunches, drained, gasping.

SCOTT   (THROUGH GLASS) Come on, come on, man, standing there like a tailor's dummy, get the beggar out.

OATES   (TO NO ONE, QUITE AUDIBLE) It's Bill Lashly's birthday today. (PAUSE) Forty-four.

Scott pockets the glass, moves to the sledge, sinks against it to rest. In close shot, he looks feverish, sweat pouring from him.

SCOTT'S LETTER   (VO) It is most awfully trying — I had expected failure from the animals, not from the men — I must blame Lt Evans much, he shows a terrible lack of judgement. (PAUSE) For your own ear, I go with the best of them, so that I am not ashamed to belong to you . . . It is a pity the luck doesn't come our way, because every detail of equipment is right and arrangements are working exactly as planned.

A ragged cheer from below.

PO EVANS   I think they've fished him out, sir.

Scott pushes himself upright, a massive effort of will. Takes his place in the traces. The others follow in a limp straggle. The strain is taken once, twice, three and four times before the runners budge.

68. *Ext. Montage of the two sledges, over several days, as their race with each other develops. Teddy Evans drives his team relentlessly. Scott is as resolute, pushing to exhaustion. Once sledge no. 2 actually overtakes Scott's on the march. Evans's face gleams. Slowly Scott overhauls them. Sastrugi, bare ice, driven snow, fog, brightness: whatever the terrain, the deadly match goes on apace. There is deep fatigue showing now, pain no longer quite hidden.*

69. *Ext. Summit Camp. The tents are pitched an unusual distance apart. Snow-gathering and other breakfast activities about the mouths of the tents. Bowers takes his morning readings by theodolite. Wilson and Scott perform their ablutions in silence some way away.*

WILSON   (INDICATING THE ACTIVITY) Fine crowd we put together, Con.

SCOTT   (WIPING FACE) On the whole I'd agree, Bill.

He watches Teddy Evans leave his tent and urinate.

WILSON   Look at old Birdie there, morning, noon and night, on the go.

SCOTT   Yes, Birdie's a great little worker. (BEAT. CASUALLY) He'll be a great loss to us.

Silence. Wilson rubs snow around his teeth with his finger.

WILSON   (SLOW) You've made your mind up, then.

SCOTT   Our team goes on.

Wilson looks away quite sharply, stabbed by elation.

SCOTT   I said we'd do it together, didn't I, Bill? And so we shall. We're the better team. Evans's lot simply can't keep up.

Wilson watches Oates crawl stiffly and slowly from his tent to urinate.

WILSON   (CAREFULLY) When do you intend to tell the others off?

SCOTT   Two or three days. We need to squeeze the last drop out of them and they're not jiggered yet. (STUDIES WILSON'S FACE) You seem doubtful, Bill.

WILSON   Well, I know you'll have your reasons, but *medically* speaking I have some doubts about Titus, I'd say he was pretty well spent.

SCOTT   Soldier's fine, Bill. Hard as they come. He'll not flinch. (PAUSE) And it's important the other great service is represented at the Pole . . . It's a part of the decorum of things. Just as Edgar Evans must go to represent the lower deck.

WILSON   Atch thinks old Lashly's a better bet.

SCOTT   (ABRUPT) Really. Then it's as well Surgeon Atkinson is not in command: PO Evans is the strongest man around and quite indispensible.

He walks down the incline towards the tent. Approaches Teddy Evans, who's helping Crean and Lashly unpack their ski at the sledge.

SCOTT   You won't be needing those, Lt Evans. I want you to depot them and come on foot.

He walks on towards the tent. Teddy Evans glances at the POs, then hurries after Scott.

LASHLY   (SOTTO, TO CREAN) That's us, boy.

Crean sucks his pipe, says nothing.

Evans catches Scott by the mouth of the tent.

EVANS   I don't quite understand the order to depot ski, Captain.

SCOTT   (PEREMPTORY) It's perfectly simple. If your people could use them properly the ski would earn their passage. As it is, you spend half the day dragging them behind you on the sledge. That's fifty-odd pounds dead weight, Lieutenant. Without them, and with a shortened sledge, it's just possible you'll manage to keep up. I hope so, anyway. We are still not up with Shackleton's dates and that does not please me. Depot your ski.

He ducks into the tent, audience over. Evans turns, whitefaced, fists opening and closing. Cannot face Lashly and Crean, who watch from the sledge. In close shot, Evans's face hardens and darkens.

LASHLY   (CALLING) What do we do, sir?

EVANS   (FINALLY) We go on foot.

70. Ext. The second sledge, in biting wind. The four stump through deep drift. In the far distance, the leading four go on ski.

The second sledge scarcely moves. The men lose their footing constantly, pitch forward on their traces. Teddy Evans urges them on with manic pressure: 'We'll show them eh, lads, we'll show them what we're made of . . .' Gradually all momentum dies; they hang in their traces, crows on wire. Teddy Evans sobs with anger.

SCOTT'S JOURNAL   (VO) Today has been a plod for the foot people and pretty easy going for us.

71. Int. Tent. Night. Crean and Lashly sleep. Teddy Evans lies in his bag, eyes the canvas roof bitterly. Birdie Bowers works out his navigational sums in a notebook in the low light of a paraffin lamp. Evans stirs in his bag, looks at Bowers briefly, turns away.

BOWERS   Sorry about the light, old man. If I don't do it tonight the Owner won't know how to steer us tomorrow. I'm still in the dirt tub over that broken thermometer, I don't want to get in any deeper. (EVANS SAYS NOTHING, BOWERS THINKS) You know, Teddy, the next New Year's Eve we spend in England, we'll gather a whole crowd of poor kiddies and give 'em a slap-up party, what do you say?

Evans grunts, pulls the bag up over his head. Bowers resumes his task, the innocence painful.

72. Int. Morning. Same tent. Bitter wind. PO Evans, Lashly and Crean shortening the sledges. It's freezing, barehanded work and hard enough to make them sweat. PO Evans seems gaunter, wolf-like, skin tight across the bones of the face. He works in sour silence. Lashly's sphinx-like. Crean sings discontinuous snatches from the Irish anti-recruiting song, Arthur McBride.

Teddy Evans appears in the doorflap. The POs work on. Evans checks the progress, exchanges a baleful look with his namesake, leaves.

PO EVANS   (GESTURING VICIOUSLY WITH HIS PLANE) Tight-arsed little bastard. Fuck!

Blood spurts from a slit in his thumb. Lashly hands him a handkerchief. Crean spits tobacco goo over the wound and Evans wraps it. On the sledge, the beads of blood are already freezing.

73. Int. Scott's tent. Scott, Oates, Wilson at work on letters home. In VO, three fragments:

SCOTT: I have led this business — not nominally but actually — and lifted the other people out of difficulty, so that no man will or can say I wasn't fit to lead through the last lap.

WILSON: This may be the last you hear of me for another whole year. All fit and strong and well and only 148 miles to go. We ought to be there in less than a fortnight now.

OATES: My feet are giving me a bit of trouble. They've been continually wet since leaving Hut Point and walking the hard ice has rather made hay of them. I want to start working for my major's exam on the way home. What a lot we'll have to talk about.

Teddy Evans crawls though the flap and across the tent to resume his place. No one speaks. Evans picks up Bowers's theodolite: fiddles with it. Scott finishes a sentence, looks up inquiringly at Evans.

EVANS They're still on the first one. Several hours, I'd say.

Scott looks at Wilson. Wilson sympathizes. Scott resumes his letter. Oates watches the theodolite in Evans's hands.

OATES I'm glad I don't have to bother with that brute. We'd be going round in circles. Thank God we have Birdie, say I.

Scott and Wilson have the same thought at about the same time. Another look, more concerned.

EVANS No problem for a Navy man, Titus. (A DELIBERATE GLANCE AT SCOTT) Provided he's not rusty.

Evans begins to show Oates how it's used. Scott watches the instrument being handled, a stain of fear inside the fascination.

Birdie Bowers squeezes in out of the wind. Flops down beside Oates. Scott and Wilson watch him carefully as he takes a notebook from his personal bag and begins his calculations.

74. *Ext. Morning. The two shortened sledges stand on the ice, gear all around them, Bowers in the thick with a clipboard. Oates helps. Scott leaves his tent, begins the walk to the second one. Stands outside a moment, bracing himself; listens to Crean coughing his throat out within; stoops, enters.*

75. *Int. Evans's tent, full of Crean's tobacco smoke. Evans, Crean and Lashly finish their morning mug of chocolate. Crean's taken some into the trachea, coughs violently.*

LASHLY Morning, sir.

SCOTT Morning. (CREAN'S COUGHING EASES) Bad cold you have there, Crean.

CREAN Not really, Captain. But I believe I understand a song half-sung, sir.

SCOTT You were always a sharp one, PO. (CASUAL) I've decided to take my own team on to the Pole. The second sledge will return tomorrow. You've pulled hard and have nothing to be ashamed of at being fagged. That's all. I'd like a word with Lt Evans, if you don't mind.

The POs slowly get to their knees in silence, leave the tent. Evans sits on, mug below lip, face white, impassive. Stress, fatigue and weather have shrivelled the handsome features, dulled the eyes.

SCOTT You'll have a list of instructions for the base camp. Meares will need to bring supplies at least as far as the Beardmore now. (EVANS'S SMILE IS THIN, DISCOMFITING) Now. I propose to make a modification in the plan. Do you think you can make it back with a three-man team? (EVANS' EYES WIDEN) I need to take Bowers on. If you can spare him.

EVANS (SOFTLY) Why don't you just make it an order, captain? (BEAT. FROM SOMEWHERE ELSE) I had your word.

SCOTT I'd prefer you to agree. There was no word, Lieutenant.

EVANS Fine.

SCOTT You agree?

EVANS If you say so.

They stare at each other for some moments in silence.

SCOTT (MOVING TO GO) Good luck.

He leaves. Evans sits on, face mask-like. Tears grease his face. He touches one.

6. Ext. Scott approaches his sledge. Wilson and PO Evans have

243

joined Oates and Bowers restacking. Scott calls Bowers away from the group.

SCOTT I've decided to take my team on, Birdie.

BOWERS (PERFECT; PREFECT) Very good, sir.

SCOTT Plus you. Move your things into my tent this evening, tomorrow you sledge with the Owner.

BOWERS Thank you, sir. (HE FROWNS)

SCOTT Something wrong, Mr Bowers?

BOWERS No, sir, I was wondering about the food and fuel out in the depots — they're in four-man units and there'll be problems dividing them five and three. I'm afraid we brought neither scales nor fluid measure . . .

SCOTT Well, you've got a day to sort all that out, Birdie. Anything else?

BOWERS I'm most obliged, sir.

SCOTT Cut along and have a word with Teddy there. Naturally he's disappointed.

Bowers leaves smartly. Scott proceeds to his sledge.

SCOTT (CALLING FOR ATTENTION) Gentlemen . . . I have decided that my team will go on from tomorrow for the Pole.

PO EVANS God bless you, sir, God bless you.

Scan of the listening faces: Wilson's, calm; PO Evans, agleam; Oates's remote.

SCOTT (CONTINUING) Birdie Bowers joins us. It'll be a squeeze in the tent but an extra oar at this stage of a race can prove invaluable. Carry on, gentlemen.

He walks off towards his tent. Wilson glances at Oates briefly, then jumps from the sledge and catches him up. Scott doesn't stop.

WILSON (ON THE WALK) I imagine you've thought all this through, Con. (SCOTT NODS, DECISIVE) We carry food and fuel for four, can it stretch to five?

SCOTT I don't see why not, with careful husbanding. And a bit of short commons won't kill us. In any case, we need a navigator.

WILSON (SLOWING DOWN, THE MOOD SENSED) Birdie has no ski, remember.

Scott slows, ten paces away. In CU his eyes are wide with panic for a moment. Turns, in control again.

SCOTT (TERSE) Birdie didn't so much as raise it. Why should you, Bill?

He turns, disappears into the tent. Oates arrives at Wilson's shoulder. They exchange a look for a moment.

WILSON Well, Titus, how do you feel?

OATES (IMPASSIVE) I'll go as far as any Navy man, Bill . . . if those are the orders.

He limps away.

77. Ext. Plateau. Caption: Plateau, 87°48′South, 4 January 1912. *Scott's sledge, loaded for five, points south. Evans's, for three, faces north. Lashly, Crean and Teddy Evans give the first sledge a push; the haulers — Scott and Wilson, Oates and PO Evans, and Bowers in the middle, the centre dot on a five-dice — take the strain. It moves. The going is soft drift: Bowers sinks to the knee with every stride. The pushers detach.*

LASHLY (TO TEDDY EVANS) Three cheers is it, sir?

Evans, introspective, broken, takes off his hat and raises three cheers. The sledge moves away down a slight incline. The three wave headgear. Crean's close to tears. Lashly puts on his hat, spits in the snow, moves to their own sledge.

LASHLY'S DIARY (VO) Captain Scott, Captain Oates, Dr Wilson, Mr Bowers and Evans, these are the people going to the Pole. Today have been a very cold wind and low drift, but we have done twelve mile.

78. *Ext. Shot of the receding Pole sledge, the sky ominous ahead.*

79. *Sequence using date-captioned mapping device showing the respective journeys to and from the Pole, together with essential images of those two separate processes: Amundsen's shows speed, ease, organization; Scott's, obduracy, will, correct passion. The Norwegians eat well, the British lick their mess tins; the Norwegians throw water away, the British share a mug of it to the last drop, following its progress with anxious eyes. On the map, the Norwegians descend the Heiberg Glacier in two days (5–6 January) and arrive on the Barrier on the 7th.*

80. *Ext. High biting wind on the plateau. Tent and sledge. Bowers takes his evening reading, huddled against a snow wall.*

81. *Int. Tent. Scott in his bag, beginning his journal by lamp-light. At the top of the new page he writes in bold capitals:* **Tuesday, 9 January: RECORD.** *In medium shot, he riffs through some loose typed pages, finds what he's seeking, reads a moment.*

SCOTT (SOTTO) We've walked Shackleton down. And do you know what he wrote in his diary, three years ago to the day, at this very latitude? I have it here: 'We have shot our bolt and the tale is latitude 88°23'. Whatever regrets may be, we have done our best.' Ha.

Slow pan across the cramped tent. Evans and Oates sleep deeply

In the corner Wilson lies on his back in his bag, his eyes bandaged.
His lips move as if to speak, then fall still. PO Evans fidgets, cries out
briefly, flexes his bandaged hand. The pan returns through this to
Scott, who scribes on, aware of nothing.

82. Ext. Plateau. Fine. The dead march continues. Sweat cascades
from them. Tongues begin to hang, as thirst bites. The sledge nudges
forward across the globe of white.

PO EVANS   (TO OATES) God, I could take a drink of water, sir . . .

SCOTT   You'll have a drink of water when we camp, PO, and
not before. The fuel will not stretch to mid-afternoon
guzzling.

PO EVANS   Aye, aye sir.

83. Int. Tent. Evening. Scott dishes out the pemmican hoosh and
biscuits. It's taken in silence, eaten fast, tastelessly, the biscuits
crumbed into the swill. Scott studies the group.

SCOTT   (EVENTUALLY) One more day like today, good weather
and hard pulling, and the goal will be ours — the end of the
earth. And pray God our efforts will be rewarded with
priority.

PO EVANS   Hear, hear.

Bowers crawls in, frozen, removes his mitts, dumps the theodolite,
gathers his mess tin of hooch and eats.

SCOTT   How's the hand, Taff?

PO EVANS   (HOLDING UP BANDAGED PAW) Coming along, sir. No
problem.

SCOTT   Good man.

84. Ext. Morning. Cold, still. Good visibility. They tie themselves to

247

the sledge. Scott counts to three and they take the strain. Shots of faces creased with effort, as the sledge fails to move. End on Bowers, in the middle, head to one side, straining. His eyes very slowly tighten, as something in the distance catches his attention.

BOWERS   Captain Scott!

SCOTT   (TURNING) What is it?

Bowers points ahead and to the left. Scott and the others follow the arm. Each tries to see, understand. Scott's face is blank. Cut to

85. Ext. Shot of Amundsen's black flag, foregrounded. As the focus loosens, we see Scott's party hauling towards it.

86. They stare at the flag, the dog turds, paw and sledge marks. Bowers unharnesses himself, removes the pouch from the runner, hands it to Scott. Scott takes it, holds it limp in his hand. Oates stares with dour detachment; Wilson is dazed; PO Evans is dazed, hostile. Bowers feels for his Captain.

SCOTT'S JOURNAL   (VO) It is a terrible disappointment. Many bitter thoughts come . . . We must march on to the Pole. All the daydreams must go. It will be a wearisome return.

87. Ext. Slowed-down mute sequence of Scott's approach to the Pole. One by one the flags and markers left by the Norwegians are encountered. The Union Jack is hoisted; a photograph of the five is taken, Bowers pulling the string. In a last image, they arrive at the tent at Polheim. The cross of St Olav flaps in the wind.

88. Int. Scott on one knee inside the spruce brown tent, in Amundsen's praying posture. He studies the book Amundsen has left. Holds two letters in his hand. Stares at the open page, face quite blank. Speaks the names out loud: Hanssen, Hassel, Bjaaland, Wisting. *A pause.* Amundsen. *We see the page; the name. Slow mix to CU of Nansen, staring out of hotel window onto dark snowy street below.*

89. Int. A Hotel in Berlin. Bedroom Suite.

NANSEN   (TO SOMEONE IN ANOTHER ROOM SOMEWHERE BEHIND
HIM) I had a dream. The night before you came to Berlin. A
glacier, white, unending. And a funeral, Kings, Kaisers, in
mourning weeds, on ski. And a coffin, the lid not secured. I
was looking at myself, it was me there, a corpse, elegantly
embalmed, at rest. They carried it through the dignitaries
to the grave — a crevasse, bottomless. And you were there,
across the crevasse, the other side, strong and bold and full
of the future: I saw you from my coffin. You said: Each age
is a dream that is dying, Or one that is coming to birth.

WOMAN   (OOS) See, Fridtjof.

*Nansen turns slowly. In the shadow, his eyes gleam, burn. Kathleen
Scott stands naked in the bathroom doorway, lit from behind. They
stare at each other across the dark room.*

KATHLEEN   (LOW, INTENSE) Tonight you must talk of *life*, Fridtjof.
No dreams of dying.

*Slow mix begins as he crosses the large room to lift her into his arms
and carry her to the bed.*

*90. Ext. Amundsen in close shot, staring at something ahead. He
turns, waves to the approaching sledges, who arrive to share the
crest of the slope with him.*

*Below, on the reverse, we see Framheim, neat and tidy in the clear
air, a mile or so away. Smiles exchanged, simple, relaxed, unshowy.
Caption: 25 January 1912.*

*91. Int. Amundsen collects a paraffin lamp from the galley, leads the
others down the hut. Johansen, Prestrud, Stubberud and Lindstrom
asleep. Amundsen shines the lamp on Lindstrom's face. Lindstrom
comes to. Sees the ring of peering faces.*

LINDSTROM   Oh, you're back. I'll get some food.

He sits up in the bunk, scratches his head, yawns and stretches.

249

AMUNDSEN   It's a Friday, too.

LINDSTROM   (STRUGGLING INTO SHIRT) Is it?

Lindstrom takes the lamp, leads them in his long shirt to the galley, lights a flame under a large pot, pours coffee for the five.

BJAALAND   (PLAYING ALONG) How's the weather been, Adolf?

LINDSTROM   Dreadful. Dreadful.

AMUNDSEN   Ship back?

LINDSTROM   Came by yesterday.

The men drink their coffee in silence, playing the game. Lindstrom busies himself, waiting to hear.

LINDSTROM   (FINALLY, CASUAL) Well, did you get there?

The men frown inquiries of each other.

HANSSEN   The Pole? Oh, yes.

Lindstrom looks around their solemn faces. Smiles suddenly.

LINDSTROM   Good.

92. *Ext.* Fram's *horn sounds, CU.*

93. *Ext. Amundsen stands on the Barrier, watching the embarkation get under way. Thorvald Nilsen stands with him.*

AMUNDSEN   What does the world say, Thorvald?

NILSEN   The British press have cast you as the villain, Chief.
        Predictably, I suppose.

AMUNDSEN Nansen?

NILSEN Defends you to the hilt.

*Silence. Nilsen watches Amundsen sketch something in the snow
with the ski-stick.*

NILSEN What was it like, Chief?

Amundsen looks out at the Bay.

AMUNDSEN (FINALLY) A terrible place.

*A shout from the ship for Nilsen. He waves he's coming. Amundsen's
returned to his sketching.*

NILSEN Did you see anything of Scott?

AMUNDSEN No.

*Nilsen leaves. Amundsen looks down at the drawing he's done. Skis
off. We stay with the snow-figure: it's a Greenland dog.*

*94. (Via dated mapping device, nudging Scott back north from the
Pole to Three Degree Depot, 30 January 1912) Int. Tent. The five sit
as if dead. Scott has his journal open on his lap; sits with eyes half-
closed. Wilson clears the snow-compress from his shin, uncovering a
huge and vivid bruise, swollen, tight, skin red and oedematous.
Oates eases a boot off, eyes clenched against the pain. Bowers, nose
deeply frostbitten, peels Evans's hand-dressing away. Two finger-
nails come away with the gauze. Evans stares at Scott with baleful
intensity, unaware of place, time or self.*

*Oates's sock is off. The foot is desperately swollen, almost black.
Oates covers it with his bag lest it be seen.*

*Scott takes up his journal. Stares dully down at it, trying to make
sense of it.*

SCOTT'S JOURNAL   (VO, HALTING) So it's goodbye to most of the daydreams . . . and a desperate struggle to get the news through first. We have only three days food with us and shall be in queer street if we miss the depot.

95. *Ext. Depot, Lower Glacier. Lashly and Crean dig their way into the ice-cairn, drag boxes from within, prise them open feverishly. Their eyes are raw, sunken; faces shrivelling with hunger. Lashly tries to measure oats, sugar and pemmican. Crean tells him to get a move on, grabs several handfuls into a tin. They move off to the sledge. Teddy Evans lies in his bag on top of the gear, physically broken. Lashly pushes a pieces of chocolate and a biscuit into Evans's hand. Evans tries to find his mouth with them. The biscuit pushes the upper lip up, reveals the bloody gums. Lashly and Crean note it grimly.*

96. *Blizzard from the south. Scott, Wilson, Oates, Bowers and PO Evans have resumed their dead march, blind to everything.*

VI

REJOICE!

Pretitle: Fram, *in pack ice, heading north. Beck in crow's nest calls down directions to Gjertsen at wheel. Caption: February 1912.*

Amundsen, Hanssen, Hassel, Wisting and Bjaaland sprawl in the sun, eyes closed, on the upper deck; seamen's gear and soft slippers.

Title: THE LAST PLACE ON EARTH

CU Amundsen, eyes closed, sun warming the face.

AMUNDSEN   (VO; TAP OF TELEGRAPH KEYS BENEATH) Askeladden has scaled the glass mountain. The Lady is ours.

A shadow falls across his face.

STUBBERUD   (OOS, QUIETLY) Chief?

Amundsen opens eyes, props himself upright. Studies Stubberud's face. Sees the vivid bruise below the eye.

STUBBERUD   Mr Nilsen'd like a word, Chief.

Amundsen nods; Stubberud leaves. Amundsen stands.

HASSEL   (PROPPED) See his face? (AMUNDSEN SNIFFS, NODS)

Johansen. Drunk as a pig last night and handing it out.

Amundsen nods, lips clipped in thought.

Terra Nova, *Cape Evans, on ice-anchors, preparing to unload. Rennick organizes seamen around the eight Indian army mules on the lower deck. Pennell scans the littoral, Cape Evans, sea-ice, through the Goetz-glass. Picks up Meares and Simpson speeding towards them on a dog-sledge, waving and shouting from a mile away. Pennell relays the news to the men below. Scans south across the sea-ice in direction of Hut Point; picks up a four-man hauling party, stopped and waving.*

Sea-ice. Atkinson, Wright, Cherry-Garrard and Keohane stand in their traces, cheering the boat. The exhaustion has bitten deep into their gaunt, blackened faces. Cherry sinks to his haunches, crying with relief, his glasses steamed over.

One-Ton Depot, Barrier. Tent. sledge, cairn. Crean painfully digs out the depot-cairn; stacks provisions in the snow. Inside the tent, Teddy Evans lies in his bag, mid-way between agony and coma. Lashly, bitten black by frost, patiently prepares the primus. Crean in, with gallon paraffin tin, face grim. He shakes the can.

CREAN   This bugger's half empty, Bill.

Lashly looks up, listens to the thin swill of fuel.

LASHLY   Well, Tom. Take our share. No more, mind.

Crean leaves. Lashly places a pannikin of snow on the primus, turns the flame down.

EVANS   Leave me. Save yourselves.

LASHLY   (SLOW, NOT LOOKING) We'll not do that, sir.

Upper Beardmore Glacier. Edgar Evans hangs, at the full stretch of his harness, down a large crevasse, in thick weather, singing hymn,

VI   REJOICE!

The Message *(from opening of Part III), and talking to the air around him. His face is ravaged by frost, the nose frozen dough. Above, Oates and Bowers prepare a rescue rope to draw Evans back to reality.*

EVANS   Oh we'll get there first, PO, you trust in me, he says, I'll see you through. (SINGS A LINE OF THE HYMN) So we're lost, you see, we're lost, *he* doesn't know the bloody way, we're goin' round in circles. (ANOTHER LINE) God, my old lady makes a grand apple pie. Beautiful, brown, crisp, fragrant, and that sharp juice below the crust. O Bronwen. O Bron. Hungry, Bron. I eat the same as them and I'm twice the size. Pulling this rock as well, you see, specimens . . . forty pounds of it . . . for Science, see . . . half-starved and lost and pullin' rock for Science, Bron . . .

He sings on, quite lustily now, aware of nothing. Scott appears at the lip of the crevasse.

SCOTT   (HARSH, NAVAL) PO Evans!

EVANS   (FAST, REFLEX) Sir!

SCOTT   Take that rope!

Evans removes his mitts, takes the rope they've lowered and ties it round his shoulders and waist. We see the gangrenous hand through the threadbare bandage. He begins the mutter again.

Long high shot of the Polar party, effecting the rescue, in a chaos of crevasses. 'Horrible light, which made everything look fantastic.'

SCOTT'S JOURNAL   (VO) In a very critical situation . . . In the afternoon, refreshed by tea, we went forward, confident of covering the remaining distance . . .

Polar party pitching camp in the ice.

VI. Rejoice!

SCOTT'S JOURNAL   (VO) . . . but by a fatal chance we kept too far
to the left and arrived in a horrid maze of crevasses and
fissures. Divided counsels caused our course to be erratic
after this. Finally we decided to camp . . . and here we are,
after a very short supper and one meal only remaining in
the food bag; the depot doubtful in locality. We *must* get
there tomorrow . . . Pray God we have better weather.

*1. Int. Tent. The biscuit tin is handed round: one each. When
Bowers takes his own, the tin is empty. Mugs are half-filled with tea.
The five men eat in silence. Oates is retruded; carapaced; eyes
closed. Evans shifts across several levels of reality with seamless
transilience. Wilson's eyes are bandaged and hurting. Bowers is
bright, whistling in the dark, missing Wilson's benedictory glances.
Scott prepares to write up the day.*

BOWERS   I make it about ten miles, sir. With a decent day's
weather we could be there tomorrow evening . . .

SCOTT   *Must*, Mr Bowers. No 'could be' about it. (INDICATES
BISCUIT TIN) Of course, if we hadn't found ourselves
inexplicably deficient of a full day's biscuit allowance,
we might have afforded ourselves the luxury of 'could
be's'.

*Bowers bows his head, disturbed by the mention. Scott begins his
journal.*

EVANS   (SUDDEN; A PARROT) Pretty polly. Pretty polly.

*He subsides as suddenly. Scott looks at him, then on a reflex at the
bandaged Wilson, who sips his tea impassively.*

SCOTT   Still, if Meares and Dmitri do get the dogs out as far as
Southern Barrier Depot, say, none of this will seem of the
least importance . . . Isn't that so, Bill? We had problems on
the *Discovery* journey too, eh?

WILSON   (SLOWLY) Indeed we did, Con. (PAUSE) Though to tell the truth, I rather hoped I'd had my fill of short commons.

Scott flicks a look at Wilson, sensing criticism.

EVANS   (QUICK; IN AND OUT) It was old Shackleton then, wasn't it . . .

Taps his dough-white nose with dark green finger. Closes his eyes. Dozes. Oates chuckles softly, eyes closed still; dreaming, perhaps. Scott watches Wilson a moment longer. Wilson's face signals nothing behind the eye-bandage.

SCOTT   (EVENTUALLY) Birdie, if you're planning another shot at getting some readings before we turn in, I suggest you get on with it.

BOWERS   Yes, I'll do that, sir. (HUNTS FOR THEODOLITE, ADJUSTS HIS HOOD AND MITTS)

SCOTT   You might hunt out a set of finneskoe for me, while you're at it, old chap. (WAGGING FEET) These are pretty well shot.

Bowers crawls stiffly from the tent, dismissed. Scott fiddles gear from the medicine chest. Huddles closer to Wilson.

SCOTT   (SOTTO) Let's take a look at those eyes, shall we, Bill.

WILSON   Kind of you, Con.

Scott angles Wilson, lays the back of his head in his lap, removes the bandage. Looks down into the ghastly visionless eyes. Prepares the dropper with cocaine solution. His hands are gentle, deft, caring. Their faces come close: inverted lovers, in their way.

SCOTT   (ALMOST A WHISPER) Dear, dear friend. I don't know what I would have done without you. Ready? (HE RELEASES A DELICATE DROP INTO THE RIGHT EYE. WILSON CHEWS ON

THE SCALDING PAIN FOR SOME MOMENTS) And the other. (A SECOND DROP) Now keep your head back for a minute or it'll run out again.

Scott's hands caress Wilson's face, gentling temples and eyelids with the pads of his thumbs. He glances down the tent. Oates's eyes are still shut. Evans is laboriously attempting to remove his left boot, but the procedure seems to have been erased from his muscular memory.

SCOTT We'll see this thing through together, Bill. We always have. The dogs will be our salvation, you'll see. Meares and Dmitri . . .

WILSON Meares?

SCOTT Meares? Did I say Meares?

Scott's exhausted mind struggles panickily to sort things out. Wilson's snow-blind POV of Scott's stupefied face.

EVANS (OOS) Ah, there's pretty.

Scott looks down the tent. His eyes shrink in disgust from the sight. Behind him, Bowers crawls wearily in.

BOWERS I have the finneskoe, sir. Afraid we still have the cloud COV . . .(HE SEES EVANS'S PRETTINESS) Oh God.

Evans holds his boot and sock in his hands. His foot bears a grisly tumid blister the size of a fist. Oates opens his eyes; studies the foot rather clinically.

OATES Well, you've made a bugger of that, haven't you, Taff?

Evans smiles, almost proudly. CU Scott, Wilson's head in his hands.

2. Mapping device and images of heavy hauling push through to Mid-Glacier Depot. Bowers digs out the cairn in mist.

SCOTT'S JOURNAL   (VO) The fog still hung over all and we went on for an hour, checking our bearings. Then suddenly Wilson saw the actual depot flag. It was an immense relief and we were soon in possession of our three and a half days food. The relief to all is inexpressible.

Oates and Wilson exchange a grave look across the sledge they're unpacking. Evans lolls against the sledge, face bloated with scurvy.

SCOTT'S JOURNAL   (VO) We ought to have kept the bearings of our outward camps; that is where we have failed.

3. Ext. Lower Glacier. Scott, Wilson, Oates and Bowers pull on in silence. From a distance behind them, the rise and fall of Evans's voice as he follows in their tracks.

EVANS   (OOS) Daisy, Daisy give me your answer do
I'm half crazy all for the love of you
It won't be a stylish marriage
We can't afford a carriage
But you'll look sweet
Upon the seat
Of a bicycle made for two.

Cut to

Evans, twenty-odd paces behind, precariously on ski, stooping to pick up a fallen mitt.

EVANS   Every little helps, as the old lady said when she pissed in the sea. (SHOUTING AHEAD) Piss off, go on, why dontcher. You always pissed more than you drank, dintcher. I shoulda known you'd bugger us all one day. You couldn't find the way through a garden gate. It was the same the last time. Yes sir no sir three bags full sir. Snotrag. Food, Food. (THE SHOUTS ECHO DOWN THE GLACIER; THEN SOFT) I need food.

Cut to the group ahead, hauling grimly. The voice behind wells and washes, its meanings fractured but unavoidable.

259

SCOTT'S JOURNAL   (VO) A very trying position. Evans has nearly broken down in brain, we think. He is absolutely changed from his normal confident self and has become impossible.

4. *Ext. Lower Glacier. Pitching camp, unloading sledge. The work is slow, bitter, silent. PO Evans is slumped against the sledge, incapable. The four work round him. Scott's lips are tight. Oates stands over Evans for a moment, looking down; sees the urine darken the crotch.*

5. *Int. Tent. Scott writes his journal by thin lamp. The others sleep. Scott flicks looks at Evans from time to time. Stops writing occasionally, to listen for breathing.*

6. *Lower Glacier. Forenoon. The four pull on. Dim behind them, the wandering Welshman, his voice dying on the still air.*

7. *Ext. Lunch camp. Sunshine. The four sit downwind of the tent, in its mouth, preparing the last of their pemmican over the primus. Bowers makes calculations in his notebook.*

SCOTT   (TO BOWERS) Well?

BOWERS   Three miles, perhaps four. As long as we can light on it easily, we'll be there well before evening.

Scott nods, watches Wilson dig the thawing pemmican with a spoon. Silence.

OATES   (SLOW) Shouldn't we see where Evans is?

No one speaks. No one looks. Bowers pockets his notebook.

SCOTT   (EVENTUALLY) Time enough when we've had our hoosh. He'll probably have caught us up by then. (LONG PAUSE) We'll need all our strength to get us to the depot.

Wilson begins doling out the stew. Oates's eyes follow Scott's. Scott does not look at him.

8. Ext. Evans, on hands and knees, ski abandoned. He searches the sky, looking for something. Finds it. Snarls, baring his bloodied gums. A shout, from the distance. Another. Evans begins to weep.

EVANS (DISTINCT) Don't let them find me please. Please don't let them find me. Please.

He lowers himself face down in the snow, shrivelling his frame, begins to undo his clothing.

9. Int. Tent. Scott and Bowers, in tacit vigil, stare down the dim tent. Oates, across from them, watches them sardonically.

Scott's POV of Wilson, on his knees, holding a mirror to Evans's lips. He takes it away, studies it, runs a finger across the surface, places an ear to Evans's chest, his face to Scott. In that position, his eyes meet Scott's and the word is passed.

10. Ext. Rear view of the four, some distance away, hauling north. Very slow track back gradually reveals a four-foot cairn, a crude ski-cross in the roof.

SCOTT'S JOURNAL (VO) It is a terrible thing to lose a companion in this way, but calm reflection shows that there could not have been a better ending to the terrible anxieties of the past week.

Slow mix to

11. Int. Tent. Six biscuits and four sticks of chocolate spread out on a handkerchief. A hand divides them into two halves. Another hand comes in to take its half.

12. Ext. Tent. Sledge. Crean crawls out of the tent. Lashly follows. Both immensely worn. Crean gets onto his ski. Lashly studies the clear sky for signs of weather.

LASHLY Last chance, Tom.

CREAN   No, no Bill. You're better here doin' the doctoring, my love. Besides, a bit of a walk'll do me good.

LASHLY   I'll fix a marker somehow, so's you can find us. (CREAN SAYS NOTHING, STARING NORTH) I'll pray you have good weather too.

CREAN   Aye, I may have one or two words meself.

LASHLY   Here. (HE HANDS CREAN ONE OF HIS BISCUITS. CREAN LOOKS AT IT FOR SOME MOMENTS)

CREAN   (TAKING IT) Thanks, Bill.

They shake hands, a formal moment. Crean stifflegs off over the Barrier snow. Lashly watches a while; checks the time on his watch (10 a.m.); hobbles back to the tent.

13. Int. Tent. Teddy Evans in CU, eyes closed. His face is bloated with scurvy. There is dried blood around his lips and nose. He could already be dead. Noise of Lashly returning. The eyes slowly open. Lashly crawls down the tent to look at his patient.

EVANS   (QUITE LUCID) Where are we, PO?

LASHLY   A bit short of Hut Point, sir. Crean's walked on to get help. How're you feeling, sir?

EVANS   How far?

LASHLY   Thirty-odd mile, sir.

Silence. Lashly breaks a stick of chocolate.

LASHLY   Try some chocolate, sir.

Evans shakes his head. Begins to shiver, a brief but violent spasm. Lashly waits till it's over, then moves to his own bag-area.

EVANS You should have gone with him.

Lashly gets into his bag, lies down to rest.

LASHLY I'm going to take a nap for an hour, if you don't mind, sir. Then I'll ski back to that motorsledge, there's a few things back there could come in handy.

He turns on his side to sleep. Evans stares at the canvas above his head.

EVANS Do you happen to know the date, PO?

LASHLY 19th February, sir. 110th day out.

Cut to

14. *Ext. Cape Evans. Hut, surrounded by newly unloaded supplies. Mules.* Terra Nova *on ice-anchors at the edge of the ice.*

Atkinson checks provision boxes on the two sledges. Dmitri and Meares harness the two dog-teams. Meares says something in Russian to Dmitri, moves to the back of the sledge, as Atkinson enters his last ticks on the inventory sheets.

MEARES It's possible I'll have left by the time you get back, Atch, so I'll say goodbye now. Good luck. (HE HOLDS HIS HAND OUT)

ATKINSON (TAKING IT) Thanks, old chap. And a safe journey home.

MEARES I erm . . . I hope you understand my reasons, Atch . . .

ATKINSON (GENTLY) Don't be silly, Cecil. You made your intentions crystal clear before we even set out and the Owner must have considered every angle when he decided to keep the dogs on an additional six weeks.

MEARES   It's just that . . . I never imagined it'd all fall to you like this.

ATKINSON   (CHEERFUL) No more did I, old chap. But Campbell's still out and Simpson's recalled and Dr Muggins is I/C everything. (LAUGHS) Be a good chap, have a word with Dmitri, tell him I'm a capital fellow and one he may trust . . . I have to say my farewells within.

He walks off to the hut. We go in with him.

15. Int. Hut. Unpacked provision boxes litter the floor. Pennell, Cherry-Garrard, Wright and Simpson lounge around the gentlemen's table, finishing the luncheon-wine amid the debris of their meal. The atmosphere is relaxed, good-natured, the young at their ease. Cherry rests his glass on a film-reel can on the end of the table.

PENNELL   Ah, here's the new Owner, any last minute instructions, Captain?

The others laugh. Atkinson grins along with them, the mildest of men.

ATKINSON   I'll see some of you blighters later on, no doubt. Jim. (SHAKING SIMPSON'S HAND) It's been a pleasure. Safe journey home.

SIMPSON   You're a gentlemen, sir. I wish you well, Atch.

ATKINSON   Penny. (THEY SHAKE HANDS) Give Campbell as long as you can to rendezvous, won't you, even if it means carting him off to New Zealand without letting us know.

PENNELL   I daren't risk being iced in, Atch, but I'll do everything I can to get them aboard before leaving.

ATKINSON   Don't worry about Griff. They can come home on their own paddle. (PENNELL NODS REASSURANCE. ATKINSON LOOKS AROUND, RELUCTANT TO LEAVE) Cherry. Silas. I'll see you anon. Don't stray too far, there may be need of you.

WRIGHT   Oh Atch, there's a film arrived for the Owner, we wondered if we might put it on one night for the men.

ATKINSON   What is it?

WRIGHT   (READING THE STICKER) No idea.

ATKINSON   (THINKING IT THROUGH BY THE BOOK) Well, Silas, if it's addressed to the Captain I fancy he might prefer it unopened when he returns. (LOOKS AROUND THE LITTERED HUT FLOOR) I know you'll have this place in spanking order by then. Hut Point awaits.

He turns. They follow him outside, glasses in hand, to wave their goodbyes. Meares shakes hands with Dmitri, gives him a pouch of tobacco, stands to one side to wave them off.

Dmitri leaves, driving well. Atkinson's mild urgings have no effect on his dogs. Meares clubs the leaders into life and the sledge jerks forward. Ironic cheers and banter from the hut party. Atkinson hangs on grimly, shaken around by the unfamiliar procedure.

16. Ext. Night. The sun has gone at midnight. The sky is filled with its eery underglow. Deep cold.

Crean shuffles forward, as if from memory. He's scarred, bitten, almost shot. He builds a rough mound of snow with mittened hands, climbs labouringly up to scan ahead. Sees next to nothing. Slumps to a sitting position by the mound. Fumbles his pocket for a fingerful of fluff and biscuit crumbs to chew on. Checks the time on his watch (3.30 a.m.) Draws himself painfully to his feet.

A dog barks. Another. Crean lumbers off, listening for the dogs' directions.

Stops. Blinks his eyes several times. His POV of Hut Point, lights in the window, a quarter of a mile away.

SCOTT (VO) I don't understand it. It's quite beyond my comprehension.

17. Int. Scott's tent. Southern Barrier Depot. Bowers prepares pony hoosh over primus. Scott has a gallon paraffin can in his hands, the lid off. He swills the fluid around the can. The others sit in their bags in their separate silences. Wilson's eyes are red-raw, leaky; Bowers's face is trenched by frost. Oates bends forward, slowly cutting the front of his boot-upper with a pair of scissors.

SCOTT First it's biscuit, now it's fuel. Quite unaccountable. What a miserable jumble.

He looks darkly at Bowers, who stares at canvas, unhappy. Wilson holds up the can-stopper he's been examining.

WILSON See. The leather washer. Rotted.

Bowers takes it, looks briefly, hands it to Scott, who replaces it on the can without looking.

SCOTT That flame's too high, Birdie. We're going to have to be *very* saving on fuel from now on.

Birdie cuts the flame by half. The still half-frozen hoosh in the pannikin subsides almost immediately.

SCOTT I think I shall need to instigate a thorough investigation into these shortages before next season, Bill. It's not good enough.

Silence, save for the reduced primus-hum.

OATES (FROM NOWHERE, STILL NUMBLY SCISSORING) Never mind. There's always the dogs.

Scott and Wilson exchange glances. Scott looks down the tent at Oates. Oates cuts laboriously on.

18. Ext. Southern Barrier. The four slog on, over vicious sastrugi, snow crystals feathering the air. Shots of the four in turn, closing on Scott.

SCOTT'S JOURNAL (VO) A little despondent again. We had another really terrible surface and only covered four miles. It really will be a bad business if we are to have this pulling all the way through. Have ten days provision from tonight and shall have less than seventy miles to go to Mid-Barrier. I don't know what to think . . .

Slow mix to

19. Int. Hut Point. A mug held up for cocoa; a second. CU Wright; Cherry-Garrard; Dmitri, pouring. The new arrivals are chilled, raw-faced; huddle over the stove and sip their drink. The wind howls outside. Cherry's glasses begin to steam up.

Dmitri returns to the table, resumes peeling and chopping several pounds of onions on a board, over which he slices half a dozen limes. Wright watches, frowning, as Dmitri carries the board down the room. By the bunks, Atkinson tends Lashly's and Crean's frostbitten feet. Teddy Evans lies in a coma in the furthest bunk, death-like. Dmitri puts the fruit and veg on a stool by Atkinson's medical box. Lashly and Crean dip in at once.

Atkinson stands, makes his way to the stove, begins to wash his hands in the can of warming water.

ATKINSON Thank you for coming, both of you. As you can see, I've hit a bit of a snag.

CHERRY-G Poor Teddy looks pretty grim, Atch, what happened?

ATKINSON (TAKING A STOOL TO JOIN THEM) Broke down. The POs hauled him forty miles and more to save him. (WRIGHT WHISTLES) I hope it won't have been in vain. (HE LOOKS TOWARDS EVANS'S BUNK)

WRIGHT The boat'll be here tomorrow as requested. (BEAT) Is he bad? (ATKINSON NODS TERSELY) Scurvy?

Atkinson's index-finger goes to his lips in perfect naval reflex.

ATKINSON Let's just say he's . . . a very sick man.

They sit in silence for some moments. Atkinson picks up a clipboard: chart of the Barrier, notes on the Original Plan, additional notes from Scott delivered to Simpson by returning parties.

CHERRY-G. (CHECKING THE BUNKS: HARDLY DARING TO ASK) Where's the fourth, Atch?

Atkinson blinks, follows Cherry's gaze down the room.

ATKINSON Five went on. They came back a three-man party . . .

WRIGHT (EMPHATIC) Really! My God!

The silence hums with meaning. Wright looks down the hut at the POs in disbelief.

ATKINSON (MILD; DELIBERATE) Well, the thing is, chaps, one of you is going to have to do the dog-run with Dmitri in my place. It really *is* touch and go with old Teddy there, and as the only doctor around I feel it's my clear duty to stay with him.

Cherry and Wright exchange looks briefly. Atkinson studies his chart and notes again.

ATKINSON I've undertaken a complete analysis of the times and distances of all the returning parties and have no reason to suppose the five-man Polar party will be travelling less fast than those already back at base did . . . I've also analyzed their requirements for the journey back against provisions awaiting them at the depots; and am quite certain that the earliest they can need for additional supply is One Ton

Depot at 79° 30', which on my reckoning they cannot reach before March. (PAUSE) Captain Scott's instructions . . . (HE WAVES THE CLUTCH OF NOTES AND PLANS) are not wholly clear on the question of the dogs and their role at this juncture — or at least I can't make too much sense of them. What they seem to boil down to is to shift food and fuel 'as far south as possible', hoping to meet the Polar party and 'hurry them home' for the ship, but in no circumstance to 'risk the dogs' for another season's work, should there be one. Well, all that's a little like squaring the circle, but given the state of the pack-ice I think we can forget about hurrying them home for the ship and concentrate on getting provisions out to One Ton to await them should they be required. The only matter of substance to decide is which of you will make the journey. Cherry, did you ever take that navigation course we talked about in the winter?

CHERRY-G.   Afraid not, Atch. The Captain said I'd be wasting my time.

Atkinson chews his lip a little, the burden of command taking its toll.

ATKINSON   (TO WRIGHT) But *you* know how to navigate, Silas, is that right?

WRIGHT   Absolutely. But I'll be running a dozen different experiments at Cape Evans single-handed once Sunny Jim takes the boat. (SARDONIC) Of course, losing half a season's scientific results mightn't matter one jot if Scott's got priority at the Pole, but if he hasn't . . . Science may be the only thing we have to take back with us. (PAUSE) You know I'll go if you tell me to, Atch, and willingly.

ATKINSON   (UNCERTAIN) Mmm. It's difficult.

Silence again. They stare at the stove.

CHERRY-G.   (WHITELY) No it isn't, Atch. I'll do it. Happy to.

ATKINSON   You're a brick, Cherry.

CHERRY-G.   (GIGGLING) Never driven a dog in my life, can't travel ten yards without cleaning my specs and couldn't find my way through a garden gate, but we'll get by, won't we, Dmitri, old sport?

Dmitri smokes his pipe at the table, nods his head impassively. Atkinson shows Cherry the chart of the Barrier, the route pencilled in.

ATKINSON   It's a routine journey. Dmitri knows what to do. No need to break your neck, as long as you're there by the 4th. You are a brick, Cheery-Blackguard.

A sob, a moan, from Evans down the room; a fevered jumble of instructions. Atkinson moves down the room to calm him. Wright follows, curious. Cherry-Garrard sits on whitefaced before the fire. Flicks a glance or two at Dmitri. Smiles when he catches his eye.

Slow mix to

20. Mapping device tracking Cherry-Garrard's route from Hut Point to the Barrier, with images of Cherry's desperate attempts to drive dogs. Over this:

CHERRY-G.   (VO AS IF COMMITTING ORDERS TO MEMORY) One Ton Depot as far possible leave the food there . . . If Scott not yet there judge for self what to do. Scott not in any way *dependent* on dogs for his return . . . dogs not to be risked for next season.

The mapping device tracks on ahead in broken line to One Ton Depot; pauses; continues south 120 miles to reveal the position of the Polar party at Mid-Barrier Depot.

Images of camp-pitching invade the white chart.

21. Ext. Mid-Barrier Depot. Cold, bright, cloudless plain. Scott and Wilson labour to pitch tent. Bowers digs out the depot-cairns. Oates

*leans against the full-sail sledge, incapable. Wilson and Scott work
around him.*

*Bowers fumbles, a little feverishly, for the fuel stock in the base of
the gouged cairn. Locates the paraffin can, draws it out, swills it
around, removes the cap to reveal the rotted leather washer. Over
this:*

SCOTT'S JOURNAL   (VO) Lunch. Misfortunes rarely come singly.
    We marched to the Middle Barrier Depot fairly easily
    yesterday afternoon and since then have suffered three
    distinct blows that have placed us in a bad position. First
    we found a bare half gallon of oil instead of the full; with
    most rigid economy it can scarce carry us to the next depot
    on this surface: seventy-one miles away.

*22. Int. Tent. CU of primus flame, very low. Shot of pemmican in
pannikin, barely thawing.*

SCOTT'S JOURNAL   (VO) Second, Titus Oates disclosed his feet,
    the toes showing very bad indeed, evidently bitten by the
    late temperatures . . .

Wilson wordlessly inspects Oates's bloated, hopeless toes.

*23. Ext. On the march, three men pulling, Oates labouring behind
on ski.*

SCOTT'S JOURNAL   (VO) Worse was to come. In spite of strong
    wind and full sail we have only done 5½ miles . . . We are
    in *very* queer street since there is no doubt we cannot do
    the extra marches, and feel the cold horribly. Amongst
    ourselves we are unendingly cheerful but what each man
    feels in his heart I can only guess. Providence to our aid!
    We can expect little from man now except the possibility of
    extra food at the next depot — a poor one.

*24. Ext. Blizzard, clearing. One Ton Depot. Two sledges, still heavily
loaded. Caption: One Ton Depot, 4–10 March. Cherry-Garrard*

stands a few paces from the tent staring south into the wind. The face is raked by frost; eyes made anxious by responsibility. He sees nothing. Turns towards the tent.

25. Int. Tent. Dmitri sits immobile in his bag, smoking his pipe, staring at canvas. There's tea on the primus. Cherry-G. pours a mug, squats concernedly just inside the entrance.

CHERRY-G.   How's your arm, old chap? (HE GESTURES WITH HIS ARM. DMITRI POINTS TO HIS RIGHT ARM, THEN TRACES THE PROBLEM DOWN THE WHOLE OF HIS RIGHT SIDE AND LEG. SHAKES HIS HEAD) Fact is, I'm not sure what to do for the best. (LOOKING FOR HELP) I believe it may be clearing . . . (PICKS UP HIS HALF-FOLDED CHART, STUDIES IT) It's another sixty miles to the depot at Mount Hooper, a hundred and ninety from there to base. (HE TRIES TO INTEREST DMITRI IN THE CHART, THE PROBLEM. DMITRI SITS STONEFACED, QUITE UNHAPPY) If we go on, we run the risk of simply missing them on the march — and then they'll arrive here to find the depot unreplenished. In any case, we have only two days surplus ration ourselves, not enough to get us there and back again. On the other hand, in the remote event that they're already experiencing some difficulty . . .

DMITRI   (TURNING HEAD, SUDDEN) Go Mount Hooper, Mister? Easy. Dmitri knowing how.

CHERRY-G.   (FROWNING, INNOCENT) Tell me.

DMITRI   Dog eat dog, mister.

A wide grin. Cherry-Garrard's smile is rictal, the face ghastly with wear and worry. Dmitri lies down in his bag, turns on his side, his back to the gentleman explorer.

26. Ext. Night. Five-foot depot cairn, dug out. Sledge, tackle. Tent. Dense swirl of snow and ice-crystals.

SCOTT'S JOURNAL   (VO) 9 March. Mount Hooper Depot. Blizzard.

272

Cold comfort. Shortage on our allowance all round. I don't know that anyone is to blame, but generosity and thoughtfulness have not been abundant. The dogs which would have been our salvation have evidently failed. Meares had a bad trip home, I suppose. It's a miserable jumble . . .

27. Int. Tent. Low light. Much silent agony. The cold is intense, the scurvy signs unmistakable. They sit in a stupor of fatigue and pain. Still Scott pushes pencil across paper, creating the myth. Oates watches him dully, as if down a tunnel.

SCOTT'S JOURNAL (VO) Titus Oates is very near the end, one feels. What he or we will do God only knows. We discussed the matter after breakfast; he is a brave fine fellow and understands the situation, but he practically asked for advice. Nothing could be said but to urge him to march as long as he could . . .

He closes the pencil in the book, lays it aside, glances round the tent.

SCOTT How does it look, Birdie?

Bowers surfaces slowly. Opens the notebook in his lap.

BOWERS (MECHANICAL; SPRING GONE) Well, it's getting a bit tight, sir. At our present rate of travel, we'll still be thirteen miles short of One Ton when the food runs out. Even then we're going to need the weather on our side.

The wind howls. Nobody speaks. Scott thinks about lighting his pipe. Picks up journal again.

SCOTT Haven't seen you doing much scribbling of late, Bill.

WILSON (INTURNED) Used up all my pages.

Oates lies painfully down in his bag. Scott watches him a moment, then reads over what he's written, closes the book and begins to signal time to turn in by preparing for bed. Wilson and Bowers follow the instruction, boys in the dorm. Scott dowses the lamp. They lie in the near-darkness.

SCOTT (EVENTUALLY) Bill, would you happen to know whether the opium tabloids are in the sledge-box or the bag?

WILSON (SLOW) I have them. Why do you ask?

SCOTT I think it might be a good idea to divide them up for our private keeping. In the event that matters grow hopeless . . . for one of us . . . or all, each should have the means of expedition to hand, to use or not as he sees fit.

Wind howls. Dies a little.

WILSON I'm afraid I could only do that under protest, Con . . .

SCOTT Protest noted, Bill.

Silence, between wind's rage and lull.

OATES (HALF-SLURRED BY SLEEP) If One Ton Depot had been laid where we'd intended — at 80° South, we'd be all but there already, wouldn't we, Birdie?

BOWERS (SLOW) I suppose that's right, Soldier.

OATES (ALMOST DREAMY) Seems a high price to pay . . . for a pair of ponies who were down to die anyway. . .

Slow mix to

28. Int. One Ton Depot. Calm, cold. Cherry-Garrard packs snow with a spade onto the enlarged depot cairn.

Dmitri puts dogs into traces. The sledge-loads are vastly reduced. Cherry-Garrard stows his spade, takes out a Goetz glass, scans south for some moments. Dmitri watches him.

DMITRI   (CALLING) All ready for going now, one minute, mister.

Cherry closes the glass, closes on the sledge.

GARRARD   How's the arm, old chap? (HE POINTS TO HIS OWN ARM BY WAY OF ILLUSTRATION)

DMITRI   Better a bit.

He cracks his whip over the dogs, to get them to their feet. Both teams set up a din. Dmitri badmouths them in fierce Russian. Cherry-Garrard stands by, in his hands.

DMITRI   To home, yes, mister?

Cherry looks south briefly, the moment come.

GARRARD   I suppose so.

He gathers his reins; watches Dmitri assault the dogs into action, the right arm doing its full share of the work.

Slow pan through 180° from empty north to empty south, taking in the distant Worcester mountains to the west.

29. Montaged in the dead white, nightmares images of Scott's party on the march, spanning several days:

a) Wilson unable to get off his ski at the end of the day;
b) Bowers's nose dead, doughy;
c) Oates unable to place foot in boot in the morning; the others waiting;
d) The sledge capsizing; being righted;
e) Oates, one leg after the other: his feet.

SCOTT'S JOURNAL   (VO) Our fuel dreadfully low and the poor Soldier nearly done. It is pathetic enough because we can do nothing for him; more hot food might do a little, but only a little I fear. We none of us expected these terribly low temperatures . . . We are two pony marches and four miles about from our depot.

The last line reverberates across separate images of the four men. On Oates, the 'two pony marches' rhythms the depot-laying dialogue within:

SCOTT   I have had more than enough of this cruelty to animals and I'm not going to defy my feelings for the sake of a few days' march.

OATES   (AFTER THOUGHT) I'm afraid you may regret it, sir.

SCOTT   Regret it or not, my dear Oates, I've made up my mind like a Christian.

f) the desperate, slow-motion business of unloading sledge and pitching camp;

SCOTT'S JOURNAL   (VO) If we were all fit I should have hopes of getting through, but the poor Soldier has become a terrible hindrance, though he does his utmost and suffers much, I fear. We hope against hope that the dogs have been; then we might pull through.

g) Scott cooking supper over almost dead primus in the dark of the tent. They sit huddled, frozen hulks in the gloom. Oates sobs a little under his breath.

30. Int. Tent. Meal ended. Bowers lies, on his back, lips flickering in prayer. Wilson is slumped, head over hands, dozing, dreaming, waking. Scott blows on his pencil hand, the book open and ready to receive. Oates stares at the greens, blues and reds of his elephantine left foot.

OATES   (DISTINCT, SUDDEN) Do we have a gun?

Scott's head jerks. Wilson bobs to the surface. Both look at Oates: face, foot.

WILSON   There's no gun, I'm afraid, old fellow.

OATES   This foot's . . . (THE PAIN CUTS HIM LIKE WIRE) no good.

Scott begins writing up. Oates looks from Wilson to Scott and back again.

OATES   Help me, will you.

WILSON   Not much we can do, old chap.

OATES   Leave me. Tomorrow. In my bag.

The pain greases his face. He begins to sway, seeking ease somewhere.

OATES   I need. Your help.

WILSON   We can't do that, Titus.

OATES   Give me a gun.

WILSON   There is no gun. (BEAT) I can give you something for the pain.

He takes out a syringe and a tube of morphine, begins to prepare them. Scott watches, huddled over the record.

WILSON   Lie down, Soldier, there's a good fellow.

Oates lies down in his opened bag. Wilson ponders where to inject; decides on the thigh. Draws Oates's trousers down; reveals the gaping hole of his ancient wound, the scar-tissue melted without trace, devitaminized. Wilson injects the morphine into the other one, rather jerkily, watches the immediate and growing effect on Oates's face.

WILSON   Please God you don't have another day like this, Soldier. Or any of us.

BOWERS   Amen.

Scott flicks a look at the still huddle in Bowers's bag.

Oates is tranced.

Wilson looks at Scott. Scott takes the stare.

31. Ext. The tent, under drift. Blizzard building, the sledge already almost invisible.

SCOTT'S JOURNAL   (VO) It must be near the end, but a pretty merciful end. No idea there could be temperatures like this at this time of year with such winds . . .

32. Int. Tent. Scott and Bowers stare down the tent. Wilson has his ear on Oates's chest, a mirror in his hand. Scott and Bowers wait for the signal. CU Oates, eyes closed. CU Wilson, listening for death. CU Oates, eyes open. Wilson's eyes are drawn to them.

WILSON   Morning, old chap . . .

Wilson withdraws a little. Oates levers himself upright with a huge effort. Looks in turn at the three watching men. Bowers turns out the primus, spoons half-frozen pemmican into tins.

BOWERS   Just in time for breakfast, Laurie.

OATES   (ACROSS HIM) What's the date?

No one knows. Scott checks his journal.

SCOTT   16th . . . or 17th March.

OATES   I think it's my birthday.

He works himself onto all fours, drags himself by them to reach the tent entrance, begins very slowly to unfasten it. Bowers watches in horror, staring at the bare feet.

BOWERS (ALMOST UNDER BREATH) Soldier? Soldier? Please don't . . . No. No. No.

Oates half-turns in the entrance. Looks once at Wilson. Once at Scott. Bowers.

OATES Call of nature, Birdie.

He crawls out. Snow howls through the flap for a second, then stops. Bowers begins to weep, an anger building. He looks at Wilson, who reaches for his mess tin and spoon; at Scott, already eating.

33. Ext. Blizzard. Scan of terrain.

SCOTT'S JOURNAL (VO) I take this opportunity of saying that we have stuck to our sick companions to the last. In the case of Edgar Evans, when absolutely out of food and he lay insensible, the safety of the remainder seemed to demand his abandonment, but Providence mercifully removed him at this critical moment . . . We knew that poor Oates was walking to his death, but though we tried to dissuade him, we knew that it was the act of a brave man and an English gentleman . . .

The blizzard clears.

The three appear through the dank cold half-light, pulling blindly.

SCOTT'S JOURNAL (VO) We all hope to meet the end with a similar spirit, and assuredly the end is not far . . . My right foot has gone, nearly all the toes — two days ago I was proud possessor of best feet. Foot went and I didn't know it. Amputation is all I can hope for now, but will the trouble spread?

34. Ext. Last camp. Blizzard.

SCOTT'S JOURNAL (VO) Got within eleven miles of depot Monday night; had to lay up all yesterday in severe blizzard.

279

Today forlorn hope, Wilson and Bowers going to depot for fuel. Tomorrow last chance — no fuel and only one or two of food left — must be near the end. Have decided it shall be natural — we shall march for the depot with or without our effects and die in our tracks . . .

35. Int. Tent. Scott sits in sleeping bag, writing journal. Wilson lies prone in his bag, suffering. Bowers tries to make a burner from the oil-lamp, but his hands have almost gone.

Over this, the wind begins to drop, the howl subsides, the canvas stills. Scott's pencil creaks on; Wilson's breathing rasps on the dead air.

BOWERS   Uncle Bill? You awake?

Wilson's eyes open. He struggles to raise himself. Scott writes on.

BOWERS   (TO SCOTT) Take a look, sir?

SCOTT   It's but a lull, Birdie. (PAUSE) This is how it is . . .

Bowers slides slowly down into his bag, turns on his side, face averted. Wilson struggles to lift a hand-sized piece of muraine rock onto his lap, face dazed with effort.

SCOTT   . . . Don't you think, Bill? (WILSON ISN'T FOLLOWING) If our effects are lost, *all's* lost, wouldn't you say? Letters to loved ones, journals, samples. In the tent, they may still be found, survive to tell the tale . . .

Silence. Bowers whispers his way down the Lord's Prayer. Wilson runs a finger around the rock in his lap.

WILSON   How ironic. I do believe there's a layer of coal here. (HE POINTS IT OUT. LOOKS FINALLY AT SCOTT) I thought this was what I wanted. (LONG HOLD, AS HE STRUGGLES TO CONFRONT HIS MEANING) It isn't. It isn't.

Bowers murmers on. Wilson lies on his back. Scott resumes his writings.

280

VI REJOICE!

36. Ext. Blizzard. Tent. Montage of days.

SCOTT'S LETTER (VO) (THE INDUSTRY INCREASINGLY MARKED) My dear Mrs Wilson, if this letter reaches you Bill and I will have gone out together. We are very near it now and I should like you to know how splendid he was at the end. His eyes have a comfortable blue look of hope and his mind is peaceful. My dear Mrs Bowers, I am afraid this will reach you after one of the heaviest blows of your life. He had come to be one of my closest and soundest friends . . . My dear Barrie . . . No fuel and a long way from food but it would do your heart good to be in our tent, to hear our songs and the cheery conversation . . . My dear Sir Edgar . . . If this diary is found it will show how we stuck by dying companions and fought the thing out well to the end. I think this will show that the spirit of pluck and the power to endure has not passed out of our race . . . My dear Sir Francis . . . I want to tell you that I was *not* too old for this job. After all, we are setting a good example to our country-men, if not by getting into a tight place, by facing it like men when we were there. We could have come through had we neglected the sick . . . My dear Sir George . . . the real thing that has stopped us is the awful weather . . . My dear Kinsey . . . I feel that the country need not be ashamed of us — our journey has been the biggest on record and nothing but the most exceptional bad luck at the end would have caused us to fail to return . . . My dear Mother . . . indeed it has been most singularly unfortunate, for the risks I have taken never seemed excessive . . . My dear Sir Lewis . . . It's a pity the luck doesn't come our way, because every detail of equipment is right. We have decided not to kill ourselves but to fight to the last for that depot . . . My dear Kathleen . . . What lots and lots I could tell you of this journey. What tales you would have for the boy. But what a price to pay . . .

37. Int. Wilson's bag is fastened over his head. Bowers lolls against the tent wall, eyes closed, tongue swollen with thirst, gums sour with scurvy. Scott writes on, a massive act of will. CU Scott, writing.

SCOTT'S LETTER   (VO) Tell Sir Clements I thought of him much . . .

Mix to Scott at 16, midshipman, being stood at ease in the Admiral's cabin and being introduced to the handsome Markham. The scene is mute, milky; the Admiral leaves the cabin, the young Scott is drawn to a sofa, watches Markham write his name in a black notebook. Markham pockets the book, begins to flirt with the boy-hero, places his right hand on the lad's white-trousered thigh. CU Boy Scott, face frozen.

CU Scott, in the tent. He blinks. Labours to write more, the mouth open with effort, blood smearing his teeth.

SCOTT'S LETTER   (VO) Message to the Public. The causes of the disaster are not due to faulty organization . . . but to misfortune in all risks . . . which had to be undertaken . . .

BOWERS   (SHARP, SUDDEN) God save the King!

Scott looks at Bowers. Bowers dozes on.

38. Ext. Tent, half-buried in drift snow. Sun gleams on the Barrier; a beautiful day. Silence. Slow fade.

39. Int. Scott's drawing-room, Buckingham Palace Road. POV shot of framed photograph of Scott and the baby Peter.

Kathleen sits at her desk by the window, writing paper to hand. OOS, Markham handles a telephone call in the hallway, quite audible in the still house. Kathleen studies the page below the pen: we read 'My dearest Fridtjof.' *She draws a many-page letter from a bureau drawer, begins to re-read it.*

MARKHAM   (THROUGHOUT AND OVER) No, I have already told you, Mrs Scott is not available to speak to you. Like myself, she has heard nothing of her husband's progress and will not speak to the press until she has . . . Markham, Sir Clements Markham, yes . . . I'd be happy to, fire away young man . . . Well, I'll tell you: we have as yet only Amundsen's uncorroborated word for it and I'm afraid there will be those on this side of the water who will want rather more tangible proof, particularly from one who has excited, by his rather sneaky way of going about things, a fair degree of scepticism already . . . I'll tell you quite bluntly, sir, the man's a gadfly, an interloper, and a damned professional to boot, not our sort at all . . . I shall be waiting for news from the *Terra Nova* before I'm prepared to acknowledge the Norwegian's priority at the Pole.

Infolded into Markham's interview, voiced fragments of Nansen's letter:

NANSEN'S LETTER   (VO) O is it not strange how things happen in this world. As I am just writing these lines, I am called down to the telephone to get the news of Amundsen. There is a whirlpool of feelings inside me. I think of you and what you may wish, more than of him, and am in a strange mood, unhappy and uneasy. Please, please say what kind of a place you are going to arrange for us in Paris . . .

HOUSEKEEPER   (OOS) Where shall I serve it, ma'am?

Markham jabbers on in the hallway. The housekeeper waits, tray in hand.

KATHLEEN   (PALM ON PAGE) By the window, Mrs Jennings. Let Sir Clements know, won't you . . .

Kathleen returns to her blank page. Crumples it slowly. Takes a second from a small drawer, picks up her pen, face white, tense, writes. Dear Doctor Nansen. Over the white face, quite distinctly, we hear Markham's answer to the final question:

MARKHAM   (OOS) No, sir, emphatically no: if the Royal Geographical Society is so lacking in propriety as to invite the Norwegian here to crow over us, I for one shall not be in attendance . . . Good day to you, sir.

Slow mix to

40. Mute film of Kathleen and baby Peter in their home. There are caption greetings from Kathleen to Scott between sequences; each caption contains the script 'Courtesy of Pears Soap' in the bottom corner right. The child crawls, toddles, laughs, claps his hands; Kathleen hugs him, kisses him; they paint together, in her studio. Gradually we become aware of a screening. Men's faces stare whitely in the flickery gloom of film and pipe-fug: Cherry-Garrards's, Wright's, Lashly's, Crean's, Dmitri's, Atkinson's. On the table, the film-can addressed to Scott from scene 15.

The film ends. Lamps are turned up. The hut, Cape Evans. Caption: 28 October 1912.

The men, a dozen or so, sit in silence, dazed, uneasy. Wright, by the table, studies the can cover.

WRIGHT   (EVENTUALLY) Well, I'm most awfully sorry about that, chaps, I had no idea. I thought it might be some of Ponting's stuff.

ATKINSON   (GENTLE) No harm done, Silas. It's no bad thing to know the old place still exists.

Silence for some moments.

LASHLY   Bonny boy, though.

ATKINSON   (STANDING SLOWLY) Well, mightn't be a bad idea to turn in. Some of us have a bit of walking to do tomorrow.

Slow dispersion. Atkinson moves towards Teddy Evans's bed area, 2 I/C.

ATKINSON   (EN ROUTE) How're the mules, Mr Lashly?

LASHLY   Mules're fine, sir. Back 'em against any two o' them ponies. Captain Oates'd be proud of 'em, I know.

284

VI REJOICE!

Atkinson moves on through the goodnights and begins to prepare for bed. Wright replaces the film in the can; reseals it; watches Atkinson for a moment, then moves to join him.

WRIGHT   Have a word, Atch?

ATKINSON   Have a seat.

Wright sits on the bed: to his right he can see Scott's sanctum, laid out as if for inspection, not a hair out of place.

WRIGHT   Atch. I know you've devoted hundreds of hours to this question during this last winter, but I still must ask you a last time: is it what we should be doing, heading south for a party we know to be dead, when there's a party still out who have some chance of being alive?

ATKINSON   Silas, you know as well as I do, if we can make it to Campbell's party over the sea-ice, Campbell can make it back to us. I think our duty's clear. I believe the powers-that-be would want us to complete the record of the Polar party come what may; and that means finding them and their effects.

WRIGHT   It's you I'm thinking of, Atch. We're in one hell of a spot, one false move and they could lay the blame for it all at your door.

ATKINSON   I think that's unlikely, Silas.

WRIGHT   Well, I hope so, Atch. We could be out there for months without so much as a track to follow, they could be down a crevasse, dead of exposure somewhere, scurvy. You saw Teddy Evans, for God's sake. Find nothing; and all the time Campbell's party are alive but weak, waiting to be relieved. How's that going to look in the 'record'?

Lights begin to be turned down in the hut. The two men are cocooned in the light of their lamp.

285

ATKINSON   And if we go for Campbell and find him cheerfully making his way home on his own paddle, and simply ignore the dead, their effects, their account of what happened? (PAUSE) In the British Navy, nothing is ever simple, Silas. (GENTLE SMILE) You Canadians probably don't realize that, but thanks for your concern, old chap. (HE TURNS THE LAMP DOWN, SLIPS INTO HIS SLEEPING BAG) Get some sleep, eh?

Wright leaves, walks down the quiet, darkened hut to the tenements. Atkinson lies on his back, staring at the roof. Dog sounds, men's voices raised, coughing of mules. Mix slowly to

41. Ext. Long shots of the Search Party caravanning south over the ice: eleven men, eight mules, two dog teams. Gradually the movement breaks down into still frames; then photographic slides. The content of the shots changes: British to Norwegian. Lecture-room acoustic, low-voiced comment, exclamations on slide-changes, when items of 'natural beauty' are revealed.

42. Int. Slide-show ends. (RGS, London. Caption: 15 November 1912) The packed audience applauds, polite, passionless, as the lights come up. Amundsen and Curzon resume their places at the speaker's table, Curzon standing, his hand up for quiet. A liveried usher approaches, whispers a word in Curzon's ear. Curzon nods. Applause dies. Amundsen sits on, remote, aloof, a touch bitter. His brother Leon watches him carefully from the front row.

CURZON   Ladies and gentlemen, we have somewhat overrun our allotted time, and I'm informed that dinner will soon be upon us, in Great Hall; so I propose to defer questions until we are all suitably postprandial. (MURMERS OF ASSENT) More later, of course, but as President it falls to me now to offer a brief word of thanks to Captain Amundsen for his simple and uncomplicated account of what we must all now assume to have been a simple and uncomplicated journey. Pole-seeking, of course, has its own undeniable attractions, and we're grateful to the good Captain for agreeing to share his recent experiences of it with us. Equally, I feel bound to say, both he and we ourselves will look forward in excited anticipation to the day when our own Captain Scott steps up to this rostrum and delivers his report on a very different project — the British Antarctic Expedition — replete, as we know it will be, with scientific knowledge for which the whole civilized world hungers. (HUGE APPLAUSE, CHEERING FROM THE GALLERY, WHERE KATHLEEN SITS, 'INCOGNITO', UNCHAPERONED, AT THE END OF A ROW) Captain Amundsen has graciously consented to autograph copies of his recently published book *The South Pole* (HE TAPS A COPY OF IT ON THE TABLE IN FRONT OF HIM), the writing of which presumably deflected him from pursuing his widely proclaimed intention to undertake a three-year drift across the Arctic Basin . . . (SOME MURMURS) and which carries a fulsome dedication to the men who helped him in the South. In concluding this short word of thanks, and having heard what Captain Amundsen has had to say, I cannot as an Englishmen help feeling that, if our first toast at dinner is to be Captain Amundsen and his Merry Men, our second should be Three Cheers for the dogs!

Surprised laughter, becoming knowing, as it widens into applause. Curzon, applauding vigorously, smiles disarmingly at Amundsen, disbarbing the slur. Amundsen stands, whitefaced, as a few people come forward with their books for signature. Leon is already by his side.

CU dedication page, The South Pole, *Amundsen's Swan describing its jerky arcs and swoops. We read:*

To
MY COMRADES
The brave little band that promised
in Funchal Roads
To stand by me in the struggle for the
SOUTH POLE
I dedicate this book.

Roald Amundsen

Uranienborg
15 August 1912.

Over this, in clipped, unstressed Norwegian (sub-titled):

AMUNDSEN   I want you to find me another hotel, Leon.

LEON   I'll speak to Lord Curzon.

AMUNDSEN   No, just do it. I will not be the guest of these . . . ignorant people a minute longer than I must.

He scans the tiny queue of autograph-hunters. In the emptying gallery, Kathleen — in thick spectacles — shrouds herself against the night and recognition. Over her CU:

KATHLEEN'S DIARY   (VO) I wanted to avoid the Press and I do not feel sociable on the subject of Amundsen. There was scarcely anyone on the platform except Lord Curzon, Major Darwin and Shackleton. Amundsen's speech was plucky and modest but dull, and of a dullness!

Mixing through to image of Barrier (next scene)

KATHLEEN   (CONT., FADING) His accent made it very difficult to follow. The Queen's Hall was moderately enthusiastic. He did not mention you except just to say . . .

43.   *Ext. Barrier. Long, high-crane shot of the Search Party caravan, strung out across the plain. In a slow adjustment, the shot includes, as foreground, the almost buried tent, gradually excluding the Search Party.*

Over shot of tent, dogs bark in distance, a man shouts, excited, fearful, anothers answers. Tilt up again to reveal Wright and Atkinson on ski, quite close and bearing down on the tent's tip.

They arrive together. Stare sombrely down at the flap of canvas above the snow. Wright unslings a spade from his back. Atkinson signals the others.

44.   *Ext. A funereal montage of images of the discovery and disposal:*

VI REJOICE!

a) Wright digs out the entrance to the buried tent; shock on the arc of watching faces;
b) Wright, then Atkinson, then Lashly crawl through the entrance-flaps;
c) The men wait, at a respectful distance, watching the flap;
d) Inside, Lashly gazes gravely at the tent's contents; Atkinson gathers books, papers, effects; Wright stares in horror, fascination, at the condition of the dead; tries to catch Atkinson's eye; Atkinson refuses the contact;
e) Lashly emerges from the flap-hole, climbs out onto the barrier crust. He stands for a moment, lost, weeping.
f) In the tent, Atkinson has begun to read Scott's journal; Wright crouches over Bowers, studying the haemotomatous tissue of face and neck.

WRIGHT (FINALLY) So this is scurvy. Eurch! (HE SHUDDERS A
    LITTLE)

Atkinson stops reading, looks at Wright levelly for the first time.

ATKINSON Silas, forgive me, but I must ask you to refrain from
    repeating your . . . unofficial . . . lay and rather peremptory
    diagnosis of our dead colleagues' condition. (WRIGHT BLINKS,
    SINKS INTO HIS HEELS) These are critical times for us all,
    Silas, and I suspect no one will thank us for bandying
    around a lot of . . . emotional terms which in the wrong
    hands might cast doubt on the whole organization and
    conduct of the expedition.

They look at each other in silence for a while. Wright frowns; nods.
Cherry-Garrard calls down through the flap.

GARRARD Wondered if you needed any help, old boy.

ATKINSON (STILL LOOKING AT WRIGHT) No, but I'll be a little
    while. Silas will join you directly. I think we should organize
    some vittles . . .

g) Outside, two tents have been pitched, mules and dogs feed; a

*small knot of men still watch the death-tent with a sort of grave
curiousness;*

*h) In the tent, Atkinson reads on and on, the myth already
gripping;*

*i) The men stand bare-headed around the cairn, Englishmen at a
funeral, while Atkinson addresses them:*

ATKINSON (VOICE RAISED, DISCREETLY EMOTIONAL) At the
express wish of the Captain, I am asked to read the following address to you. It is headed: Message to the Public.

He begins to read, 'The causes of the disaster are not due to faulty
organization, but to misfortune in all risks which had to be
undertaken,' *over the watching faces of the others: Wright,
Cherry-Garrard, Gran, Crean, Lashly, Dmitri, Nelson, Keohane,
Williamson, Hooper. Gradually Atkinson's voice fades seamlessly
into Scott's, the message ground out remorselessly over the tiny
British huddle in the vast white plain.*

SCOTT (VO) 1. The loss of pony transport in March 1911 obliged
me to start later than I had intended, and obliged the limits
of stuff transported to be narrowed. 2. The weather throughout the outward journey, and especially the long gale in
83°South, stopped us. 3. The soft snow in lower reaches of
glacier again reduced pace. We fought these untoward
events with a will and conquered, but it cut into our
provision reserve. Every detail of our food supplies, clothing
and depots made on the interior ice-sheet and over that
long stretch of 700 miles to the Pole and back worked out to
perfection. But all the facts above enumerated were as
nothing to the surprise which awaited us on the Barrier. It
is clear that these circumstances come on very suddenly,
and our wreck is certainly due to this sudden advent of
severe weather, which does not seem to have any satisfactory cause. I do not think human beings ever came
through such a month as we have come through, and we
should have got through in spite of the weather but for the

290

sickening of a second companion, Captain Oates, and a shortage of fuel in our depots for which I cannot account, and finally, but for the storm which has fallen on us within eleven miles of the depot at which we hoped to secure our final supplies.

We are weak, writing is difficult, but for my own sake I do not regret this journey, which has shown that Englishmen can endure hardships, help one another, and meet death with as great a fortitude as ever in the past. We took risks, we knew we took them; things have come out against us, and therefore we have no cause for complaint, but bow to the will of Providence, determined still to do our best to the last. Had we lived, I should have had a tale to tell of the hardihood, endurance and courage of my companions which would have stirred the heart of every Englishman. These rough notes and our dead bodies must tell the tale, but surely, surely, a great rich country like ours will see that those who are dependent on us are properly provided for.

End on cairn cross. Mix to giant cross on Observation Hill, the actualization of Scott's premonitory hallucination on arriving at Cape Evans in episode III.

45. Ext. Over the hill cross in long shot, the inscription in VO: 'In memoriam. Captain R.F. Scott RN, Dr E.A. Wilson, Captain L.E.G. Oates, Inniskilling Dragoons, Lt H.R. Bowers RIM, Petty Officer E. Evans RN, who died on their return from the Pole, March 1912. To strive, to seek, to find and not to yield.'

On the reverse, we see Atkinson by the hut at Cape Evans, staring at the cross across the Sound. Men shout from close by, beckon South. Across the sea-ice, a group of men trudge towards them. An eerie silence for some moments, then cheering sets up, excitement and waving, men set out to meet them. Atkinson joins them, walking at first, then breaking into a run, as the excitement fills his lungs. The Terra Nova, *back in the Sound, blasts off her greetings.*

46. Ext. Campbell's party (Campbell, Levick, Priestley, Abbott, Browning, Dickason), on the sea-ice, almost home. They wear their desperate ice-hutted winter on their frames and in their shoe-black blubber-stoved faces. Others free them from their loads, help them in over the ice. Campbell and Atkinson shake hands gravely.

ATKINSON   Welcome home, Victor.

CAMPBELL   Dear old Atch. Good to be back.

They walk in towards the hut, old friends on a chance meeting.

CAMPBELL   Reach the Pole, did we?

He stops. Stares at the huge cross on the hill across the Sound.

ATKINSON   Five men, the whole party: Scott, Wilson, Oates, Bowers, Seaman Evans.

Campbell nods, sniffs phlegmatically, continues to stare at the cross.

ATKINSON   They weren't even first.

Campbell turns, looks hard at Atkinson.

CAMPBELL   Never looked like being, Atch. Lambs to the slaughter.

They ski on towards the hut, their voices receding.

CAMPBELL   How'd they die, do we know?

ATKINSON   (VOICE FADING) Want and exposure just about covers it.

The shot edges left, clears hut and ship, centres yet again on the distant cross. Below the slowly growing clatter of telegraph keys.

47. Ext. Night. Ship-deck, Pacific Ocean, between Tahiti and Rarotonga. Kathleen stares at the brilliant moon-lit sea. Caption:

19 February 1913. Dim, high-frequency whining from nearby wireless room.

KATHLEEN'S DIARY (VO) I joined my ship for New Zealand without selling out any stock, I couldn't bear to sell out, everything was so low. Several reporters, and the Mayor and so on, saw me off. This ship smells.

MAN (OOS, BEHIND HER) Mrs Scott?

She turns, sees the captain, dressed for dinner.

KATHLEEN Captain Graham?

GRAHAM (SCOTS, DOURISH) I have some news just in, ma'am. I wonder if you'd mind stepping into my cabin?

KATHLEEN (STUDYING HIS FACE, THE MESSAGE PAPER IN HIS HAND) The Expedition? (HE NODS, LOOKS AROUND HIM DOWN THE DECKS) Well, let's have it.

The Captain chews his lip a little, hands her the paper. She reads it for some time.

CAPTAIN I'm deeply sorry, ma'am . . .

KATHLEEN Ah well, never mind. I expected that. Thanks very much. I'll go and think about it.

CAPTAIN If there's anything I can do, Mrs Scott.

KATHLEEN No, I can manage perfectly, thank you.

He dwells. She turns to the sea, hands on rail. Watches it swirl and bubble down below. He leaves.

KATHLEEN'S DIARY (VO) My God is godly. I need not touch him to know that. Let me maintain a high, adoring, exaltation and not let the contamination of sorrow touch me. Within I shall be exultant. My God is glorious and and could never become less so . . .

48. Int. Wireless room. The operator, Irish, copies out the condolences, hands them in silence along the desk to Kathleen, who sits by him, a stack by her hand already consumed. We see the senders' names: heads of governments, monarchs, the great and the good (Asquith, Marconi, Artie, Muriel Paget, Lord Liverpool, Barrie, Markham, Curzon and the RGS; Ory Wilson; Teddy Evans; Admiral Beaumont; Reginald Smith; Lt Atkinson on behalf of the BAE.

KATHLEEN'S DIARY (VO) The operator is an Irishman; we have never had any conversation . . .

She takes the next batch: Fridtjof Nansen's name on the top one. Tapping of telegraph keys, buzz of wireless, bridging to

49. Madison, Wisconsin. Int. Large hotel bathroom suite. CU Amundsen, eyes closed, water to his neck.

LEON (OOS INITIALLY, LISTING PRINCIPAL ITEMS TO BE DEALT WITH) Christiania are offering you a professorship in something or other, with a regular salary, I suppose you'll decline. (AMUNDSEN'S HEAD NODS ONCE. LEON, ON A CHAIR SOME YARDS AWAY, IN THE CORNER OF THE VAST ROOM, TAKES IT PHLEGMATICALLY, RETURNS TO THE HEAP OF CORRESPONDENCE IN HIS HAND) More honours; the American Geographical, the German Geographical, the French, the Italian. (NOTHING FROM AMUNDSEN) Receipts from the book royalties, nothing to shout about . . . Letters from Hanssen, Lindstrom and Wisting, they'll go with you as and when, you have only to say. And a cable from Bjaaland . . .

AMUNDSEN (EYES OPEN AT ONCE) What does he say?

The phone rings, quite loudly, in the adjoining bedroom.

LEON 'North not for me, but congratulations on your triumphal progress around the world.'

Amundsen nods, sad suddenly; gestures Leon to answer the phone. Leon leaves. Close on Amundsen again, the eyes shut, a thin, indistinct telephone mutter relaying from the next room. Mute images of comradeship on the journey home invade his eyelids: welcomes, dinners, freedoms of cities, royal receptions, farewells.

LEON   (OOS, QUIET) Roald.

Amundsen's eyes blink open, focus on his brother, just returned to his chair in the corner, the sheaf of correspondence on his knee. Amundsen studies him. Leon sits thinking, face uncertain, a touch uneasy.

AMUNDSEN   Who was it?

LEON   (TERSE, ABSTRACTED) Nansen. From New York. I took his number, said you'd call him.

AMUNDSEN   (WEARINESS DEFUSING ANGER) Will he never give me peace? I'll go north when there's money for the journey and when the Norwegian government agree to honour their pledges. I *know* it's a point of honour to complete the journey, why can he not understand I cannot *move* on the matter?

Silence.

LEON   Scott's dead.

Amundsen blinks, looks towards the still open connecting door, then back to Leon. Says nothing.

LEON   The whole party. Five of them. Perished on the Barrier coming back from the Pole. Starved to death in their tent, I don't know. The ship just broke the news from New Zealand. Nansen wants to discuss a statement. He's . . . anxious you shouldn't say anything . . . undiplomatic.

Amundsen sinks lower, head barely above water. He lies behind closed lids for a fair time. Opens eyes finally. Leon remains, solid, questioning.

AMUNDSEN (SOFT) True, you mean? (PAUSE) What is there to say? (PAUSE) It's quite a coup. (PAUSE) He wins at the last.

The phone rings again, shrill, insistent. They ignore it.

AMUNDSEN (GESTURING) Have we done with the mail?

LEON More or less: a note from Shackleton, one from Peary, another from Cook.

AMUNDSEN Good old Fred.

LEON (SCANNING) 'Looking forward to meeting you in New York in the fall.'

The phone starts up again. Again it's ignored.

AMUNDSEN Dear old Fred . . .

LEON That'll be the Press.

AMUNDSEN (BITTERING UP) Thirty years on the ice, never lost a single comrade's life . . . and already the world's forgotten him. Never learnt the British habit of dying, the glory of self-sacrifice, the blessing of failure, that's where he went wrong.

He looks at Leon. The phone stops ringing. CU Amundsen.

AMUNDSEN (THE DEATHS HITTING HIM SUDDENLY) Horrible. Horrible.

50. London. Int. CU Atkinson. Mid-afternoon light through glass. Voices drift from a nearby room. L.S. Atkinson, in naval uniform, an attaché-case on his knees, seated rather stiffly in a high-backed chair in Markham's large marbled hall. A door opens down the hall, the voices lift and drop, he watches Kathleen Scott approach, stands for her arrival.

KATHLEEN   (SHAKING HIS HAND) It's extremely good of you to come and see us, Dr Atkinson.

ATKINSON   Only too pleased, ma'am. I'm er ... (HE FINDS IT HARD TO SPEAK FOR A MOMENT. SHE PLACES HER HAND ON HIS GENTLY)

KATHLEEN   I was so happy it was you found him, Lieutenant. Your quietness and ... tact ... and reverence in this matter are widely admired and much appreciated. (HE BLUSHES) If I say more I'll only embarrass you, come and speak with my committee.

She links his arm like a friend and leads him into the room down the hall.

51. Int. The committee sit around a table covered with galleys, typescripts, manuscripts, journals, photographs and other expeditionary artefacts. Atkinson sits with them, though a touch removed, reading aloud his report in manuscript ('The Last Year at Cape Evans'). Shots of Markham, Lord Curzon, Admiral Sir Lewis Beaumont, fearsome in full uniform, Sir Reginald Smith, Kathleen Scott chairing. They each have pad and pencil, make a note from time to time.

ATKINSON   '. . . It was a sad homecoming for them after their hard time. I can only here say that I can never be sufficiently grateful to all the members of the Expedition who were with me during this bad season for their entire loyalty and good-fellowship; never one moment's trouble and always cheerful and willing.'

He removes his glasses, looks shyly round at the others.

MARKHAM   Splendid.

CURZON   First class.

SMITH   I agree. Would you happen to know how many words?

ATKINSON   (HOLDING MS PAGES UP) I'm afraid not. I suppose it's quite a few . . .

SMITH   No matter. It may be a bit long, but a little judicious trimming here and there won't damage its excellence.

Atkinson sits, shy, pleased, still wary.

KATHLEEN   I have one or two tiny things. I suspect we all have, but I'm sure they can wait. Sir Clements, anything?

Markham takes her look briefly, makes a business of checking his notes.

MARKHAM   Fairly minor stuff, really. Ah yes. (ISOLATING A NOTE WITH HIS PENCIL) Your reference to the cause of death — 'want and exposure', I believe you said?

ATKINSON   That's right, sir.

MARKHAM   I do not seek to pry, Dr Atkinson, but may I ask whether you have yet submitted your medical report for the Admiralty?

ATKINSON   I put it in last week, sir.

MARKHAM   May one assume a similar factual and unsensational diagnosis there as here?

ATKINSON   There is only one diagnosis, sir. You have heard it.

MARKHAM   Thank you. (HE TURNS TO KATHLEEN, HANDING BACK)

KATHLEEN   We're most grateful for your work and your support, doctor. *The Last Year at Cape Evans* could not have had a better or more loving chronicler. My husband's book will be the better for it.

Atkinson has stood, says his goodbyes, Kathleen leads him from the room.

KATHLEEN (IN DOORWAY) I think we should move on at once to the main text, gentlemen. Sir Reginald knows my general feelings, I'll see Dr Atkinson to the door.

They leave. The men remaining begin to finger their galleys.

CURZON Charming man.

BEAUMONT Man's a fool. Couldn't tell his arse from a pineapple. Damned lucky he's not facing a court martial. (PAUSE. SOME TENSION IN THE OTHERS: BEAUMONT IS NAVY, NOT WHOLLY DEPENDABLE) Doesn't mean he won't go far. Damned clever report-writer.

SMITH (CLEARING THROAT, DANGER OVER) Well, gentlemen, last week there was some discussion of whether it would prove of any real benefit to the Expedition to press for a full public enquiry into the cause of the deaths, as a way of countering any criticism that may have arisen as to the organization and leadership displayed.

BEAUMONT (PEREMPTORY) Have no truck with inquiries, no one knows where they might lead.

SMITH (SILKY) I was about to say, Admiral Beaumont, that by the end of that discussion there was general greement that the best course by far was to publish the book as quickly as possible and let Scott speak for himself. You've now all had a chance to read the journal in its entirety, I believe, and will probably agree with me that it's a masterpiece. (NODS, CLUCKS ALL ROUND) Nonetheless, I've taken the liberty as publisher, in consultation with Mrs Scott, of drawing up a list of very minor trims and excisions for your approval. The criteria are in the main two: lacking interest for the general reader or causing hurt to fellow-members of the expedition. Page 3, gentlemen (THEY TURN ON), the reference to PO Evans being drunk and disgracing the ship etc: of no interest and damaging.

BEAUMONT   (STANDING) Excuse me, gentlemen, I must go to the lavatory.

He ambles from the room. They watch him in silence.

MARKHAM   Don't worry, Reggie. He always does that. He'll come back when we've finished and say not a word.

52. Int. Evening light. CU Teddy Evans. LS shows him on Atkinson's high-backed hall chair, an attaché case by his feet. Smith's voice drifts half-audibly from the committee room. We hear 'Page 568, take out line 16 et seq: "We ought to have kept the bearings of our outward camps, that is where we have failed."' Another quotation is lost, then 'Page 589, line 11 et seq: "but generosity and thoughtfulness have not been abundant . . . " and just below: "It's a miserable jumble".'

KATHLEEN   (oos) My dear Teddy, I had no idea you'd arrived, it's so good of you to come.

He stands, kisses her hand. She takes his arm, leads him down the hall.

KATHLEEN   Come, dear man, come and meet my committee . . .

Bring up sound from next scene: metallic clanks, echoing footsteps, hollow acoustic.

53. Int. Two men, one uniformed, one in bowler hat, walk away from camera down long, booming, institutional corridor. They stop at the far end, the tall one sits on a bench, at the other's gesture. The second man leaves. The seated man takes out a book; begins to read.

54. MS Amundsen, seated on bench, reading, held in the building's echo-system. He looks old, worn. Several time-mixes: he turns the pages, calm, stolid. Footsteps. He looks up. The warder's returned.

WARDER (AMERICAN) Follow me, please.

Amundsen follows. Is shown into a room with no windows in the walls, divided down the middle by a wire-grille. He's shown to a chair, the warder presses a buzzer, a door is opened on the other side of the grille and a man enters and takes the chair opposite Amundsen.

WARDER When the bell goes, that's dinner, he has to go. (HE LEAVES)

AMUNDSEN Hello, Fred.

COOK Hello, Roald.

AMUNDSEN I expected you at my lecture.

COOK Yes. I couldn't make it.

AMUNDSEN I thought I'd look you up.

COOK Bad idea. I'm stinking fish right now, if the press find out they'll give you a roasting.

Amundsen smiles, says nothing. Cook scratches his head.

AMUNDSEN Want to tell me about it?

COOK (SHRUGS) I went into stocks and shares. Seemed the thing. Formed a partnership with a couple of fellows. They cleared off one day, took the lot, left me holding the baby. I'm charged with fraud, bail set at 20,000 dollars, and no one in the whole wide world to post it. You wouldn't have that sort of money, I suppose? (AMUNDSEN SMILES WANLY) No, I thought not, you're much too honest . . .

Silence. Amundsen looks at the book he carries. Cook scratches his head.

COOK So. You took my advice. (AMUNDSEN DOESN'T AT ONCE

301

FOLLOW) The South Pole. I knew you would. Quite a coup. How was it?

AMUNDSEN   Cold.

COOK   I bet.

Silence again.

COOK   Weren't you supposed to go north? What happened?

AMUNDSEN   No cash. I've been stalking the globe lecturing just to pay off my debts. All the money's marching to war just now. (COOK WATCHES HIM CAREFULLY, WAITS FOR THE REST) That's part of it. Partly I wanted something else.

COOK   What was that?

AMUNDSEN   I thought I might go and live with Esquimaux for a few years, try and learn what they have to teach. (LONG PAUSE) But I don't suppose I'll ever stop doing this. It's all I know. All I can. So I'll go north, in a year or two, and see what's there. (HE LOOKS AT COOK, SMILES GENTLY) I brought you a book, the guard says I can leave it at the office (HE HOLDS THE SPINE UP TO THE GRILLE: Scott: *The Last Expedition, Volume one.* COOK'S LIPS PURSE IN DISTASTE) Read it anyway, it'll help to pass the time.

COOK   (SCRATCHING HEAD) I'd sooner count bugs. Besides, I read the reviews and I stopped reading fiction years ago.

AMUNDSEN   I'll leave it anyway.

A bell begins ringing in the corridor. Cook's door slams open behind him.

COOK   You must be proud. (AMUNDSEN NODS) You've earned it.

AMUNDSEN   One each.

COOK You believe that?

The bell stops ringing. Amundsen's door slams open behind him.

GUARD One minute, Bud.

The door remains open.

AMUNDSEN (STANDING) If you say so, Fred.

He puts his hand to the grille. Cook covers it with his, finger-pads touching where they meet.

AMUNDSEN I'll do what I can about all this . . .

COOK Thanks. (AMUNDSEN WALKS TO THE DOOR, ON HIS WAY) Roald. (HE TURNS) Don't brood. (INDICATES HIS OWN CONDITION) Scott killed *himself*, it's what the British do best, they have such contempt for the work it's just as well they do. (HE GRINS) Let Scott have the glory. You keep the Pole.

Amundsen smiles, leaves.

55. Int. Long shot from rear of Amundsen and guard walking the high corridor, their conversation resonant in the barrelled hollowness.

GUARD You really the guy who got the South Pole?

AMUNDSEN That's right.

GUARD Hmm. Swede, aren't you?

AMUNDSEN Norwegian.

GUARD Norwegian, right. I heard about that, coupla years ago mebbe. You always wear a bowler?

AMUNDSEN No.

303

GUARD Edmonston, someat like that, hunh?

AMUNDSEN Amundsen.

GUARD Edmonson, right. Ate the dogs.

AMUNDSEN You have it.

GUARD God damn. And who was the guy committed suicide
— Johnson?

AMUNDSEN Oates?

GUARD No, I know about Oates, one o' your guys, Johnson,
read about it in the paper, last week sometime. Went to a
hotel, Europe somewhere, puts a gun in his mouth and
blows his head all around the room. Johansen, that's it.

*Amundsen has stopped, stares out of a grimy window at a courtyard
below.*

GUARD You knew him?

AMUNDSEN Yes, I knew him.

He walks on.

GUARD Jeez, bud, you know some funny people.

*Peal of bells, loud, sonorous, picked up by others, spread across a
city.*

Mix to

*56. Montage of mute images of grave rejoicing: St Paul's, smoulder-
ing censi, rich copes, school assemblies, unveiling of Scott sculptures
by Kathleen, unending of copies of* The Last Expedition. *The
sequence settles finally into Buckingham Palace and Palace Yard.
The members of the BAE pose for a group photograph, South Pole*

medals proudly displayed, the King in their midst. Wives, families and friends watch; crowds have gathered to peer and cheer through the railings. In three-quarter speed and very gradually slowing, the group session ends and the group splits into smaller knots standing, talking, promenading. They are the last of these English — or so it once seemed; a dream that is dying. Evans, Atkinson, Kathleen, Markham, Cherry-Garrard, Wright, Campbell, Pennell, Lashly, Crean, Keohane, Clissold and the rest and their families perform the ritual dance of class and Empire in their gowns and uniforms and sober best suits.

Discreet caption, over this:

> The real value of Scott's expedition was spiritual, and therefore in the truest sense national. It is proof that in an age of depressing materialism men can still be found to face known hardship, heavy risk and even death, in pursuit of an idea . . . That is the temper of the men who build empires and while it lives among us we shall be capable of maintaining an Empire that our fathers builded.
>
> *The Times*

Sound bursts onto the screen, artillery flashes and cannonades from the Great War. Another dance begins, in grisly slow-motion, men dying by the millimetre in their millions. The camera tracks mildly on through mud and blood, but their numbers remain undiminished. The roller begins, listing first all those who served in the Great War and what happened to them; other notables from the BAE and their supporters; and ends on Amundsen's list of achievements and death, black on white.

Over this:

WOMAN'S VOICE   If nothing else, Scott showed his countrymen the way to die. We have so many heroes among us now, so many Scotts, holding sacrifice above gain . . . and we begin to understand what a splendour arises from the bloody fields of Flanders and Gallipoli . . .

Fade.